G·R·
EXPECTATIONS

Baby
Sleep
Guide

Sleep Solutions for You
& Your Baby

Marcie Jones & Sandy Jones

Foreword by Wendy Middlemiss, PhD

STERLING

New York / London
www.sterlingpublishing.com

STERLING and the distinctive Sterling logo are registered
trademarks of Sterling Publishing Co., Inc.

Library of Congress Cataloging-in-Publication Data

Jones, Marcie.
  Baby sleep guide : sleep solutions for you and your baby / Marcie
Jones & Sandy Jones ; foreword by Wendy Middlemiss.
      p. cm.—(Great expectations)
  Includes bibliographical references and index.
  ISBN 978-1-4027-5815-7 (pb-with flaps : alk. paper)
  1. Infants—Sleep. 2. Toddlers—Sleep. 3. Sleep—Physiological
aspects. I. Jones, Sandy. II. Title.
  RJ506.S55J66 2010
  618.92'02—dc22

2009028381

2 4 6 8 10 9 7 5 3 1

Published by Sterling Publishing Co., Inc.
387 Park Avenue South, New York, NY 10016
© 2010 by Sandy Jones and Marcie Jones
Distributed in Canada by Sterling Publishing
$^{c}/_{o}$ Canadian Manda Group, 165 Dufferin Street
Toronto, Ontario, Canada M6K 3H6
Distributed in the United Kingdom by GMC Distribution Services
Castle Place, 166 High Street, Lewes, East Sussex, England BN7 1XU
Distributed in Australia by Capricorn Link (Australia) Pty. Ltd.
P.O. Box 704, Windsor, NSW 2756, Australia

Sterling ISBN 978-1-4027-5815-7

For information about custom editions, special sales, premium and
corporate purchases, please contact Sterling Special Sales
Department at 800-805-5489 or specialsales@sterlingpublishing.com.

Dedication & Acknowledgments

To Matthew, who always took the early shift. And to Zoë and Max, who taught me everything. And to all the tired parents who shared with us.

Our gratitude to Jennifer Williams, Hannah Reich, and Michael Fragnito for their tireless efforts. We couldn't have done it without you!

Contents

Foreword by Wendy Middlemiss, PhD / vii

Introduction: If You're Reading This Before Your Baby Is Born / ix

1   The Sleepy Fetus / 3

What's Going on In There? / 5

2   Newborns in "The Fourth Trimester" / 11

Understanding Your Baby's Sleep Cycle / 13
How Your Baby's Brain Is Different from Yours / 14
A Closer Look at Adult Sleep / 17
To Sleep, Perchance to Dream / 19
Your Baby's Sleep Cycles / 20
Common Medications That May Affect Your Baby's Sleep / 21
Baby Wake Cycles / 24
It Pays to Answer Promptly / 24
Decoding Your Baby's Cries / 25
The Swaddling Option / 26
Drowsy But Awake / 27

3   Where Should Baby Sleep? / 29

The Great Debate / 31
Bed Sharing: The World's Oldest Sleeping Arrangement / 33
The Biology of Mother-Baby Night Closeness / 38
Bed-Sharing Negatives / 39
Bed-Sharing Safety Checklist / 43
How and When to Stop Bed Sharing / 46
Co-Sleeping / 47
All About Cribs / 48
Setting Up Your Baby's Room / 59
Baby Soothers / 62

4   Six Weeks: The Crying Peak / 65

The Six-Week Crying Peak / 67
Sudden Infant Death Syndrome (SIDS) / 71
Colic: The Waking Nightmare / 79
Dealing with Exhaustion / 90

5   Three to Four Months / 97

Developing a Daily Routine / 99
What's Happening in Your Three-Month-Old Baby's Brain / 100

Feeding and Sleep: The Big Differences Between Breast
and Bottle / 102
Nap Routines / 107
Charting Your Baby's Day/Night Patterns / 113
The Nighttime Put-Down / 116
Tips for Handling Your Unique Baby / 120

6   Four to Six Months / 125
The Four-Month Sleep Shift / 127

7   Six to Nine Months / 137
Your Baby's New Sleep Patterns / 139
Is It Time for a Change? / 139
What Is Sleep Training? Does It Really Work? / 141

8   Nine to Twelve Months / 155
All About Toddler Sleep / 157

9   Twelve Months and Beyond / 163
The Challenge of Toddler Sleep / 165
Exercise Is Important / 165
Handling Delaying Tactics / 166
Twenty Tips for Toddler Bedtime / 167
Coping with Your Early-Morning Riser / 170
The Changing Nap-time Scene / 170
Containing a Roaming Toddler / 171
Monsters and Night Fears / 172
Moving from Crib to Bed / 174
Bed-wetting / 175
Sleep Problems When Traveling / 177
Family Upheavals / 178
A Distant Memory / 179

Glossary / 181
Resources / 185
Endnotes / 187
Index / 191

Foreword

One of the most pressing concerns for most new moms and dads is getting baby to sleep (and grabbing a little shut-eye themselves). It is also one of the most controversial aspects of parenting; every expert and veteran mom or dad has an opinion about how long—and where—a baby should sleep, what to do when their baby wakes up in the night, and how to determine if he or she is sleeping well. Like so many other aspects of parenting, however, opinions about sleep—particularly how soon a baby can be expected to sleep through the night—are very often contradictory and downright confusing.

In *Great Expectations: Baby Sleep Guide*, baby experts Marcie and Sandy Jones give parents all the tools and information they need to assess the latest research about sleep, naps, and feedings. With their customary thoroughness, the authors explain the basic facts of infant sleeping patterns and how these patterns change during the first year of a baby's life and on through the toddler years. In addition to describing every stage of development, Marcie and Sandy make helpful suggestions and assure parents that, other than some very clear dos and don'ts associated with how to handle infant sleep, much can be left to the discretion of individual parents and the particular needs of each child.

Building on this foundation of information and reassurance, Part I helps parents understand how babies' sleep patterns are established and develop over time. With a helpful focus on the importance of mothers' sleep during pregnancy, the authors present a considered discussion of how new parents can approach the last trimester of pregnancy in a way that may help their infants' sleep patterns *after birth*. At the same time, they take a practical look at navigating the emotional and financial ins and outs of maternity leave, always with an eye to helping parents-to-be make decisions that are best for their own family.

Next they explore how infants sleep, with a focus on the developing brain and the changes that influence patterns of sleep, giving parents a thorough understanding of what they might expect in the normal course of infant sleep. For example, babies don't generally sleep for long periods, especially if they breastfeed. Regardless of whether a baby is bottle- or breastfed, the fact is, all babies take time to develop the mechanics of sleep, which explains why parents are so tired, especially in the early months. But take courage—Marcie and Sandy have looked deeply into the factors that may be hampering a baby's sleep, and parents can benefit from this knowledge. In fact, the authors offer many practical ways to help parents get through this challenging period (often described as "the fourth trimester"). The discussion of the benefits and methods of answering a baby's cries when he or she awakens will help new parents cope with the uncertainties of how best to respond to their baby's needs while getting some sleep too.

And then there's the ongoing debate over the best and safest place for a baby to sleep. Once again, Marcie and Sandy take a practical approach to this hot-button issue—always with a baby's best interests in mind—and discuss the pros and cons of myriad sleeping arrangements, whether co-sleeping, sleeping in the family bed, or putting him or her down in a crib, bassinet, or cradle. In every environment, Sandy and Marcie point out sleep scenarios that might place an infant at risk and they help parents understand the options they have that can make each sleeping space safe for their baby. They also cover difficult subjects, such as Sudden Infant Death Syndrome (SIDS) and colic, giving parents a lucid and useful distillation of the latest findings and research and how they can apply it to help keep their babies as safe as possible. The authors' thorough discussion of the issues at the heart of these very personal decisions will help families make the best choices for their own situations.

And, at 3 to 4 months, when a baby's physiological patterns of sleep change, parents will learn how to understand and adapt, because as soon as a baby has established a pattern—and parents have gotten used to it—it will change. Marcie and Sandy have the good sense to point out that no matter how well-informed you may be about the science of baby sleep (and you certainly will be after reading this book) it will be of limited use to you unless you've developed some flexibility and a good sense of humor along the way.

Concerns about sleep take a different shape as a baby develops into a toddler, not the least of which are the subjects of mobility and child safety. What do you do, for example, if your baby is now capable of climbing out of a crib and exploring the house in the wee hours? In the last two sections of the book the authors explain the developmental changes that support the growth and expansion of a toddler's thinking and goals, and help parents understand what's going on and how to adapt to their toddler's new needs.

Throughout this eminently useful, thoroughly researched, reassuring book, Marcie and Sandy's advice, tips, and caveats not only help parents build healthy sleep routines for their babies, they also lay the foundation for a parent-child relationship that will be satisfying to the parent as well as the child. At every step Marcie and Sandy show their respect for differences in family styles and encourage parents to make decisions that are best for *their* family. They accomplish this by giving new moms and dads the tool they need the most: clear, easy to understand, and well-supported information.

Wendy Middlemiss, Ph.D.
Department of Educational Psychology
University of North Texas

If You're Reading This Before Your Baby Is Born

If you're reading this before your baby is born, especially if you're a first-time mom-to-be, it's probably because all the sleep-deprivation horror stories you've heard from new parents are making you a bit nervous. Even if you haven't heard the one about the time hubby brushed his teeth with hemorrhoid cream by accident, you're no doubt familiar with the stereotype of the unshowered, zombiefied new mom, sleepwalking through the day and barely managing not to drop the baby. You're probably wondering, "Does that really have to be me?"

The answer is no! In spite of what you may have heard, it *is* possible to get through baby's first year without being chronically sleep-deprived. But it takes planning, support, compromise, and a little bit of luck.

If you want to wake up a room of drowsy parents, bring up the emotional hand grenade of baby sleep. People—including people who have never met a baby—are rarely neutral about when, where, and how babies should be put to sleep. A parent's attitude about baby sleep somehow becomes not just about sleep, but the epitome of your parenting attitude and approach.

Should you co-sleep? Crib sleep? Let the baby cry it out? Pick her up whenever she cries? Let her cry for a while and then pick her up? Should she be on a schedule? Is it okay to nurse her to sleep? When should your baby sleep through the night? Are you creating good sleep habits? Adding to new parents' anxiety is the specter of SIDS and conflicting advice from books, magazines, friends, and family. What's a worn-out parent to do?

Great Expectations: Baby Sleep Guide to the rescue. We've read hundreds of pages of sleep studies, parent surveys, and pretty much every baby sleep book on the market. We've surveyed sleep-related products to find out what works and what's a waste of money. And we've taken some of the hundreds of sleep-related questions parents have asked us to determine what tired parents and worried parents-to-be really want to know.

What we found was surprising—there's a lot that the other baby sleep books don't tell you! For instance, breastfed and formula-fed babies have completely different sleep patterns, and even need different amounts of sleep in a 24-hour period. We'll tell you how much sleep you can expect your baby to need, based on his or her age and diet, and how often you can expect your baby to feed.

And, believe it or not, there are things you can do *even if you're newly pregnant* to ensure that, for your baby's first year of life, both you and your baby have healthy amounts of the best-quality, safest, and most restful sleep you can.

This book is not a go-to-sleep system or a training manual, although we do promise that if you read this book from cover to cover, your baby will be able to put him- or herself to sleep quickly at a developmentally appropriate time with minimal tears and will be able to sleep for a reasonable amount of time.

Instead, our book is designed to provide you with an unbiased source of information on why babies sleep the way they do, how their sleep needs change over time, problems parents encounter, and evidence of what works and what doesn't, based on credible scientific studies.

Here's what you'll find inside:

- **For sleepy readers.** Straight-to-the-point guidance structured with you, the sleep-deprived parent, in mind.

- **Information on baby sleep.** An explanation of the complexities of baby sleep, and how it differs from a child's sleep and an adult's sleep.

- **When to worry.** When your baby's sleep patterns could indicate a medical problem.

- **Sleeping gear reviews.** A guide to sleep gear: cribs, bassinets, mobiles, monitors, sleep sacs—

what works and what's a waste of money.

- **Coping strategies.** Easy-reference tips on how to manage your baby's sleep—and your sleep deprivation.

- **Fast facts.** Summaries of recent sleep research findings and surveys to help you decide what to do and what to avoid.

- **Advice from other parents.** Moms and dads share their frustrations and their practical strategies for putting baby to sleep, dealing with too little sleep, and getting the critical rest *you* need.

- **The big "Q."** Q&As throughout the book will help you find the best answers for the most common sleep questions parents ask.

- **Web savvy.** A roundup of Internet resources, including research centers, shopping sites, support organizations, and sleep-related parent blogs and hotlines.

- **Word sense.** A glossary of critical sleep and medical terms.

G·R·E·A·T
EXPECTATIONS

Baby Sleep Guide

The Sleepy
Fetus

1

What's Going on in There?

YOUR BABY'S SLEEP PATTERNS

Before your baby was a baby, she was a fetus, and even back then, her sleep patterns were in place! While your baby is still in the womb, her brain will grow an average of 250,000 new cells every minute. At several developmental points, she will have generated more than 50,000 new brain cells per *second*. Starting at 14 to 18 weeks, fetuses show a pronounced **circadian rhythm** in their activity level, and after a mere 4 months, a human fetus is already having bouts of sleep, usually lasting less than 5 minutes at a time—the first of what will be *millions* of sleep-wake cycles over your baby's lifetime.

Most moms begin to first experience brief fluttering feelings around 16 to 18 weeks of pregnancy. Then, stronger and more distinct sensations of movement will begin to "kick" in starting at around 20 weeks. By the time you can detect your baby's first movements, her brain will already have created 200 billion **neuron**s.

By about 21 weeks, your fetus will have begun a regular schedule of movement and rest. Fetuses as young as 23 weeks of age and weighing a single pound have been found to have **rapid eye movement (REM)** sleep states that are critical to the process of growing and cutting back brain connections.[1] By 26 weeks, only about 50 percent of those 200 billion brain cells that developed just 6 weeks earlier will have survived. This pruning process is the way nature ensures that your baby's brain is customized to provide the exact mental equipment she requires to survive in her environment.

What you're exposed to during the second half of your pregnancy may have a vital affect on your baby's health—and her sleep—later in life. The toxins in cigarette smoke in utero are especially dangerous during this period, because they can change the behavior of brain cells that will play a critical role in regulating breathing, sleeping, and waking. Babies younger than 6 months of age whose mothers smoked during pregnancy have *triple* the risk of **sudden infant death syndrome (SIDS)** of babies whose mothers did not smoke while they were pregnant. (For more on SIDS, see page 71.)

PLANNING AHEAD WHILE YOU'RE PREGNANT

Believe it or not, we've heard moms ask, "Do I really have to take the full 6 weeks of maternity leave my doctor recommends?" We know that bills need to be paid, health insurance benefits must be maintained, and that for some families, taking extra time off is not an option. We know some of you are super-resilient physically and love your jobs, too. But promising your boss or clients that you're going to be back from maternity leave asap, ready to tackle a huge project, is

Your Baby's Sleep and Activity Stages in Utero

By the time you can feel your baby really move, she will already have developed 4 different rest-activity stages, which are collectively called **non-rapid eye movement (NREM) sleep,** that you can learn to detect.

1. During episodes of **deep sleep,** moms report that their babies are unresponsive to outside noises or motion. This stage can be alarming, because the baby seems so still. If seen on ultrasound, a deep-sleeping fetus may keep her head in the same place, while floating motionlessly.

2. During **light sleep,** your baby will seem to be very quiet but may have momentary bursts of arm and leg movements. She might even hiccup! Remarkably, Dutch researchers have found that the REM patterns of pregnant women during sleep change as a function of how far along they are in their pregnancies and appear to be synchronized with their babies' sleep patterns. Women's REMs at any stage of late pregnancy were found to be similar to REMs observed in premature babies at a similar gestational age.

3. If you happen to be having a sonogram, you may see your baby literally climbing the walls of your uterus during an **active-awake** period! In this stage, you will feel strong, vigorous bursts of arm and leg kicking.

4. When your baby is **active and alert**, her movements will have pauses, as if she's waiting for something outside to happen. She might respond with kicks and movements to a sound, music, a touch on the belly, or other motions.

setting yourself up for total burnout, and, instead of proving your hardcore loyalty, will demonstrate your ability to fall asleep with your nose in a coffee cup.

How much time should you plan to take off after you give birth? How about *as much as you can get away with.* It's unlikely you'll ever kick yourself and say, "I should've gone to work for those 6 months!" Don't plan to work from home, either, unless you have a babysitter.

Taking time to bond with your baby and meet her needs during those first months will make her more independent later on, and that translates into a baby who is more capable of independent sleep, too. And on the biological front, the older she is, the more consolidated and predictable her clusters of sleep will become. All newborns wake up multiple times at night, but

> *"It seems like she rarely sleeps in utero; sometimes at night, but generally she's awake. Like, all the time. One night I lay on my side and snuggled up to my husband and he said she was keeping him awake! Him! Most people ask me if she's most active at night. No, she's active all the time."*
>
> —Heather H.

by 9 months, 70 percent of babies sleep through the night.

And, while sending a 6-week-old to day care is usually expensive and emotionally difficult, it becomes more manageable on both fronts the older your baby is. Once she gets to be 9 months to a year, she'll start pulling up, cruising around, and grabbing whatever she can reach and sticking whatever-it-is into her mouth. By that point, the structured naps that day care provides (not to mention all the new toys and the change of scenery) might turn out to be just the thing to help everyone sleep better.

In the meantime, can you simplify your lifestyle? (It's not worth it to have an extra family car if you're just going to get sleep-deprived and drive it into a ditch.)

Could you work fewer hours or take extra time off without pay?

What might happen if you straight-out quit your job and looked for another one later?

What if your husband or partner took leave when it was time for you to go back to work?

You don't need to make any of the big decisions right this minute, but do read the section on adult sleep deprivation (page 90) to get a realistic sense of what you'll be facing. The longer you can wait to go back to work, the more sleep you will get because a baby's ability to sleep through the night takes time to develop.

DON'T GO CRAZY OUTFITTING BABY'S BOUDOIR

When it comes to furnishing your baby's bedroom, less is more. In fact, we'd go so far as to advise you not to even buy a crib while you're pregnant. You read it right: You don't need to run out and get one. The American Academy of Pediatrics recommends that babies sleep in their parents' room for the first few months.

You may also find out, after your baby is born, that your equipment needs are different from what you anticipated. Your baby may have reflux, for instance, and be better soothed by a hammock-style crib than a more conventional one. Or someone may offer to give you a crib. You may also come across a great used crib.

Safety Tips for Used Cribs

A sturdy used crib may be an economical alternative to buying, but only if it has the following:

- **Fresh mattress.** Replace the used mattress with a new, very firm one so your baby isn't exposed to mold or corrosion on the surface of the mattress.

- **Directions.** Make sure that the crib still has the assembly directions—and follow them to the letter.

- **Intact hardware.** Check that all the original screws and mattress support hardware are there and in perfect condition.

- **Perfect condition.** Test that all the crib's parts are in perfect working order—that the bars, teething rail, and endboards are solid and no part has been rigged or glued back together.

- **No recall.** Check www.recalls.gov and know for certain that the particular crib model has not been recalled for dangerous flaws.

- **Proper storage.** Make sure the crib has been kept somewhere climate-controlled, not in an attic or garage where temperature and humidity changes could have caused the wood to warp and hardware or glues to corrode.

As for all the baby-bedroom furniture, keep in mind that anything beyond the basics is really for you, not the baby. The baby will not care one whit if she has a hand-painted mural of Paris on her wall, or a miniature leather chair, or curtains that match the diaper keeper. If you want to give your child the gift of interior design, put that money in the bank and wait until she's old enough to help you pick things out herself! (For more about cribs, see page 51.)

REST, REST, REST

A lot of moms-to-be try to work all the way up until their due date to maximize their allotted leave after the baby is born. That's a personal choice, but do keep in mind that in the last month of your pregnancy your sleep cycle will begin to synch with that of your baby-to-be (plus, getting comfortable gets more difficult the larger your belly is), so you may be sleeping in stretches that are just a couple of hours long. When you're pregnant, you should never feel guilty about taking a nap!

DON'T LISTEN TO THE "SHOULDS"

When it comes to sleep, you'll find that (1) everyone, even people who don't have kids, will think that they know when, where, and how

If You're Pregnant and Working

- Know your rights under the law.
- Extend your maternity leave as long as you can.
- Talk to your boss, or whoever's in charge of vacation and sick time at work, about your options while you're still pregnant.

FIND OUT IF YOU CAN:

- Take more time off without pay and still keep your position.
- Find someone to fill in temporarily.
- Return part-time and still retain your health insurance.

your baby ought to be sleeping, and (2) even doctors and pediatric sleep experts have vastly different opinions about what ought to be happening in the family bedroom at night.

As you prepare to embark on the various controversies of your parenting career, make it a habit to learn the facts, respect the individuality of your child and your family, and not get caught up in all of the "shoulds" and "supposed tos," as in "He should be sleeping through the night by now!" "He shouldn't need a pacifier to get to sleep!" "He's supposed to nap for a half hour every 3 hours!"

Not only do these rigid "shoulds" undermine your confidence as a parent, but they can actually cause sleep and behavioral problems if you take them so seriously that you stop looking and listening to your baby's cues and start trying to follow an externally imposed regimen.

Yes, this book is chock-full of all sorts of statistics having to do with what *most* babies are doing—where they sleep, how often they feed, how often they wake up at night—but as you'll soon find out, there is a wide range of normal and healthy behavior.

Some 1-year-olds will still wake up at night. For those individual toddlers, that *is* normal and healthy behavior. Waking up doesn't mean that a baby or child is emotionally or physically immature, or that if parents don't start implementing some sort of behavioral modification program their child will never learn to sleep through the night on her own. Sure, there are things you can do to help a baby sleep longer, but like so much in life there are costs and benefits, and you and your family are the only ones qualified to decide if a particular course of action—or inaction—is worth it. What parents expect from a baby in terms of sleep often has less to do with biology than what they hear from other parents.

The reality is, during the first year, a baby's sleep needs will be constantly evolving as her hormonal cycles develop in response to the environment. She will need to sleep every 2 to 3 hours for the first few months, and will spend a lot of that time in a half-awake state, nursing or sipping a bottle and going ballistic if someone tries to put her down.

Developing an independent, all-night sleep routine is not an "overnight" process for babies, who are born preprogrammed with a drive to be physically attached to a parent for every conscious moment, and needing to feed every 2 to 4 hours. Over time, as babies grow, they become able to sleep in longer stretches. But in the meantime, a baby's needs can leave parents having to choose at 4 a.m. between putting the baby down in a crib to cry until she finally passes out, only to wake up again 2 hours later; to stay awake holding the baby in a rocking chair for much of the day or night; or to go against the advice of most pediatricians and bring the baby into bed, or have dad or someone else give the baby formula. These are rough choices, and there's little consensus to be found about what the "right" way is. What is right for one family may not be right for another.

The good news is that after 6 months, as solids gradually become a greater chunk of her diet, your baby will become ever more capable of longer stretches of sleep. With help from both parents, she will be able to develop healthy sleep habits for a lifetime, and that means quality sleep for parents, too.

Newborns in "The Fourth Trimester"

Understanding Your Baby's Sleep Cycle

You can expect your newborn to get 13 to 16 hours of sleep within a 24-hour period, with 6½ to 8 hours of 45-minute to 3-hour naps throughout the day and night. It takes 5 to 25 weeks for a baby to establish a day-night pattern of sleep and wakefulness.

Of all the mammals on earth, humans are born the least developed, with only one-quarter of the brain volume of an adult. The human brain is huge compared to other animals, but the pelvis through which human babies are born is relatively narrow. This means that humans have to finish their gestation after birth.

Neurologically and biologically, a newborn is not very different from a fetus. The first 90 days or so of a baby's life serve as kind of a "fourth trimester." Your newborn is, after all, the same person who was kicking inside you just a little while ago. Although he is now outside your body, he really isn't a separate individual—not yet. He can't communicate except with cries, and is totally helpless to protect himself from predators, dogs, children, and neighborhood busybodies; his caregivers are his only defense. Unlike most animals, he could hardly survive a day were he left to fend for himself.

The most important thing to know about your newborn's sleep cycle is that it is based on the need to feed. Once he is born, your baby will continue to develop at the rapid pace he did while he was inside you. Though he's now separated from the all-nurturing placenta and umbilical cord that kept him alive during the third trimester, he is still following the rhythm he experienced in the womb and requires feedings around the clock to keep his body and brain running at top efficiency.

Your newborn will come equipped with a high-performance, milk-guzzling engine, but a fuel tank that's only the size of a walnut. While an adult's sleep/wake cycles operate within a 24-hour time frame, or a little longer,[1] depending on the individual and on factors such as exposure to artificial light and cappuccinos, your baby's

Average Daily Feedings

Bottle-fed babies: Seven feeding sessions every 24 hours until 2 months, then usually three to five times a day after that. (The general recommendation is that infants consume 2½ ounces of formula per pound of body weight each day.)

Breastfed babies: Eight to twelve feeding sessions, every 2 to 4 hours, out of every 24 hours during the first year.

sleep/wake patterns will occur in a 90-minute framework, mirroring his need for almost continuous nourishment.[2] It is *not* a sign of maturity if a days-old baby is able to sleep for 4- or 5-hour stretches a night: If your newborn doesn't wake up at least every 4 hours, it's actually a *bad* sign. He may not be receiving sufficient nourishment, and you ought to wake him up for feedings. Your baby's stomach is simply too tiny to hold enough milk to meet his body's nutritional needs for any longer than that.

The second most important thing to know about your baby's sleep cycle is that breastfed and formula-fed babies sleep differently.

In a 24-hour cycle, healthy, full-term newborns sleep an average of 15 hours of every 24. Premature infants born at 32 weeks post-conception will sleep about 18 hours out of 24, and if your baby was born at 37 weeks, you can expect an average of 15 hours and 15 minutes of total sleep per day,[3] but, again, these are simply estimates and every baby is unique.

Soon after birth, though, formula-fed and breastfed infants begin to develop very different sleep cycles. Every baby's individual sleep needs are slightly different, but formula-fed babies on average begin to sleep in longer stretches.

By 1 year of age, the average formula-fed baby will sleep about 1½ to 2 hours *more* out of every 24 hours, in stretches that are more than twice as long as breastfed babies, on average. This is probably because a baby's body must work harder to get nutrients from

formula, and formula also stretches the baby's stomach and increases its capacity.

If you're combining breastmilk and formula, figuring out how much to feed your baby, and how long you can expect your baby to sleep, becomes a little bit more complicated. There simply haven't been enough studies that combine the two feeding methods to come up with any conclusions about how they affect infant sleep. Also, once formula is introduced into your baby's diet, the weaning process begins. Your baby's stomach will stretch to accommodate the formula, and your breastmilk production will slow down in response to feeding your baby less frequently.

If you plan to combine breast and formula feeding, give your baby no more than one bottle of formula every 24 hours to prevent a decrease in your milk production. Wait until your baby is 3 to 4 weeks old and breastfeeding is well established before introducing the first bottle. Then, pump when you bottle-feed if you do not want to risk a reduction in milk supply.

How Your Baby's Brain Is Different from Yours

Our daily sleep/wake cycle, the circadian rhythm, is a combination of Latin words that mean "around the day." Generally, it takes between 5 and 25 weeks for a baby to begin to establish a 24-hour circadian pattern of sleep and wakefulness.

Circadian rhythms are controlled by the **hypothalamus,** a gland that is smaller than the size of an almond, which is located deep in the center of the brain behind the eyes. This important gland serves as the commander of your biological clock and is responsible for maintaining daily body cycles based on environmental cues, such as light, temperature changes sensed by nerves in the skin, and odor.

Sleep cycles can also be influenced by internal body cues, such as fatigue. The gland's operation can also be affected by medications that artificially induce sleep or provoke alertness. Research appears to show that exposure to natural light and dark can help cue a baby's day-night sleep and wake rhythms; some animal studies seem to show that mothers play a strong role in providing babies with cues about when to sleep and when to be awake.

The power of the circadian control system inside an adult's brain can easily be demonstrated by the phenomenon of jet lag, when the body's circadian rhythms are disrupted by traveling across one or more time zones, which can result in insomnia or overtiredness, a feeling of malaise, and problems with simple daytime tasks, such as efficient decision making.[4]

Newborns, on the other hand, don't have this established rhythm, and their sleep patterns are different because the entire structure and chemistry of their brains are different from an adult's, and even from an older baby's. A newborn is basically a blank slate when it comes to sleep, and he is ready to adapt to the sleep/wake cycles of the environment he is born into.

Your baby's brain will continue to forge some 1,000 trillion neural connections over the next 2 years. A human brain, already huge at birth compared to other animals' brains, will more than double its weight during the first 12 months after birth. As a newborn, his brain is only about one-fourth the weight of an adult's, but it will grow to 60 percent the size of an adult brain by his first birthday.

Sleep serves a vital role in brain growth for fetuses, infants, and

Dehydration Danger

It's perfectly normal and healthy for newborns to have very erratic sleeping patterns. Sleeping too much, though, could signal a more serious medical concern. Be particularly concerned if your newborn sleeps for more than 4 hours in a row and seems difficult to rouse.

Excessive sluggishness could be caused by dehydration, which can be due to feeding problems or a fever. This can be serious and even deadly for newborns. If your baby has not wet a diaper in the past several hours and has slept for longer than 4 hours in a row, and is difficult to rouse, contact your pediatrician immediately.

What Happens During Baby Sleep?

- Cells in your baby's body and brain multiply rapidly, and growth hormones are stimulated.
- Connections are built between brain cells.
- Calories from milk convert into energy and build body and muscle tissue.
- White blood cells are produced to help the immune system fight infection.

grown-ups, too. Aside from feeding and dirtying diapers, the most important job your baby has during his first 3 months of life is to grow brain cells and build connections between his neurons and synapses. Researchers theorize that a baby's brain, just like his eyes, must stay continuously active to grow.

Newborn sleep is far from a passive state, and a newborn's awake and sleeping states may look a lot alike. A newborn often feeds in marathon sessions for what can seem like hours, opening his eyes to look around from time to time, then nursing some more, then closing his eyes again, cycling back and forth between semi-consciousness and sleep. A sleeping newborn can be clinically asleep but still have half-open eyes, fluttering eyelashes, and twitchy muscles, and can make a cacophony of grunts and squeaks.

This awake-sleeping/sleepy-awakeness is the result of the newborn brain not going through the same daily stimulating and sedating hormonal cycles that adults or toddlers experience. Two critical hormones in the sleep/wake cycle, **melatonin** and **cortisol,** have not yet started to flow in a consistent daily rhythm, as they will later on.

Melatonin, the light-sensitive "sleep" hormone, doesn't kick in until about 4 months of age. Cortisol, the "stress" hormone that increases blood pressure and blood sugar and that jump-starts children and adults at wake-up time, doesn't begin its daily rhythmic work until some point between 2 weeks and 9 months.[5] (See page 100 for more on melatonin.)

During this formative stage, your baby's experiences will have a strong effect on his brain. Bonding and interactive experiences, such as being held by you, hearing your voice (as well as those of others), and being soothed and rocked, can actually make permanent changes to the structure and chemistry of his brain. Babies who are deprived of exposure to human language have delayed speech and difficulties mastering the intricacies of language later on, even if they have the right physical equipment for speaking.

Formula feeding also causes neurological changes, due to differences in nutritional content between formula and breastmilk and also possibly because the effort required to digest formula promotes deeper and longer sleep bouts, giving your baby less time each day to interact in the waking world.

A Closer Look at Adult Sleep

In contrast to a newborn's changeable sleep states, the brains and bodies of adults predictably travel through five stages of sleep for every 90- to 110-minute sleep episode. Each stage has its own muscle tone, eye movements, brain waves, and changes in electrical current in the brain.

During the earliest phase of sleep, you are still relatively awake and alert. If you were connected to a brainwave machine, others would observe that your brain was making small, fast beta waves, as shown on a video screen or by a pen jiggling up and down on a roll of graph paper.

As your brain begins to relax and slow down, slower wave patterns, known as alpha waves, begin. Although you are not fully asleep, you may experience strange and extremely vivid sensations, known as **hypnagogic hallucinations**. For example, as a kind of sleep paralysis

Newborn Sleep

- **The feeding drive.** A breastfed newborn may need to feed multiple times—even constantly—in a waking hour. A formula-fed newborn will need to feed about every 3 hours.

- **Changeable states.** Newborns enter deep sleep more rapidly than children or adults.

- **Different hormones.** Newborn babies don't have the same daily hormonal patterns and fluctuations that older babies or adults have.

- **No day/night patterns.** A newborn typically sleeps as much at night as during the day.

- **The mom connection.** Newborns aren't aware that they are separate individuals from their mothers and show signs of distress when separated from their mothers for more than brief periods.

- **The need for rapid response.** Responding immediately to a newborn's cries will shorten the amount of time it takes to soothe him.

- **Sleep "training" can harm.** Sleep training or attempting to enforce strict sleep schedules on a newborn isn't helpful, and can actually harm your baby, possibly even to an **apparent life-threatening event,** if it stresses his body's coping resources or deprives him of desperately needed fluids and nutrition.

Grown-up Naps

Adults in most parts of the world sleep once during a daylong cycle, although many countries in warmer climates have a traditional rest in the heat of the day. In some cultures, such as the Efe of Zaire and the !Kung of Botswana, it's not unusual for people to sleep in three or four episodes over the course of a day.

begins to set in, you might suddenly imagine yourself falling, experience the sensation of earthquake tremors, hear sounds that startle you, or notice your body making involuntary, jerking movements.

Next comes *stage 1 sleep*, which is real sleep, or light sleep. These brain waves are called theta waves. They look distinctly different from alpha waves and are much slower. This stage only lasts a very brief time, around 5 to 10 minutes, during which you may not be aware that you are asleep, even if someone awakens you.

Then *stage 2 sleep* arrives, a deeper form of light sleep. This phase accounts for about 50 percent of an adult's sleep on any given night. Your brain will produce bursts of rapid, rhythmic brain waves called sleep spindles. Your breathing and heart rate will slow down and your body temperature will also go down.

During *stage 3 and stage 4 sleep*, you will move from light sleep into very deep sleep and your brain will produce slow waves known as delta waves. Stage 3 and stage 4 sleep set in after you've been asleep for about 30 minutes, and each stage lasts about 15 to 30 minutes. These are the deepest

levels of sleep and can be identified by the slowest brain waves.

It is during these two stages (stages 3 and 4) that growth hormone secretions are at their highest. This is when your body goes to work to repair itself from the wear and tear of the day. Body temperature, heart rate, and blood pressure decrease, muscles relax, and the body's metabolism—its burning of fuel—slows down. During these stages you will be the most sluggish and hard to wake up.

Finally comes *stage 5*, or **REM (Rapid Eye Movement) sleep**. This particular sleep stage is remarkably different from all previous stages. Sometimes this stage of sleep is referred to as *paradoxical sleep* because your muscles become more relaxed, even paralyzed, while at the same time all your other body systems are busily at work, with your brain and internal body operations as active as if you were awake. Your eyes dart back and forth beneath your closed eyelids. You breathe faster, your heart rate speeds up, and your blood pressure rises as your brain actively repairs itself, and as the connections for language are being forged.

All five of these stages repeat themselves approximately five or six times a night, but they don't always progress in a direct 1-to-5 sequence. Typically, sleep will start in stage 1 and then progress to deeper stages 2, 3, and 4, but then cycle back to lighter but longer stages 3 and 2 before entering REM sleep. Once a cycle of REM sleep has completed, the body will revert to lighter stage 2 sleep. Earlier stages repeat themselves approximately four to five times a night. Hard work!

To Sleep, Perchance to Dream

When it comes to comparing grown-up and baby sleep, the most active form of sleep—stage 5 or REM sleep—is the most important cycle to know about. Brain growth and body repair in babies and adults occurs during this stage, along with active dreaming.

During dream cycles, body metabolism fluctuates. Heart rate, blood pressure, hormonal secretions, and many other functions seem to go along with the events that are shown on your internal movie screen—your dreams.

Even though you will not remember *all of* them, you will undergo four or five periods of REM sleep every night with the length of REM episodes getting longer as the night goes on. Dreams for grown-ups can last anywhere from 11 to 25 minutes. Some superficial dreams can occur during other stages of sleep, but REM dreams are the memorable ones, the going-to-school-in-your-underwear type of episodes.

It's also thought that dreams are one way the brain files away the lessons and experiences of the day; another explanation is that REM dreams serve as a "screen saver"—the way a bored brain entertains itself while interior growth and repair work are in progress.

The jury is still out on whether dreams have important prophetic or symbolic significance or have some other deeply meaningful function in helping us to understand human predicaments.

Adults' Waking Body Changes

When you're awake, your heart rate, blood pressure, core body temperature, and hormonal output vary depending on the time of day and your activity level. Your lowest temperature occurs in the deepest stages of sleep. Generally, as people's core body temperature goes down and they get colder during wakefulness, they get sleepier, and when it goes up, they become more alert.

Your Baby's Sleep Cycles

Scientists have narrowed down newborn sleep to two primary sleep stages: quiet, or light, sleep and active (REM) sleep.

A newborn will become drowsy and spend about 10 to 20 minutes in light sleep, and then sink into REM sleep for another 20 to 30 minutes at a time. During those first 20 minutes of sleep, your baby will likely appear to be dozing soundly. He will look relaxed, his eyelids will be shut, but, as you will soon discover, if you jar him or try to lower him down into his crib, he's likely to startle, awaken, and start crying.

While grown-ups spend about one-fourth of their nights in active REM sleep, babies spend nearly half their sleeping lives in this highly active state. Premature babies may spend as much as 80 percent of their sleeping time in REM. Over the course of your baby's first year, the proportion of time he spends in REM sleep compared to other stages of sleep will change, with REM sleep decreasing and the time spent in quiet sleep increasing.

In the REM sleep stage, your baby's eyes will show the typical back-and-forth movements associated with dreaming. He may also snuffle, cry, move, and make sucking motions with his lips. At times, his eyelids may be weirdly half open, with only the whites showing, like an extra in an old zombie movie. With older children and adults, unless someone has a sleep disorder like **night terrors** or sleepwalking, muscle impulses go into a state of paralysis during sleep. But in infants, some thrashing and jerking is normal during the REM phase.

REM sleep isn't simply about falling off into dreamland—it also plays a critical role in how well we function during waking hours. For both adults and babies, brain connections are actively created during REM. Adults who are deprived of sleep, especially REM sleep, are apt to perform poorly on memory tests compared to people who have had sufficient REM sleep. And when babies and toddlers are chronically deprived of their REM sleep over a long period of time, behavioral problems, permanent sleep disruption, and even decreased brain size can result.

Sleep-deprivation studies show that REM sleep plays a key role in something called procedural

Breastfeeding and Baby Sleep

Breastfed babies awaken more readily than formula-fed babies do. This may be a reason why breastfed babies are less at risk than formula-fed babies of dying from sudden infant death syndrome (SIDS). (For more on SIDS, see page 71.)

Citalopram (Celexa®). Reported cases of excessive sleepiness, decreased feeding, and weight loss in infants.

Clemastone (Tavist®). May cause drowsiness, irritability, and loss of appetite in infants.

Codeine. Potentially sedating in high doses.

Diazepam (Valium®). Lethargy, sedation, and poor feeding have been reported.

Diphenhydramine (Benadryl®). May cause sedation in an infant; and there have been reports of reduced milk supply.

Doxepin (Adapin®, Sinequan®, Zonalon®). Taken orally as an antidepressant or applied to skin to control itching—either way can cause dangerous sedation and poor sucking and swallowing.

Doxylamine succinate (Unisom® Nighttime). May cause sedation.

Heroin. May cause tremors, vomiting, poor feeding.

Hydrocodone (Vicodin®). May cause sedation, apnea, and/or constipation.

Nefazodone HCL (Serzone®). May cause drowsiness, lethargy, and failure to thrive.[6]

Smoking, Breastfeeding, and Baby Sleep

Not only does smoking significantly increase a baby's risk of dying from SIDS, it also affects a baby's sleep patterns. A 2007 study published in *Pediatrics* found that babies who nursed immediately after their mothers smoked slept an average of 54 minutes, while those whose mothers had abstained from smoking immediately prior to breastfeeding slept about 85 minutes. Nicotine and chemicals in cigarettes were found to affect both the babies' quiet sleep cycles, but REM sleep was affected the most, and this is the period when the most brain growth happens.[7] This could be one reason why children of smoking moms score lower on intelligence tests.[8]

Baby Wake Cycles

Not only is it important to understand how babies sleep; you need to know about their wake cycles, too, which can help you become a more effective baby manager. While babies basically have two sleep states—deep sleep and light sleep—their waking can be divided into four separate states: drowsy, quiet alert, active alert, and crying. This brief primer should help you decipher awake-baby cues:

A drowsy baby has heavy eyelids, breathes irregularly, and may startle occasionally. There are two basic options for handling the drowsy state: If you want your baby to go back to sleep, keep things quiet, don't stimulate him, and don't make any sudden movements. On the other hand, if you want to rouse your baby, perhaps because he's due for a feeding or needs a diaper change, then you can stimulate him by picking him up, talking to him, or gently rubbing his back or tummy, which will wake him up, at least temporarily.

In the *quiet alert* state, your baby will be calm and have wide-open eyes. Unless he is very premature or underwent a stressful birth, he will have his first quiet alert state outside the womb during the first hour or two after birth. In the quiet alert state, your baby's body will be still, his breathing will be regular, and he may make eye contact with you or fixate on some object or place in the room.

The quiet alert time gives you an excellent opportunity to talk to your baby, hold him close, snap some pictures, or just quietly let him look around and take in his new world. (If your baby is preterm, he may not be sufficiently mature to sustain a quiet alert state or interact visually quite yet.)

In contrast to the calm cuteness of the quiet alert state, the *active alert* state is what parents quickly learn to recognize as the "starting-to-get-fussy" stage. Your baby will become squirmy and restless and will appear less attentive. This happens when one or more of your baby's needs are not being met. It could be that he wants food, a diaper change, or comforting. If he's still fussy and unsettled, try rocking, soothing, swaddling, or changing his environment.

If your baby goes into active alert when he's in a room with too much noise or too many people, you need to intervene, because if he isn't comforted or fed during the active alert state, he'll soon enter the fourth state on the list: *crying*. A crying baby is trying to tell you that he's reached his limits: He's hungry, tired, uncomfortable, or had enough stimulation.

It Pays to Answer Promptly

As you will soon learn, it's much easier to prevent crying by intervening when your baby begins to reach a fussy, active alert state than it is to stop a crying jag once it's underway. Studies have shown that the longer you wait to answer your baby's cries, the longer it will take to soothe him.

The critical cutoff point for answering a baby's cries appears to be a mere minute and a half! If it takes a caregiver longer than that to respond, then the amount of time required to quiet him begins to multiply. Researchers found that when a response was delayed, it took between three and fifty times as long to quiet the baby again.

Also, Johns Hopkins researchers found that babies whose caregivers responded quickly to their cries during the first few months after birth cried less often and for shorter periods of time in later months, too. Instead of becoming clingy or demanding toddlers, they were more likely to demonstrate age-appropriate maturity,[9] perhaps because they learned to develop communication skills other than screaming to have their needs met.

Decoding Your Baby's Cries

For the first month, your baby's cries will sound similar no matter what's wrong—"tired," "gassy," "hungry," "bored of sitting in my car seat," and "this shirt has a scratchy seam" all sound exactly alike. Most parents use the context in which their babies are crying to help them decipher what the baby is trying to convey; for instance, "I'm tired" cries are easiest to interpret if you know your baby hasn't slept in a while.

Soon, however, your baby's cries and vocalizations will begin to sound different to you, and you'll be better able to tell what they mean. For instance, you may notice that when your baby is hungry he'll make a sound like "eh, eh." A cry of pain will be more high-pitched and intense, and your baby may be saying "I'm tired" when his cries have a lower pitch.

If your baby is fussy and starting on the downward slope toward crying, quickly run down the list of potential problems: Is he hungry or tired, is his diaper dirty, is it too noisy, is he over-stimulated? If none of these is the likely problem, then you will need to go through some soothing strategies— trial-and-error style—to see what works.

If your baby is hungry but it's been less than an hour since his last feed, consider that he may not have nursed long enough on a particular side to become satisfied. Make sure that he stays on one side for at least 15 to 20 minutes to get enough nourishment (as he matures, he'll become a more efficient feeder and won't need to nurse as long).

The first milk your baby gets during a nursing session is called **foremilk**, but could be called "skim" milk. It's high in milk sugar (lactose) and low in fat. If you pump milk, you will be able to see the thinner ribbons of fat in the milk become thicker as the pumping session goes on. Only after your baby has nursed for a while does your body supply him with what's called **hindmilk**, the human version of cream. The longer you let him nurse on one side, the more fat he will receive, and fat is an indispensable food for baby brain growth. The cream helps him to feel full and calm, and his nursing will naturally slow down.

If your newborn is bottle feeding, let him establish his own feeding schedule and try not to fret about how many ounces of formula he drinks. Also, check the flow of formula. Make sure bottle nipple holes are not so small that your baby has to strain to get milk, or so large that he chokes.

Some bottle nipples allow you to correct the amount of milk flow by how tightly you screw on the bottle ring. It may help, too, to hold the bottle at an angle to keep air from getting trapped in the nipple. Even with precautions, bottle drinkers usually swallow more air than breastfeeders, so your baby will need to be burped during feeds to relieve his discomfort and to make room for more milk.

The Swaddling Option

If your newborn is crying and you know that hunger isn't the problem, or he seems to be having trouble settling down because the motions of his arms and legs are startling to him, then enfolding him in a "baby burrito" could be just the solution!

Tummy Time

"Tummy time" is when you place your baby onto his stomach during play times to help him strengthen his neck, back, and trunk muscles—an important activity that helps him prepare for crawling and walking. The American Academy of Pediatrics now recommends that babies get at least two or three sessions of tummy time that last three to five minutes every day, with grown-up supervision during waking hours.

Since 1994, the American Academy of Pediatrics has been urging parents to put babies to sleep on their backs to help prevent sudden infant death syndrome (SIDS). Previously, most babies slept on their tummies. Even though placing babies on their backs has succeeded in decreasing SIDS deaths by as much as 40 percent, the position has been linked to delayed motor development, including crawling and walking.

The back-sleeping position has also caused babies to have cranial asymmetry, or a misshapen head. Because babies' skulls are still somewhat soft during the first year, continuous back positioning for babies during sleep can cause the back of the skull to flatten over time.

So, tummy time is important, even for newborns. The good news, though, is that lying awake on a parent's chest in the **prone position** counts. Most newborns far prefer that to being tummy down on a floor or hard surface.

No Feeding Schedule!

The American Academy of Pediatrics (AAP), the World Health Organization (WHO), and La Leche League International (LLLI) all agree: You should feed your baby on demand, and not attempt to put your newborn on any kind of feeding schedule. There have been numerous reports of failure to thrive, poor milk supply, dehydration, involuntary early weaning, and underweight babies as a result of "parent-directed feeding" or harsh "infant management" programs. The AAP stipulates, "Newborns should be nursed whenever they show signs of hunger, such as increased alertness or activity, mouthing, or rooting. Crying is a late indicator of hunger. Newborns should be nursed approximately 8 to 12 times every 24 hours until satiety. In the early weeks after birth, non-demanding babies should be aroused to feed if 4 hours have elapsed since the last nursing."

Swaddling is a soothing method that involves wrapping up your baby in a specific way to restrict the movements of his arms and legs. Many pediatricians believe that babies should only be swaddled for the first month of life. After that, swaddling can inhibit motor development because it restricts arm movement (you'll probably find that your baby begins to resist having his arms restrained around this time anyway). Swaddling is not recommended if you are bed sharing, however, because it may cause him to become overheated, and will also inhibit him from using his arms or legs should bedding cover his face.

Swaddling can also be helpful if your newborn is going to be put down to sleep in a crib or co-sleeper, since babies tend to feel insecure in open spaces.

Commercially made swaddling wraps are available in stores that sell baby products. Most feature a pouch for baby's legs and have Velcro tabs to make the job of swaddling a little easier.

Drowsy But Awake

Should you wait until your baby is completely asleep to put him down, or should you put him down "drowsy but awake"? Some experts are against putting a baby who is sound asleep into a crib because when he wakes up he will be disoriented, not knowing where he is and how he got there, just as you would be if you fell asleep in your bed and woke up in the front yard.

However, waiting until your baby is "drowsy but awake" is a principle that doesn't really apply to most newborns. Biologically, a baby's very survival has always depended on being in close contact with mom, so typically, putting a baby down while he's drowsy but awake will only make him wake up fully and begin to cry in protest.

Not only does the half-awake or half-asleep state promote brain cell growth in newborns, it may also be a survival mechanism that young babies have adapted to keep them from being abandoned. Newborns also depend on adults for much of their temperature regulation. So putting your baby down while he's deeply asleep—and while he's unaware of where he is—may be the only way you can put him down at all!

If you can put your baby down "drowsy but awake," then by all means, do so. But most newborn babies are the no-put-down type, and you will need to wait until he's a little older—between 3 and 6 months of age—before you can put him down without waking him.

One simple trick to tell if your baby is sound asleep is to do the limp-limb test: Pick up his arm and let go. If he's still awake, he'll reflexively pull his elbow in toward his body. But if his arm plops down limply, he's sleeping deeply enough that you may be able to put him down. Make sure you lower him gently, however, so that you don't set off his startle reflex and wake him up.

After you've put down your baby, keep a hand on his belly for a few moments. This will help keep him from being startled by the change in temperature.

Swaddling Baby

1. Fold down one corner of the blanket and place your baby in the middle of it. His shoulders should be in line with the fold and his head should be above the edge of the fold.

2. Put your baby's right arm close to his body, then pull the left side of the blanket snugly across his chest and tuck it beneath his left arm.

3. Fold the bottom of the blanket up and over your baby's feet.

4. Take the left side of the blanket and pull it snugly across your baby's body, then tuck the blanket under him.

Where Should Baby Sleep?

The Great Debate

Even before you bring your baby home from the hospital, you have to make a major decision on your baby's behalf: Where is she going to sleep? In a crib? A bedside sleeper? In your bed? A bassinet in your bedroom? In the family bed at night, but in a bassinet for naps during the day? Where babies are "supposed to" sleep is a raging hot-button topic for expectant and new parents: blogs, message boards, and parenting groups practically burst into flames when this subject comes up.

To vehement pro–bed sharers who believe in bringing their babies into bed with them, crib sleeping approaches child neglect. To the pro-crib camp, bed sharers are indulging in a bad habit that will endanger their babies and their marriages.

The truth is, there are advantages and disadvantages to every type of baby sleeping arrangement, and your relationship to your baby is not going to be made or broken based on where you choose to put her to sleep.

In this chapter, we look at all the different places where babies can sleep, and the pros and cons of each. We'll start with bed sharing, the world's oldest baby sleep arrangement, discuss crib sleeping, then co-sleeping, and finally, the "buffet" in which baby sleeps in multiple places. We will then discuss specific sleep-related products and how to shop for them, from cribs and bassinets to night-lights and rockers.

WHERE DO MOST BABIES SLEEP?

According to the National Sleep Foundation's Sleep in America poll, about 60 percent of infants under the age of 1 sleep most of the night alone in their own rooms, 24 percent sleep in a parent's room but in their own bed, and about 12 percent sleep in their parents' bed.[1]

An Informal Survey

We posed the question, "Where does the baby sleep?" on the bulletin board of a popular parenting Web site,[2] and found the response revealing: Parents use a surprisingly wide variety of sleeping arrangements for their babies, such as:

- **Crib.** "Our daughter slept in the crib as soon as we got home from the hospital. It has never been a problem for us. She's 10 months old now and still sleeping well in her crib."

- **Crib and bassinet to crib.** "My first child slept in a crib and had no problems. My second child slept in a bassinet for a couple of months in my room and then went to a crib. I think it all depends on the child."

- **Crib, swing, parents' bed, car seat, crib.** "For my first child I was determined that she sleep in her crib from day one. That started a yearlong sleep battle as she was not a big fan of the crib. She spent most of her day asleep in her swing. For my second I was much too tired to battle the issue. I tried a bassinet, which he hated. So he alternated sleeping in my bed and sleeping in his car seat on the floor next to my bed. At about 4 months old he became a very squirmy sleeper and none of us could sleep in bed at night. When I would wake up I would find him asleep under my bed as he had slid under there from his car seat. My pediatrician suggested the crib at that point. It took a few nights but he has been comfortable there ever since."

- **Bedside co-sleeper, crib.** "My now 9-month-old daughter slept in a co-sleeper next to me until she was 16 weeks and then we moved her into her crib. Prior to 16 weeks, she would never nap in her crib and I was very worried that we were going to have a fight on our hands. She made the transition like a champ, though."

- **Bassinet, portable crib, and parents' bed.** "All three of my kids started out in a bassinet or portable crib next to the bed. When they were nursing in the night I would bring them into the bed with us."

- **Bassinet, portable crib, car seat, crib.** "We started with my son in the bassinet, but he was 9 pounds when he was born, so he only got to stay in the bassinet until he was about a month, I think. We then started putting him in his portable play yard

to sleep. I know that sounds strange, but my husband and I took sleeping shifts. Once Dave got home from work at about 5 we'd eat dinner and then I'd nurse the baby. By about 7 I'd go to bed. My husband would feed the baby expressed milk at about 10 and wake me up at 12 or 1 for the next feeding and we'd switch. Needless to say he was very sleep deprived since he left for work at 6:30 a.m. and I wanted to give him as much peace during his sleep as possible. So I slept on our couch next to the playpen until morning. It's a VERY comfortable couch. My son was also a marathon eater and would nurse for 20–30 minutes at a time. Being in front of the TV was nice for me, and I was able to hear him breathe all night, which gave me peace of mind. Oh, I forgot, we had a 2-week period in there somewhere where he slept in his car seat, I think at about a month old. He had a really nasty cold, and the doctor said it would help him breathe easier. Shortly after 2½ months, he started sleeping through the night (I know I'm really lucky), and we put him in the crib."

- **Parents' bed.** "Our son has slept in our bed from day one . . . and still does at 20 months!"

- **Parents' bed, crib.** "My child slept with me. When he was first born we lived in a one-bedroom apartment. Because my husband had to get up early to go to work, I put him in bed with us instead of fussing and waking everyone up. Then we moved when our baby was 10 months old and he got his own room."

- **Parents' bed, bouncy seat, and crib.** "We set up a bassinet next to our bed for my daughter and I think she slept there for about 10 seconds. She was just one of those babies who needed to be more secure, so she slept in my arms in our bed for about 2 months . . . She napped well in a bouncy seat, so she slept in the bouncy seat, at the foot of our bed, for about a month, and slowly we moved the chair from our room into her room at the foot of her crib. I think she was about 4 months when she finally slept alone in her crib."

- **Parents' bed, portable play yard.** "Our 4-month-old feeds in bed, then we move him to a play yard in our room, but somehow we always wake up with him in our bed in the morning."

From the variety of responses, it's clear that the bed sharing versus co-sleeping versus crib sleeping debate isn't necessarily black-and-white. Many babies start out sleeping in one location and then end up somewhere else. Some babies even prefer to sleep in unusual places such as car seats, swings, or bouncy chairs. As long as your baby is properly attended and her sleep spot is safe, there's nothing wrong with letting her sleep somewhere unusual in the short term, although cushy surfaces, such as couches, waterbeds, and beanbag chairs, can pose a suffocation risk.

In fact, some parents find it helpful to have more than one baby sleep spot—for example, if you're bed sharing, it isn't safe to leave your baby alone in an adult bed, so it makes sense to provide her with a different daytime nap spot.

Bed Sharing: The World's Oldest Sleeping Arrangement

A mother sharing a bed with her baby is the most common sleeping arrangement in most of the world, but in the United States, Canada, and Western Europe it is not the norm. As recently as a century ago in the United States, however, it wasn't considered unusual for parents to share their bed with an infant—or the rest of the family, for that matter. Only very rich families could afford homes with private quarters for everyone. Back in the old days, before central heating was widely available, parents slept in the same bed with babies, older siblings slept in the same bed with each other, and family members shared bedrooms to stay warm and conserve heat.

During the post–World War II construction boom, bigger houses were built, and private bedrooms became accessible to every family member in America's fast-growing middle class. Having a separate bedroom for baby became a status symbol and bed sharing or co-sleeping was associated with poverty.

SLEEPING SAFELY

Where you decide to lay your baby down is a personal decision, but some spots are safer than others, and every location has potential safety issues that you should be aware of.

Here's a list of the many places for baby to sleep—including some of the more unusual ones—with a brief summary of the potential safety risks involved. For any used baby products that you plan to use—cribs, co-sleepers, high chairs, and even toys—it's important to check the Web site of the Consumer Protection Safety Commission (CPSC) at www.cpsc.gov for recalls and safety warnings.

BED TYPE	SAFETY ISSUES	COMMENTS
Bassinet	• Soft mattress can create SIDS hazard (see page 71). • There should be no gaps between mattress and sides. • Legs should be sturdy with no risk of collapse. • Unlike full-size cribs, no current safety standards.	Compared to a full-size crib, a bassinet conserves space. Wheels make it easy to move around in cramped bedrooms. Use only a unit that has an extra-firm mattress that fits flush on all sides. Use only the correct size fitted sheets to cover the mattress to prevent bunching and possible entrapment.
Bedside sleeper	• Gaps between adult mattress and co-sleeper potentially create an entrapment hazard. • Any gaps inside the sleeper could capture baby's head, neck, or limbs.	Bedside co-sleepers have to be strapped under the mattress of the adult bed, so parents can't exit the side of the bed where the co-sleeper is secured.
Bouncy seat	• Should never be placed on a table or other high surface, due to risk of seat falling to the floor with baby inside. • Loose straps can pose a strangulation hazard.	Safest when used on the floor, but that may leave baby vulnerable to harassment by pets or young siblings. Units that rock or offer vibration may help soothe the baby.

BED TYPE	SAFETY ISSUES	COMMENTS
Car seat	• Should never be placed on a table or other high surface, due to risk of the heavy seat falling to the floor, entrapping baby inside. • Shoulder straps should be adjusted to fit securely.	Heavy to move in and out of the house. Offers the right angle for small babies, and straps can help to hold the baby in place. Be cautious about adding any extra padding around baby's head.
Crib	• Older cribs can be killers when components fail, such as bars coming loose or when the mattress support breaks.	Usually too large to be rolled out of the room once it's installed. Newborns don't need that much room!
Non-full-size crib	• Soft mattresses, gaps, and lack of air circulation can pose SIDS hazard (see page 71).	Of all the baby beds in the "miniature" category, this is the safest and sturdiest, since it's covered by stringent federal regulations. Small enough to roll through doorways. Folds for storage in closet or pcar trunk.
Parents' bed	• Soft bedding and sheets may pose SIDS or strangulation risk. • Risk of falling out of bed. • Risk of overlaying by parents. • Poses entrapment hazards.	The age-old way that babies and parents have slept (and still do in 90% of the world). Improve your baby's safety by removing the mattress from the bed frame and springs and put it on the floor to reduce falling and entrapment risks. Keep baby away from the edges of the mattress and keep pillows, sheets, and blankets away from the baby's face.

BED TYPE	SAFETY ISSUES	COMMENTS
Portable play yard	• Mattresses are covered in a non-porous fabric that could affect the baby's breathing if she's in a facedown position. • Children playing inside the unit can dislodge add-on bassinets that fasten to the rim of the main play yard, and baby could roll out. • Folding mechanisms may fail, raising the risk of entrapping and injuring the baby.	Make sure all bars are in the locked, fixed position before using. Place baby faceup in the bed portion of the play yard, rather than in smaller, detachable bassinet unit, even though it is deeper and less convenient for putting the baby into it and lifting her out. For cleanliness, we recommend a play yard that accommodates fitted sheets.
Hammock or motion bed	• Avoid units with soft or poorly fitting mattresses or pleats. • Some hammock models have been recalled.	The soft, semi-upright angle of these beds may help babies with GER (gastroesophageal reflux), and the gentle swinging and swaying motions may be more soothing and comfortable for the baby than flat, hard surfaces

Having baby sleep alone also reflected the conventional parenting wisdom of the post-war era, which was based on the popular psychological theories of the time. Too much affection and intimacy was thought to "spoil" babies and spawn overly dependent and clingy children, while keeping emotional and physical distance from one's offspring was thought to toughen them up to face the world.

Promoting solo crib sleeping over the family bed had more to do with cultural and social notions of values and morality than it did with the actual biology of newborns, or evidence-based information on the psychology of children. Now that we know more about the biology of brain development, the evidence is clear that physical and psychological closeness to caregivers makes for more secure, attached, and resilient children and grown-ups.

Today, in the United States, bed sharing with a baby is still generally regarded with great suspicion in some circles. Safety concerns have dominated much of the debate, along with the concern that once a baby gets used to the adult bed, she'll never learn to sleep alone. And, if you're not the bed-sharing type, a baby in bed can put a serious damper on your sex life.

PROMOTING– OR HINDERING– INDEPENDENCE

Some experts have opined that independent sleep fosters self-reliance and confidence, but there has never been a single scientific study that supports that theory.

One study from the University of California at Irvine dealt with the question of bed sharing, co-sleeping, and preschool children's independence and found that children who shared a bed or room with their parents actually became more self-reliant. For instance, they were more able to dress themselves and exhibited more social independence—they were better able to make friends independently than children who had slept in a crib in their own rooms.[3]

It's important to keep in mind, though, when it comes to studies that involve the personality traits of individuals, it's impossible for researchers to take every single variable in a person's life into account to come up with a "pure" result. Maybe the bed-sharing parents were doing so because they were too poor to afford a crib, and that could also explain why their kids grew up to be more self-reliant. Perhaps co-sleeping

parents are more outgoing socially, and their kids are that way, too.

Bottom line: Be wary of anyone who claims that your sleeping choices will determine what kind of personality your child will have

"When I say to a mother or father of a day-old infant, 'we want to help her become independent,' they sometimes look at me. 'Independent? She's only a few hours old.' So I ask, 'Well, when would you start?' That's a question no one can answer, not even the scientists, because we don't know the precise moment when an infant begins to truly comprehend the world or develop the skills she needs to cope with her environment. Therefore I say, start now."

—Tracy Hogg, *Secrets of the Baby Whisperer*[4]

when she grows up, because that's a question no one can credibly answer accurately. There are plenty of healthy, well-adjusted adults who grew up with all sorts of sleeping arrangements.

The Biology of Mother-Baby Night Closeness

Only within the past few decades have scientists begun to study human infancy from the perspective of evolutionary biology, studying the interactions between mothers and infants sleeping together in labs, in hospitals, and at home. The results point to what mothers and babies have known for millions of years: Sleeping together is a natural, normal human behavior, and it offers numerous benefits. For instance, it:

- **Encourages breastfeeding.** A newborn needs to get about half her calories overnight, and at 8 weeks, a baby will still get about ⅓ of her daily calories overnight. Human milk is low in fat and protein and high in sugar to provide energy and stimulate baby brain growth, but those nutritional qualities also mean that it doesn't satiate a baby for very long. Typically, a breastfeeding newborn will feed every 1½ to 2 hours, sometimes less, sometimes more, according to her individual nutritional needs. Having a nursing baby sleep within arm's reach helps

> *"It isn't obvious to me how a baby would develop a robust sense of autonomy while being confined to a small cubicle with bars on the side and rendered powerless to influence its environment. (Nor is it obvious these days, when many kids spend 40 hours a week in day care, that they need extra autonomy training.) I'd be willing to look at the evidence behind this claim, but there isn't any."*
>
> —Robert Wright,
>   *Slate magazine*[5]

to conserve a mother's energy and provides her baby with ready access.

- **Protects against SIDS.** Some research appears to show that bed sharing may have a protective effect. Infants who share a bed with their mothers don't sleep as deeply, and it appears that a mother's exhaled carbon dioxide could stimulate infant respiration.[6]

- **Means better sleep for baby and mom.** Research shows that new babies sleeping alongside their moms tend to synchronize their sleep schedules and cycles with their mothers'.

- **Helps moms recovering from surgery.** Being spared getting in and out of bed is an especially important issue for the moms who have cesarean sections (over 30 percent of Western births are c-section) and spend the first weeks of their baby's life recovering from surgery.

- **Regulates baby body temps.** The physical proximity to a parent helps regulate baby body temperature, and studies have shown that the physiology of bed-sharing babies is more stable. For example, bed-sharing babies have more regular heart rhythms and fewer long pauses in breathing than babies who sleep alone.[7] The more time a baby spends in physical contact with her

mother, the less time on average she will spend crying.

- **Promotes touching.** Primate studies appear to show that the amount of touch infants receive during the first 6 months of life is directly related to their ability to fight illness.[8]

- **Reduces cortisol levels.** Cortisol is a stress hormone produced by adults' and babies' bodies when they encounter stress, and it can be measured in saliva. Studies have shown that stress hormones, including cortisol, are lower in mothers and babies who co-sleep and bed share. Some cortisol is necessary to wake up fully and function, but it is thought that an overabundance of cortisol in a baby's body can affect her growth.

Bed-Sharing Negatives

While sleeping next to your baby is safe, normal, and natural, certain bed-sharing circumstances can be

Breastfeeding in the Side-Lying Position

If you're bed sharing, mastering breastfeeding in the side-lying position is the key to a good night's rest. However, it may take a while before your baby masters latching on to your breast in this new position, because it's not as easy to guide your baby to the breast as it is when you are holding her in your arms. At first you may need to switch your baby from one side to the other to feed, but as you become experienced you may learn to alternate breasts while your baby stays on the same side.

When Baby Shouldn't Sleep with You

The safest sleep scenario for your baby will depend on your individual circumstances. Crib sleeping is the safest option for your baby when:

- **You smoke.** Smoking is a major contributing factor for SIDS, even if only dad smokes and mom doesn't, and even if no one smokes in the house or around the baby. Toxins in exhaled smokers' breath appear to disrupt the signals to a baby's brain that cue breathing.

- **Your adult bed is not safe for your baby.** If the adult bed has a gap between the mattress and headboard larger than two and a half inches, and you are unable to remove the mattress from the frame and put it on the floor, your baby shouldn't sleep with you in your bed.

- **Young siblings or territorial animals sleep with you too.** If other children are sharing your bed or you have territorial pets that sleep in your bed—and you're not willing to banish them from the bedroom—they pose a risk to your baby.

- **You drink or take drugs or sedatives.** Don't share a bed if you or your bed partner have been drinking or taking sedating medications before bed, or if your partner sleeps like a log. (Plenty of dads can sleep lightly in a bed, conscious of where the baby is at all times. But some dads say they're conscious when they actually aren't ["Oh, I see him, I'm not going to hit him in the head with my elbow . . . zzzzz"]). If this is the case, you'll need to put your mattress on the floor or install a bed rail, and sleep with the baby on your side of the bed with you between baby and dad.

lethal. For example, your baby can get wedged between the mattress and the wall or become entangled in bedding, or you or your partner can suffocate your baby if you accidentally roll over or lie on her. Some studies have suggested that as many as two-thirds of deaths attributed to SIDS were actually accidental asphyxiations. Although babies have always bedded down with their mothers, we now have bedroom fixtures that are a far cry from the sleeping mats and leaf nests of our ancestors. Headboards, bed frames, squishy mattress pads, elevated sleep surfaces, comforters filled with polyester fluff, waterbeds, nightstands, and sofa beds, as well as parents' sedating medications all pose a risk to the survival of babies.

For parents who smoke or drink or who are obese, sleep heavily, or use any kind of drug that inhibits awakening, bed sharing is dangerous! If you (or your partner) sleep like a log, have been drinking, are obese, or have taken sedating medications (sleeping, allergy, or anti-anxiety medication, for instance) then a crib, bassinet, or other baby bed is the safest answer.

You can sue the manufacturer of a crib if it hurts your baby, but if she is injured or dies while sleeping in an adult bed with you, you and your partner could be the subjects of a criminal investigation. If it can be proven that you were drinking or using drugs when your baby was injured or died, you can be prosecuted for criminal negligence in some jurisdictions.

It cannot be emphasized enough: If you choose to share a bed with your baby, *you must take complete responsibility for her safety while she's in bed with you*, since adult beds are not made to be safe for babies. If you have any doubts about the safety of your bed, yourself, or your partner, when it comes to protecting your baby through the night, let her sleep in the same room, but put her down in her own bed—a portable crib, for example, or a cradle or bassinet. This will protect her from adult-bed hazards while giving her some of the same benefits of bed sharing.

THE BED-CRIB CONTROVERSY

As the result of a 1999 published report of its survey of adult-bed-related baby deaths, the Consumer Product Safety Commission (CPSC) issued a warning to parents against bed sharing with children younger than 2 years old.

According to the CPSC, from 1990 to 1997, 515 babies died in adult-bed-related accidents in the United States. Of those deaths, 128 appeared to be caused by babies being wedged between the mattress and the wall; 145 were from the baby becoming trapped between the mattress and bed frame; 121

appeared to be caused by being unintentionally smothered by a parent, pet, or child; 68 suffocated on waterbeds; 31 were trapped between restraining railings placed on the side of the adult bed; and 22 were trapped between the mattress and adjacent furniture.

Is sleeping in adult beds more dangerous than sleeping in a crib? The same year that CPSC's survey results were released that appeared to prove that babies' sleeping in adult beds was a dangerous practice, a separate survey of suffocation and strangulation deaths of babies and children was published in *Pediatrics*, the journal of the American Academy of Pediatrics.[9] It appeared to show that out of 2,178 children who died over the course of the survey's 17 years, 139 died from suffocation in an adult bed, while 428 died in crib-related accidents. Of the remaining deaths, babies were in other places, such as infant beds, high chairs, or strangled by a drapery cord, or there was insufficient information as to where, or how, the deaths occurred.

In a more recent, systematic review of the benefits and dangers associated with the practice of bed sharing based on 40 highly controlled surveys of infant death, the most frequently cited association with infant death and bed sharing was smoking by the mother, either during pregnancy or afterward.[10] Babies younger than 11 weeks were found to be the most at risk for SIDS when they slept in adult beds or on soft surfaces.

Bottom line: Babies can be endangered by unsafe practices in both adult beds and cribs. Wherever your baby sleeps, it's important to take steps to protect your baby from accidental suffocation and strangulation hazards.

No studies of which we are aware have created risk ratios for baby deaths attributed to sharing a family bed with non-smoking, sober parents who have made reasonable efforts to protect their babies from suffocation and entrapment hazards.

PEDIATRICIANS AND THE FAMILY BED

In 2000, one year after the CPSC issued its recommendations, the American Academy of Pediatrics (AAP) issued its own statement that appeared to straddle the line by proclaiming both solitary crib sleeping and bed sharing to be less than optimal. The AAP suggested, instead, that during the first 6 months, babies should sleep in cribs, bassinets, or co-sleepers in the same room as adults while also using pacifiers at the time of sleep.

The AAP's recommendation states: "Although electrophysiologic and behavioral studies offer a strong case for bed sharing's effect in facilitating breastfeeding and the enhancement of maternal-infant bonding, epidemiological studies of bed sharing have shown that it can be hazardous under certain conditions. Several case studies of accidental suffocation or death from undetermined cause suggest that bed sharing is hazardous."

If you ask your pediatrician about bed sharing, he or she may inform you of the AAP's stance but add that bed sharing is a personal choice, advise you to research the risks and benefits, and then support your choice anyway. Or, your pediatrician may give you a unilateral statement about bed sharing being dangerous and say you shouldn't do it.

Unfortunately, the AAP has not issued any guidelines to help pediatricians advise parents on bed-sharing safety, perhaps out of concern that providing safety information could appear to be an endorsement of the practice. Of course, this lack of information only makes bed sharing more dangerous, because many parents don't start out intending to bedshare but end up bringing their babies into bed for nursing or after a particularly rough night.

The AAP's "just say no" approach also can have the side effect of driving a wedge into the parent/doctor/patient relationship, forcing parents to choose between being dishonest with doctors or facing their doctors' disapproval.

Why would the AAP take such a severe stance? Pediatricians tell us that dealing with babies who have been killed and injured in adult beds is so traumatic, they come away understandably determined never to repeat the experience. Also, there are so many types and styles of adult beds on the market—none constructed with infant safety in mind—so perhaps the AAP decided that the task of attempting to educate the public on sleep safety was too complicated and more of a consumer-product issue than a medical one.

This brings us to another point: Pediatricians are *doctors*, after all, which means that they are experts on the physical health of babies and children. If your baby is sick or injured, your pediatrician is of course the go-to guy or gal. But when it comes to parenting decisions, *you* are the expert on your baby. For matters of parental judgment, a doctor can tell you what's worked for other parents, recommend resources, let you know what her professional organization has to say on a given topic, and offer you an opinion based on that information. But you, the parents, are the parenting experts of *your* baby. Only you have the right to decide where your baby sleeps, and the responsibility to keep your baby safe.

Bed-Sharing Safety Checklist

Before you bring your baby into bed with you, always do a safety check. There should be:

- **No places where baby can get trapped.** Babies and young children can be killed when they get their heads wedged in the gaps in furniture. Headboards, footboards, and side rails can be unsafe, especially if a baby is left alone to sleep in a bed. Just as with cribs, head- and footboard railings should have spaces that are no wider than 2⅜ inches apart when an adult's weight is in the bed.

- **A firm mattress.** The surface you share with your baby needs to be firm. Avoid waterbeds, lambskins, fluffy mattress pads, and other soft bedding. Keep stuffed animals and toys out of the baby's sleep environment. Do not sleep on a sofa or a chair with your baby or leave a sleeping baby alone there. And, make sure there's enough room on the mattress for you, the baby, and your partner with no crowding. A king-size bed is ideal, a queen-size bed is fine, but a full (double) bed or a twin is simply too small.

- **No pillows, quilts, or blankets.** Don't give pillows to babies or young toddlers, and keep your pillow away from your baby's sleep area. Don't put a blanket over your baby at all; instead, dress her warmly enough not to need one (babies will kick off blankets, anyway). Keep a night-light on so that you can check on your baby throughout the night.

- **No swaddling.** Do not swaddle a bed-sharing baby.

- **No overheating.** Bed-sharing babies are kept warmer than solitary sleeping babies, so they need lighter pajamas. (Being too warm may be a factor in SIDS.)

- **No other children or pets in the bed.** Toddlers and young children should not be allowed to sleep near your baby. Nor should you bed share if you have a territorial pet that you're not willing to banish from the bedroom.

- **Proper restraints.** Don't try to prevent falls with pillows. If your mattress can't be taken off of the frame and placed on the floor without a box spring, then you will need to get a bed rail suitable for infants for the baby's side of the bed to prevent falls. There should be no spaces between the rail and the mattress greater than 2⅜ inches. Bed rails can be inconvenient because they block off a whole side of the bed so you have to scoot to the foot of the bed to get out, and if you remove the bed rail to change the sheets, it may be tempting to just leave it off. But, in order to work, the bed rail must be properly installed and used after every linen change.

- **No bed wedging.** Avoid placing an adult bed directly alongside furniture or a wall. Babies and young children have very vulnerable windpipes and can become trapped between the bed and other furniture or a wall and can be strangled when their throats are pressured.

- **No excuse to leave your baby alone.** Do not leave your baby unattended in an adult bed, because even newborns can scoot into a suffocation or entrapment hazard, especially if they wake up to find that mom isn't there. The strategy to sleep when your baby sleeps may be fine for the first 6 weeks or so, but as soon as your sleep needs

No matter where your baby always sleeps, place her on her back to sleep. Research clearly shows that this can help protect your baby from the risk of SIDS and the hazards of suffocation and overheating.

change and your baby's naps come in longer stretches, you will need to find a safe nap spot for her.

In addition to some of the glaring safety issues, there are some other potential downsides to bed sharing that you need to consider. Your baby will have to learn to sleep in her own bed eventually, unless you are committed to sharing the family bed for an extended period of time. Many parents opt against bed sharing because they don't intend to share for an extended period of time, and they don't want to have to go through the process of transitioning their baby to her own bed. How difficult it will be to transition your baby will not be possible to determine ahead of time. Some babies take to solo sleeping like champs after just a few nights of mild fussing; for others the transition is more difficult.

A shared bed may also mean less intimate time for you as an adult. Many couples appreciate the time before bed to talk and relax together, and enjoy the bed as one of the few kid-free zones in the house. With a new baby, grown-up time can be harder to come by, and yet such time is more essential than ever for supporting your relationship.

And then there's your sex life. Sure, sex doesn't have to be at night and in bed, and plenty of bed-sharing couples have robust sex lives that involve finding new places around the house and taking advantage of baby nap times—but for other couples who are thoroughly wiped out by the new-baby lifestyle, planning a laundry room adventure is far too ambitious.

If you're a single mom, you can run into problems if you want to have a guest over for an adult sleepover. It could be very upsetting to a tot if she's temporarily evicted because a stranger is taking over "her" place in bed.

If you've been bed sharing for an extended period and find yourself pregnant again, it's also important to transition your baby or child into her own sleep area before you're visibly pregnant. Otherwise, it may cause deep and long-lasting resentment if the new baby appears to be responsible for pushing her out of her bed and into a crib in another room. And it's dangerous to bed share with both an infant and a toddler, because

toddlers sleep deeply and don't fully grasp the concept of injuring others.

What About Co-sleepers?

Currently, there are no safety standards for the bassinet-like devices that are designed to go in between parents or alongside an adult bed. In 2008, two babies died when they slipped through an opening in the frame and were asphyxiated by the Simplicity bedside sleeper/bassinet. If you plan to have your baby sleep in the same room as you, it's safest to put a mini or full-size crib in your room.

Sleep Positioners

With both the incidence of bed sharing on the rise (or, perhaps, the numbers of parents willing to admit to bed sharing), and the growing awareness of bed-sharing safety concerns, there are some new products on the market that are designed to make adult beds safer for young babies. Sometimes called "snuggle nests" by Baby Delight, adult-bed sleep positioners are foam-lined enclosures with mesh sides designed to be used on the surface of an adult bed.

Parenting Issues and Bed Sharing

The following are the results of an informal survey conducted by *Babytalk* magazine:

11 percent of expectant parents planned to co-sleep with their babies.

42 percent of parents reported sharing a family bed once the baby arrived.[11]

Most are specified for babies up to the age of 4 months, and are designed to keep pillows and blankets from accidentally covering a baby. They also provide an extra barrier to keep an adult from rolling over on her. Some sleep positioners also come with night-lights and a wedge shape that keeps a baby positioned on an incline, ostensibly to address reflux problems (for more on reflux, see page 84).

There are serious safety concerns related to these positioners. The AAP advises, "Although various devices have been developed to maintain sleep position or to reduce the risk of re-breathing, such devices are not recommended, because none have been tested sufficiently to show efficacy or safety."

Parents have reported that babies can easily scoot or slide out of positioners that are not enclosed on all four sides, especially if the bed has an incline. *Consumer Reports*, the publication of the nonprofit group Consumers Union, has reported death by asphyxiation of at least one baby whose nose and mouth were obstructed by a foam positioning device. These positioners also potentially create a false sense of security: Parents don't make their beds baby-safe, relying on the positioner to keep the baby in place.

> *"I just don't think I would have made it through those first few months if every time he fed, I had to get out of bed, go downstairs, pick up the kid, stay awake while nursing him, soothe him to sleep, and then go back upstairs to try to fall asleep again while calculating in my head how soon I'd have to get up for the day."*
>
> —Elizabeth S.

How and When to Stop Bed Sharing

No one can pinpoint the exact age that a bed-sharing baby or child should start sleeping alone. On one end of the spectrum there are parents and experts who claim you should never bedshare in the first place, and on the other side of the fence there are families dedicated to extended bed sharing, who maintain that parents and children should share a bed until the child decides she's ready for her own room.

Both extremes are, in our opinion, perhaps a little too extreme. Never sharing the bed can be tough, especially if you're sleep-deprived, you've had a c-section, or your baby is simply the type who goes ballistic every time you put her down. And, if you opt for the "let-them-decide-for-themselves" route, most kids will opt to sleep in the parental bed until peer pressure sets in to deter them, which may not happen until grade school.

So, unless you plan to share your bed indefinitely, it's easiest to start to transition your baby into her own sleeping spot between 6 and 8 months of age. That's when your baby's stomach will be big enough so she can sleep for longer phases, you're out of the SIDS risk zone, and it's early enough to pre-empt the separation-anxiety phase (which can begin as early as six months for some babies). It will also make things much easier if you make the transition before your baby is mobile enough to climb out of her crib or toddler bed and walk into your room of her own accord, which obviously will present much bigger challenges.

Or, you may decide to transition your baby out of your bed sooner, if:

- **Sleeping positions or situations have made sharing unsafe.** When baby becomes so mobile that she can no longer bedshare safely—if you wake up and the baby has wiggled down to the foot of the bed, for instance, take that as a sign that she may need her own bed for her own safety.

- **It's affecting your relationship.** When you (or your partner) begin to resent sharing the bed, it's time to reconsider.

- **It's affecting your sleep.** When baby's noises or movements make it difficult for you or your partner to get needed sleep.

- **Your baby is sleeping in very short stretches.** It's not unusual for breastfeeding babies who bedshare to feed on and off for most of the night. To them, it's probably like sleeping next to a plate of hot cinnamon rolls—they can smell a delicious meal, and it wakes them up. If you don't mind keeping the all-night buffet open, there's nothing wrong with that, and a side effect will be that the baby will need to feed less often during the day. But if your baby is "snacking" every hour and you don't like it, crib sleeping could help everybody get more rest.

- **You know you don't want to bedshare for a long period of time, and your baby has not yet started climbing.** It's good to make the transition sometime before your baby is able to climb out of a crib—because once she is able, if she can vault herself out, she will. If your baby has not yet started pulling up on furniture, that will make the transition much easier for everyone.

Co-Sleeping

Bed sharing is when babies or children and parents share a bed, and co-sleeping is when a baby sleeps in the same room, but not in the same bed with parents (though sometimes the term co-sleeping is used as a "blanket" term for any kind of sleeping that happens in the same room).

Though the AAP favors co-sleeping as a compromise between bed sharing and crib sleeping in a separate room, if you poll parents you'll hear that the picture for co-sleeping isn't always rosy, and the phrase *worst of both worlds* will pop up a lot. Parents who are awakened by baby's sleeping noises will still be disturbed by them, and a parent will still have to get up to tend to the baby, even with the "sidecar" sleepers that attach to the side of the bed. If baby is in a crib in another room, one parent can be "on duty" to get up and tend to him, but if baby's in the same room, both parents will hear the baby's sleeping noises and listen to him being soothed and fed.

Also, babies who don't like sleeping in a crib won't like sleeping in a bassinet or a co-sleeper any better. As far as a baby's concerned, being a foot away from mom is not much of an improvement over being 20 feet away. Babies crave skin-to-skin contact.

What typically happens is that a baby begins the night in a bassinet or co-sleeping sidecar, but moves into the parents' bed for the first feeding of the night and doesn't move back. Breastfeeding is sedating for both mom and baby, so it may be unrealistic to assume you'll be awake enough at the end of every feeding to get up and put the baby back. And as you may notice, the "end" of a feeding can be difficult to determine, especially with newborns. Your baby's nursing may slow down, but then speed up

as soon as you try to unlatch her. If you wait for your baby to unlatch herself when she's done, you could be waiting for a long time. And if you unlatch her yourself before she's finished, that may wake her up completely.

So this is how "accidental" bed sharing begins, and this situation may have the potential to create the most dangerous sleeping environment of all, because parents may not make the bed baby-safe on the assumption that the baby's "real" sleeping place is somewhere else.

All About Cribs

CRIB SLEEPING PROS

- **Contains the baby.** Unlike bed sharing, where it's unsafe to leave a sleeping baby alone in an adult bed, crib sleeping allows parents to do other things around the house while baby is sleeping.

- **Sometimes is safer.** May be safer than bed sharing under certain circumstances—if parents drink or smoke, for example.

- **May be more restful for you.** If your baby is a nighttime kicker and thrasher or makes a lot of noise in her sleep, crib sleeping may turn out to be a lot more restful for you than bed sharing or co-sleeping.

- **Couple privacy.** Many parents prefer having the bedroom a grown-up-only area. Crib sleeping promotes marital harmony when one parent favors co-sleeping or bed sharing and the other doesn't.

- **Requires no transition later.** If your baby starts out sleeping in a crib, you don't have to worry about transitioning her to it later.

- **Is more travel-friendly.** If you travel, you don't have to worry if a hotel bed is baby-safe.

CRIB SLEEPING CONS

- **Could negatively affect breastfeeding.** Compared to rooming-in, crib sleeping makes overnight breastfeeding inconvenient, and feeding overnight is important to keep up your milk supply and keep the baby nourished. Skipping night nursing can lead to painful engorgement.

- **May seem inconvenient.** If your baby is sleeping in another room, that means that you (or your partner, if you're formula feeding or pumping milk) will have to get up several times a night, walk into the baby's room, feed and lull her back to sleep, and then go back to your own room to get some sleep. There is no magic age at which a baby will stop feeding at night. According to surveys, at one year of age about 80 percent of babies sleep through

the night without waking up to feed, leaving one out of five still getting up at night after the baby's first birthday.

- **May isolate baby.** Newborns rely on mom and other caregivers not only for food but temperature regulation and sleep-cycle regulation, and a healthy newborn separated from her mother will protest, loudly. After all, in hunter-gatherer times, the only time a baby would find herself sleeping alone was if something horrible happened—mom was killed by a beast—and the wail was needed so other family members could find her and come to her rescue.

- **Is sometimes physically uncomfortable.** Bending over to lower your baby into the crib and lifting her out can be a pain in the back, especially for physically challenged parents. Getting in and out of bed can be painful and difficult for moms who had c-sections.

- **Carries its own risk.** Even though they are covered by stringent federal regulations, cribs are still responsible for numerous baby deaths every year, most commonly due to malfunctioning parts, or hardware or slat failures.

PICKING A CRIB

A non-full-size crib resembles a standard crib complete with wooden (or metal) bars except at three-quarters the size. (And it may not have all of the extra features that the big models do.) Portable cribs are priced between $90 and $200.

A bassinet is a small baby bed supported by a frame with legs and usually with wheels. Bassinets come in a wide variety of price ranges from about $30 to more than $200. You can expect to pay around $50 for a bare-bones model, $60 to $150 for models with fabric skirts, a hood, and a storage compartment underneath. Models priced at $150 and above come with advanced electronic features, such as lights, sounds, vibration, and a moving mobile, as well as novel designer shapes and plush fabrics.

A bedside sleeper attaches onto the side of an adult bed and allows baby to be easily lifted from sleeper to bed, and back. Some allow the open side to be closed for use as a portable bed or changing station. Prices range from $100 to $300. The lowest-priced models are made of tubular metal and mesh; the highest-priced versions are made of wood and are convertible to children's desks and other kinds of furniture.

A cradle is a rocking baby bed, and a *bassinet/cradle* is the newest product combination. It combines the comfort features of a bassinet's basketlike sleeping area with the rocking capability of an old-fashioned cradle. Bassinets can be made of wood or molded plastic, and they offer just rockers or combine rockers with wheels that fold into the rocker frame.

Hammocks and motion beds are designed to allow parents to provide soothing motion and most offer a semi-upright position for

babies, which is especially helpful if your baby has gas or reflux.

We don't recommend *hand-carried baby beds*, sometimes called carrycots or Moses baskets, which are oval baskets with carry handles. Some safety warnings are in order for these beds because not all of them are made with the same quality and durability as full-size cribs. Often the mattresses supplied with the beds are flimsy, thin, and overly soft, and could be covered in inexpensive vinyl that isn't breathable and traps moisture. In some cases there's a gap between the mattress and the side of the basket that could allow a baby's neck to be entrapped, causing suffocation. These small, portable baby beds are also difficult to balance, since the heaviest part of the baby is her head, putting most of the weight at one end of the carrier. And some Moses baskets come with a warning that you shouldn't carry them with the baby inside, making us wonder, what's the point of buying one?

BABY BED SHOPPING CHECKLIST

No matter what type of sleep arrangement you choose—whether a bassinet, a small crib, a cradle, a full-sized crib, or a combination of products—safety should be your number-one consideration. Here is a basic checklist to make your shopping decisions easier:

❏ **Sturdy construction.** A baby bed should be firmly put together with no wobbling when jiggled.

❑ **Stability.** Childproof leg locks are especially important if there are other children in the house, particularly toddlers. Check that the bed can't be pulled over sideways. Keep casters locked except when you're moving the bed.

❑ **Quality mattress.** An extra-firm quality mattress won't create a suffocation pocket around your baby's face if she accidentally turns over—try punching your fist into the mattress to test it. And if you can fit two fingers between the edges or corners of the bed and the mattress, it could pose an entrapment or suffocation hazard.

❑ **Solid construction.** For safety, the sides of a bassinet should be made of solid, unbendable material, rather than fabric over a tubular frame. Loose fabric sides could allow your baby's neck, head, or limbs to get trapped in fabric pockets.

❑ **Washability.** Bedding and liner fabrics should be completely washable. (Read the manufacturer's instructions.)

❑ **Folding locks.** Folding components, such as legs, frame, or canopy, should lock securely with no danger of collapsing.

❑ **Safe rocking and swinging.** Beds with rounded rockers prevent it from tipping. However, they should not stick out so far that they pose a tripping hazard. Beds that hang and swing from

a frame should have a locking mechanism to make them stationary. Beds with wheels should have locking casters to make them more stable and to keep children from pushing them around.

❑ **Fitted sheets.** Elastic sewn around the corners makes fitted sheets less likely to be pulled loose and potentially entangle your baby. Buy three or four sets in exactly the same size.

❑ **Storage and travel options.** Consider a compactly folding non-full-size crib if you have limited storage space or plan to use the bed for sleepovers away from home. (Plus it can be used a lot longer than a smaller baby bed.)

CRIB SAFETY SHOPPING CHECKLIST

Here's what to look for when you shop for a crib for your baby:

❑ **Certification.** A JPMA certified sticker means the crib brand passes a voluntary safety test overseen by manufacturers.

❑ **Easy-to-use side lowering.** Try lowering the side yourself. A simple lift and knee-press action works more easily and is quieter than models that require the use of a foot pedal or a spring-action knob.

❑ **Frame and slat integrity.** Make sure the frame doesn't

rattle when shaken. The slats should be firmly fastened at top and bottom, with no twisting or moving. Glue residue spilled out onto the wood is a sign of poor craftsmanship.

❑ **Proper finishes.** All surfaces must be smooth and splinter free.

❑ **Single dropside.** A crib with only one side that can be lowered (dropside) will be quieter and more stable than models that have two sides that lower.

❑ **Teething rails.** Most models have a small plastic covering that lines the tops of the railings to prevent teething on wood or other surfaces. Make sure it doesn't have sharp edges or broken pieces and make sure it can't be pulled loose.

❑ **Mattress support.** The metal support that goes under the mattress must be sturdy with no sharp points that could puncture the underside of the mattress. Make sure it fastens to the crib with strong, thick hardware.

❑ **Locking wheels.** If the crib has wheels, they should be lockable to prevent a baby's motion from "walking" the crib.

❑ **Underside storage drawer.** Storage drawers that slide or roll out from under the crib can be useful, but check out their quality and how easily they open and close before paying extra for them.

CRIB SAFETY

Here are some tips to ensure that your baby's crib is as safe as possible:

• **Wait to tighten the bolts.** Put the crib up a few weeks before you plan to use it and let it "settle"—allow the wood to expand or contract according to the temperature and humidity, and then tighten all the bolts and hardware.

• **Inspect hardware.** Make sure the metal hardware on the crib has no rough or sharp edges, in case your baby falls against it.

• **Check teething rails.** Periodically check the teething rails, which should run the length of the railing tops, to make sure they're not cracked and don't have any sharp edges.

• **Check mattress support.** Babies can fall from their cribs if the side rails are not at the right level in relationship to the mattress surface. Periodically adjust the height of the mattress supports under the mattress and adjust it to your baby's height and abilities. When your baby learns to sit up, lower the mattress level so she can't fall out or climb over the side rail. When she learns to stand, set the mattress level at its lowest point. When she reaches a height of 35 inches or the side rail is less than three-quarters of her height, move her to another bed.

Crib Assembly 101

Crib assembly is a two-person job, and it can be a relationship-testing experience, especially if neither of you is particularly handy.

Expect it to take two people of reasonable intelligence at least half an hour for the initial assembly (although, if it turns out you have missing or damaged parts and need to order replacements, it could take a month or more!) and plan to take 5 to 10 minutes to re-tighten the bolts and screws before you put baby in it for the first time.

Make sure you have the complete parts list and assembly instructions and *all* the hardware you need to put the crib together *before* you start to put the crib together. Never attempt to use a crib that is missing slats, spindles, or hardware.

If you don't have the instructions or parts list, phone the crib manufacturer and have replacements sent to you *before* you begin to assemble the crib, so you won't end up with a half-put-together crib lying around, or a potentially dangerous disassembly.

If the baby-gear store or catalog you order from offers crib delivery and assembly for free or at a reasonable price, that's a huge perk. But be sure to keep the assembly instructions that come with the crib, because you will have to follow them backward to take it apart one day.

Make sure your crib is set up in the room where you intend it to stay, because once it's built it will be too large to be rolled, intact, through most doorways.

- **Use only fitted sheets.** Babies can get entangled in loose sheets and blankets and strangle themselves. Use only tightly fitted sheets.

- **Avoid "cushy."** Soft mattresses and padded quilts have figured in SIDS deaths and suffocations. Rather than using blankets, keep your baby warm by dressing her in a blanket sleeper. If you use a blanket, make sure your baby's head remains uncovered during sleep.

- **No crib bumpers.** The American Academy of Pediatrics does not recommend using crib bumpers, because they pose a suffocation risk and restrict the flow of fresh air around a baby; some experts believe this restriction increases the risk of SIDS. In addition, once your baby grows into a toddler and starts climbing, the bumpers will give her a foothold to climb out of the crib.

- **No blanket.** Because of the potential for strangulation, don't put a blanket in your baby's bed. All you need is a crib sheet. Your baby should sleep in a bunting (also known as a sleep sac, blanket sleeper, or baby sleeping bag), a swaddling blanket, pajamas, a onesie, or just a diaper, depending on the temperature.

Time to Play or to Sleep?

When you put your baby in her crib to go to sleep, you want her to get the message that it's time to go to sleep—not stay awake and play with toys or watch a stimulating mobile spinning around. It's okay to put your baby down when she's awake to watch her mobile or play with toys in her crib; otherwise you might never get a shower! But when it's time to sleep it's more restful for your baby—and safer—to remove the mobile and take the toys out of her crib.

- **No pillow.** Pillows are for children 2 years and up. Babies don't need pillows for head support, and like crib bumpers and quilts, they create a suffocation hazard.

- **No toys in the crib or hanging over it.** Toys can suffocate and can also be used by your baby to climb out of the crib. Crib gyms and mobiles should be removed when she starts to sit or reaches 5 months of age, whichever comes first. Mobiles become strangulation or choking hazards if a baby can reach them or fall into them.

- **Keep cords out of reach.** Keep the crib away from windows, window blinds, and/or drapery cords. Children can strangle on window cords or can fall through screens. If it's not considered a fire-escape hazard to use window guards, install them. Make sure that all drapery or window blind cords are out of your child's reach. The CPSC has received numerous reports of strangulation deaths involving window blind cords over the years. To keep cords out of reach of children, use tie-down devices or take the cord loop and cut it in half to make two separate cords. Consumers should call toll-free 800-506-4636 or visit the Window Covering Safety Council Web site at www.windowcoverings.org to receive a free repair kit for each set of blinds in their home.

HOW TO CHOOSE A SAFE CRIB MATTRESS

Your baby will be sleeping on a crib mattress for approximately 2 years—and maybe a couple of years longer if you buy a pint-sized toddler bed that has the same dimensions as her crib. Firmness is more critical than internal structure or padding.

Granted, getting a quality mattress is important, but there's no need to pay extra bucks because a salesperson convinced you that your baby needs extra back support. She doesn't. Babies' bodies are quite flexible. It's the grown-ups who carry babies around who need the help.

There are basically two types of mattresses: innerspring

and foam. Innerspring crib mattresses resemble miniature adult mattresses. Underneath the ticking are thick layers of padding, a series of metal coils, and thick metal support wires to hold up the edges of the mattress. Costlier innerspring mattresses generally have more coils than less-expensive versions, and the coils are made from higher-quality metal, such as steel. The quality and price of the mattress often depends upon the number of coils, such as 180 tough steel springs and steel-reinforced edges. Their advantage is that they offer variable support to different parts of your baby's body as she grows and gains weight, but they are substantially heavier and less flexible than foam versions, which makes sheet changing a challenge. Plus, most tots like to use innerspring mattresses like trampolines, which could lead to falls and injuries.

Foam mattresses come in a variety of prices and grades. The higher the quality of foam, the more it weighs and the denser the mattress will be. Denser versions are less "squishy" when you squeeze them, while poorer-quality mattresses are mushier, which could create a suffocation pocket if your baby turns facedown.

Quality foam mattresses are really firm, almost like bricks— an advantage when it comes to preventing potentially dangerous "suffocation pockets." They're lighter than hefty innersprings, and have clear-cut corners that help keep fitted sheets on. Choose a thick, firm version from a name-brand manufacturer.

Federal regulations enforced by the U.S. Consumer Product Safety Commission (CPSC, see page 185) mandate all crib mattresses to be the same length and width so that they fit flush against the sides of cribs. In turn, full-sized cribs must also have identical interior dimensions. But some mattresses may be deeper than others.

Sometimes manufacturers will claim that a mattress has "anti-bacterial" qualities. That means that an anti-bacterial chemical has been added to the vinyl used in the laminate to help destroy bacteria on the surface of the mattress. Unfortunately, a baby's continual wetting is more than any surface material can handle.

Some mattresses claim they are "non-allergenic," or "hypoallergenic." That simply means they're made of foam instead of cotton and other fibers that attract dust mites and that can cause allergic reactions.

Manufacturers will also use the selling ploy of a "lifetime warranty" to get parents to pay more for a crib mattress. But you'd better read the fine print, since the actual warranty may come with lots of loopholes in favor of the manufacturer, such as special conditions and a pro-rated payback scale that depends upon the age of the mattress.

We suggest using a snug-fitting washable pad to protect the mattress, turning the mattress over frequently, and following the manufacturer's directions for cleaning (usually wiping the surface down with a mild soap solution and then cleaning off the soap residue using a cloth dampened with clear water).

Organic Mattresses and Bedding: Are They Worth It?

When the term *organic* is applied to crib mattresses or bedding, it may mean that the fibers were produced using organic farming methods, or it may just mean that they are made of materials thought to be non-toxic for babies. Most are made of unbleached or "natural" cotton and/or materials that don't contain phthalates, including polybrominated diphenyl ethers (PBDEs), or polyvinyl chloride (PVC), polyurethane foam, and other fire-retardant chemicals.

By law, though, even organic mattresses must meet certain standards for flame retardancy. And that means treated with chemicals. Boric acid, formaldehyde, melamine, antimony trioxide, vinylidene chloride, zinc borate, and decabromodiphenyl oxide are all either suspected or known carcinogens or developmental toxins[12] used in making mattresses flameproof, and there's no requirement that a manufacturer of mattresses, organic or otherwise, reveal what chemicals were used to get the mattress up to standard. And, since cotton mattresses are highly absorbent (and breeding grounds for dust mites), "all-natural" mattresses will still contain plastics in their water-resistant barrier.

All-cotton sheets and blankets wick moisture away and allow your baby's skin to breathe. Some parents are concerned about pesticide residues that are thought to remain embedded in typical cotton bedding. If that's your concern, then you may want to seek out organic cotton sheets, which may be pricier than non-organic versions. Again, they may have been treated with any number of chemicals, as there is no agreed-upon definition or legal standard for what *organic* means when it comes to non-food products. For any sheets or bedding, launder in fragrance-free detergent before use.

CRIB SHEETS AND MATTRESS PADS

Start out with at least three fitted crib sheets. Don't try to use other sheet sizes, such as twin-sized fitted sheets tucked under the crib mattress, because they can come loose and create a strangulation hazard.

There are newfangled crib sheets that are easy to remove and replace. They have either zipper or Velcro tops, or have corners that snap onto the crib bars, which can be very helpful.

If you use the conventional crib sheets that need to be tucked under the mattress, select a crib with casters (pivoting wheels) or one that allows easy access for tucking in the sheets.

Crib mattresses are waterproof, but having an extra pad between the mattress and fitted sheet can help with cleanup in case of diaper leaks or spit-up incidents. However, a mattress pad will also create more laundry and one more bodily-fluid-soaked item to hassle with in the middle of the night, so consider it optional. If you use one, it should fit snugly on all corners with elastic, so there is no danger of it becoming lumpy or bunching up.

Since babies are sensitive to aromas and laundry chemicals, sheets and bedding should be laundered in hypoallergenic, fragrance-free liquid detergent. If you use fabric softeners, make sure they are also fragrance-free. Powdered detergents don't completely rinse out and may cause an allergic skin reaction and may affect the sheet's absorbency.

The biggest advantage to using a portable crib is that it will be slender enough to roll through most doorways, and unlike bassinets and most cradles, it will offer a clear, unrestricted view of the baby from all sides. Typically, such cribs can be used with a baby of up to about 2 years of age and weighing between 40 and 50 pounds, so it will be good for much longer use than a bassinet. Most offer a lowering floorboard that allows the crib to be used as a small playpen later.

On the downside, miniature cribs are heavier than bassinets and some other baby beds; they also cost more. Only a few models have sides that lower, so they may be less convenient to place baby in or lift him out. Some may require non-standard-size sheets and offer only a single mattress height. Of course, they are also subject to other safety concerns, such as soft mattresses, sharp-edged hardware, and poorly secured floorboards.

BASSINETS

Bassinets are small beds on a stand that are much more compact than portable cribs. Some come with electronic extras, such as vibrations, small night-lights, or musical features that are operated with buttons.

It's worth noting that extra electronic perks eat up a lot of batteries, and you (and your baby) may not find them all that pleasing. On the other hand, a bed that rocks itself or vibrates could help temporarily soothe your baby when you're at wit's end. Just don't expect it to convince your baby she's not hungry!

The bassinet's narrow dimensions and its wheels allow it to be rolled through doorways, something full-size cribs can't do. Some newborns appear to prefer being in small, enclosed spaces.

The negatives are that bassinets are generally limited to babies weighing up to 15 pounds. Mattress pads tend to be soft and cushy, which could affect a baby's air supply if she accidentally rolls facedown. Closed sides shut out airflow, potentially making the bed stuffier and increasing the risk of SIDS.

Fitted sheets may be hard to find in off sizes, and loose sheets pose an entanglement or even a strangulation danger. The long narrow design of bassinets makes them vulnerable to toppling and sometimes leg locks fail, causing the bed to collapse. You may strike your baby's head on the rigid hood, especially if you're using the bassinet in low-light conditions. Bassinets with tubular frames and fabric liners to keep the baby in place have been recalled when the liners allowed babies' limbs, heads, or entire bodies to become trapped between component parts.

BEDSIDE SLEEPERS

Bedside sleepers resemble small cribs or "sidecars" that attach onto the side of an adult bed and keep an open side toward the bed so a baby can easily be lifted from sleeper to bed and back. Some allow the open side to be closed for use as a portable bed or changing station.

The concept is to give parents easy access to their babies without the risks of SIDS and suffocation that occur when babies sleep in their parents' beds.

They're especially handy if you're nursing and want to be able to move the baby in and out of your bed without getting out of bed yourself. However, placing babies in a bedside sleeper after they have fallen asleep at the breast means rousing them and removing them from the warmth of their parent's body. Putting them onto the cold sleeper surface is likely to awaken them (but placing them in a crib or other bed can do the same thing).

Some parents dislike that the co-sleeper gets in the way of their getting in and out of bed, an unavoidable side effect. To get the baby in and out of the co-sleeper, you must sit up in bed, twist at the waist, and lift, which can be difficult and painful if you have recently undergone a c-section.

As with bassinets and other baby beds, these beds should have no gap between the railings that could capture and strangle a baby if her body slips through; and be sure to follow the manufacturer's instructions to the letter about how the co-sleeper is fastened to the side of your bed. Make sure it is completely flush with your mattress.

MOTION BEDS AND HAMMOCKS

One advantage to waiting to buy a crib until after you give birth is that you have ample time to explore all your infant bed options. Springing for a hundreds-of-dollars designer crib (motion bed-hammock) may seem like a wild move while you're pregnant, but if your baby turns out to be bothered by reflux (see page

Night-lights and Baby Sleep

Dimming the household lights in the evening may be one way to encourage your baby to become a more predictable sleeper, especially at night. A study of baby sleep found differences in day and night sleep patterns between 1- and 3-month-old babies exposed to bright lights at night, such as when parents turned on an overhead light to feed or diaper their babies versus those who cared for them in dim light or in darkness. Babies handled in dimness or dark developed more regular day- and night-sleep patterns than those exposed to bright lights at night.[13]

84) or to be the sort that demands constant motion to fall asleep, you may find that a motion bed is your best option.

The hammock style allows the baby's head to be higher than her belly, which can help if she has GER (gastroesophageal reflux), and its swaying motion helps soothe your baby to sleep.

Whatever model you decide upon, make sure there are no suffocation pockets or places that could capture your baby's head, neck, or limbs, and make sure that there is no danger that your baby could fall out.

Setting Up Your Baby's Room

Here are a few tips and products that can make your baby's room comfortable, safe, and conducive to sleep:

1. **Blackout shades.** Newborns spend half of their time asleep. At first, it won't matter how bright or dark your baby's nursery is. But, once the production of the hormone melatonin begins at 12 weeks, keeping her room dark may help her sleep longer in the mornings, rather than waking up like a rooster at the first light of the day. Blackout shades are also most helpful for when you have to put the baby to bed in the summer months, when it can be as bright as daylight in the evening.

2. **Night-light.** For all of those nighttime trips to the crib (at least three or four a night for the first weeks), you'll want a night-light to keep you from stumbling into furniture or having to turn the overhead lights on completely. You may have heard that night-lights can cause baby nearsightedness, but that isn't true (nearsightedness is caused by having nearsighted parents); however, light exposure, even to electric lights, can disrupt both baby and human sleep cycles, making the deep-sleep phase shorter. So you want a night-light that's just bright enough to do the job.

3. **Ventilation and humidity.** Proper ventilation and a clean environment are important for a baby's good night sleep. One 2008 study appearing in the *Archives of Adolescent & Pediatric Medicine* appeared to show that sleeping in a room with an open window cut the risk of death from SIDS by 36 percent, while sleeping in a room with a fan lowered the risk by 72 percent.[14]

Also, a dry, dusty room can lead to a stuffy nose, and that can disrupt baby sleep. Because of babies' tiny nasal passages and delicate tissues, it only takes a little swelling to cause blockage. (A few drops of infant saline solution work better than a nasal aspirator, which can cause swelling in the nasal passages.)

A cool-mist humidifier will help keep nasal discharge from drying out and backing up, especially in the winter months when household heating systems dry out the air. A fan and open bedroom door will also help air circulate in the house, and can provide some soothing "white noise," too. If weather and safety permit it, open a window to let in some fresh air also.

4. Comfortable temperature. The thermostat for your baby's room should be set to between 65°F and 72°F (18–22°C). Newborns are comfortable at the same temperature as adults,but babies have a hard time regulating their body temperature, and are less able to cope if it's too hot or too cold. Fresh air is a good thing, but position the crib away from heating and air-conditioning vents and direct drafts.

5. Toy basket. Newborns are generally uninterested in anything that's not mom. But when your baby gets to be about 3 months old she'll start to grasp objects and stuff them into her mouth, and at that point you'll want a place to toss all her loose toys. A simple basket is a great place to store them in the nursery.

6. Crib tent. If your baby is going to be sleeping in a crib and you have cats, then a crib tent is a must. Cats are naturally attracted to the cozy, safe perch a crib provides, and they're also attracted to the warmth of a sleeping baby. We know your kitty is a saint, but babies have been scratched and even suffocated by felines looking for

somewhere to nap. Employing a tent is not a good safety measure for a climbing toddler, though; children can become dangerously trapped between the crib tent and crib rails. Once your child becomes able to climb out of the crib, it's time to transition her to a toddler bed.

7. Clear path from door to crib. Your baby doesn't care how tidy her room is, but you should always have a clear path from the door of the room to the crib, even if you have to use a snow shovel to achieve it.

8. Rocking chair or glider with comfort items. You'll be visiting the nursing station one to four times a night for the first year or so, so you'll want a comfy rocking chair with a footrest. Within arm's reach: books and magazines nearby to catch up on reading; breast pads; burp cloths, and paper towels in case of spit-ups; pacifiers, if your baby uses them; powdered formula, bottles, and nipples, if you're bottle feeding; and bottled water if there's no sink nearby, for middle-of-the-night mixing and for the thirsty caregiver.

9. Arm support. Holding your baby to nurse can put a strain on your arms and shoulders and can quickly become tiring. A semi-circular nursing pillow that fits around your waist, such as a Boppy, can be an important comfort item to reduce the strain.

10. Diaper changing station.
You'll want to have a place in your baby's room (or yours) dedicated specifically to diaper changing, something you'll be doing hundreds of times over the coming months. It helps to take the diapers out of their package ahead of time so you don't have to fumble with packaging with a baby in your arms.

11. Wipes and wipe warmer.
Some parents opine that warmed wipes are the height of frippery, but we say if it helps you accomplish a quick change without fully rousing the baby, it's money well spent.

12. Paper towels. You'll want a roll of these handy for spit-ups, blowouts, and the like.

13. One-handed or hands-free diaper pail or trash can. You don't want to be wrestling with a diaper pail in the middle of the night while you're holding a stinky diaper! Before you bring a diaper pail home (or add it to your baby registry) make sure that it can be operated with one hand or with a foot pedal. Also opt for a pail that uses regular trash bags, and not special refill bags. Not only are regular trash bags cheaper, but also you're less likely to run out of them, because they're more readily available. A trash can with a lid that springs closed is even better, because it holds more diapers, and after your child is potty trained, you can put it to other uses after a thorough cleaning.

14. Plastic laundry hamper.
You'll need a place to store soiled baby clothes and linens until you can get them to the washing machine. It's always when you least expect it that your baby throws up in bed or has a diaper blowout.

15. No clocks. Do you really need to know what time it is when

Preventing Baby Nasal Congestion

- **Keep baby's room vacuumed and dusted.** During your last weeks of pregnancy, use your nesting urge to fuel giving the baby-to-be's room a good once-over, dusting surfaces such as baseboards, bookshelves, and ceiling-fan blades and vacuuming. After baby's born, touch up as necessary and your energy permits.

- **Use a fan.** Having a fan circulating air can help reduce dust and may also help prevent SIDS.

- **Buy an air filter.** If your baby's room has poor ventilation, seems to get dusty in a hurry, or your baby is constantly congested, consider buying a **HEPA** (high-efficiency particulate air) **filter** for her room.

you're up feeding the baby for the third time? No, you don't.

16. **A baby monitor with volume control.** The big plus to having your baby sleep in her own room is that you won't be awakened by every little snuffle. Unless your bedroom is so far way from your baby's you can't hear her cries, or your baby has an exceptionally weak cry, you may find that the monitor is more of an irritant than a help at night. Most babies are quite capable of crying loud enough for caregivers in adjoining rooms to hear.

However, for naps, it can be helpful to have a way to keep tabs on baby from farther away.

Baby Soothers

SOUND MACHINES AND CDS

Babies appear to be soothed by specific sounds that mimic what they heard in the womb. For some babies, monotonous sleep sounds, such as canned white noise similar to radio static, appear to encourage slumber. Infant studies show that babies can also be soothed by the sound of the human heartbeat (and are roused and start to cry at the sound of other babies' crying). The droning of a vacuum cleaner also seems to work with some babies, as does the humming of a car engine or a clothes dryer, which you can record for an hour or so, and then play back to your baby.

"It took a few months for us to realize that the baby monitor wasn't helping us, especially at night. One of us (usually me) would jump up every time there was a sound. Finally we decided just to turn it off, trusting that if our baby really needed us, he'd let us know."

—Diane M.

There are also specific "go-to-sleep" CDs that you can order online. These recordings generally contain a white-noise track along with a choice of heartbeat sounds combined with lullaby-like music and nature sounds, such as a rainfall or pounding surf. You can also download sleep sounds from the Internet in MP3 format onto your computer or iPod. And sleep machines with similar sounds are also available, but with varying sound quality.

You may discover that your baby couldn't care less about the special sounds you play for her, particularly if her wakefulness has to do with hunger, discomfort, or missing your physical contact. Some parents find that having

Dangerous Crib Toys

We don't recommend teddy bears or other stuffed animals with embedded, battery-operated heart sounds. Safety issues are the problem. Inquisitive babies and toddlers shouldn't be left alone with products that contain batteries, nor should soft objects, including stuffed animals, be kept in the crib, because of their suffocation potential. Similarly, sound makers and lights should not be fastened inside your baby's crib, since she could fall into them and get injured.

the volume loud works better than quiet sounds. On the other hand, an adult or baby machine may be helpful for a toddler's room to help mask traffic noises outside or the cries of a newborn sibling.

A potential downside to using sounds to soothe your baby to sleep is that she may get so attached to having a specific sound or CD played as she goes to sleep that she becomes dependent on it. Problems can arise when the CD becomes scratched or lost, or you need to travel somewhere without your sound machine. If you find a CD that works, it's a good idea to make copies of it right away.

BABY MONITORS

Nursery (or baby) monitors use electronic transmitters and receivers to allow you to hear your baby's every whimper and snort from another room or even when you're on the way to the mailbox. Monitors have two basic parts: a transmitter that sends a baby's sound—or sound plus image—and a receiver that you carry around to pick up on your baby's signals. It's important to remember that

monitors don't make babies sleep better, nor do they protect your baby from SIDS, but they can allow you to keep tabs on your baby when you're out of earshot.

Monitors vary in quality and sensitivity. Some have multiple channels that let you select the best "station" for your location. Their biggest problem, other than eating up batteries, is that they may make you hypersensitive to your baby's every move and snuffle as she stirs in the night, which could interfere with your dropping off into the deep sleep you so desperately need.

Some parents purchase video monitors, which allow them to see their babies as well as hear them. And some video versions equipped with special lenses can pick up the baby's image even in dim light. The question is whether you really *need* to watch your baby sleep or awaken, since most babies are quite vociferous in signaling their parents when they're awake and want to be picked up. And, as with audio monitoring, video images offer no insurance against SIDS, since you can't tell from a tiny screen whether your baby is breathing or not.

NIGHT-LIGHTS

Given that you'll be waking up over and over to tend to your baby in her first year, some type of dim lighting system is needed that won't be so glaring that it will startle your baby or keep her awake. You need just enough light to change diapers if you have to. You have a choice between lights that you have to manually turn on and those that automatically turn on when the ambient light becomes dim, which may be an advantage. Note: Night-lights attract tots as playthings and could present a shock hazard.

ROCKING CHAIRS AND GLIDERS

A good rocking chair or glider with supportive armrests can be an indispensable piece of baby equipment. Rocking, especially the vigorous kind, appears to have the powerful effect of relaxing babies and helping them to drift off into sleep. Premature babies who were rocked in small hammocks in NICUs were found in one study to gain more weight and get to go home earlier than babies planked out on flat beds with no motion, so there's something to be said for the effects of movement not only on baby soothing, but also on baby development. A comfortable leg rest, such as a footstool or hassock, will make the chair much more comfortable.

SCENT SOOTHERS

The sweet, camphor-like scent of lavender blossoms is thought to act as a potent relaxant and soother. Unfortunately, the research on the effects of lavender on babies is scant, and side effects are unknown. It's worth noting, too, that there are many varieties of lavender, with only certain types, specifically *Lavender offininalis* and *Lavender augustfolia*, thought to carry relaxation properties. Dab a small amount of oil extracted from one of these types of lavender onto the bottom sheet of your baby's crib at the opposite end of where she sleeps to see if it helps her to relax, keeping it well away from her skin and at a good distance from her sensitive nose.

Six Weeks: The Crying Peak

4

The Six-Week Crying Peak

Congratulations! You've figured out where the baby should sleep, and you're fully recovered (one would hope!) at this point from the immediate physical effects of childbirth.

Now it's on to a new milestone, albeit not a very pleasant one for many parents: a phenomenon known as the six-week crying peak.

Research shows that between the ages of 6 and 8 weeks, the average time babies spend crying, which increases from birth, hits an all-time high of 2 out of 24 hours (though a range between 1 and 5 hours of crying is considered normal, believe it or not). For reasons not yet entirely understood, most of this crying happens in the hours between 4 p.m. and midnight. Instead of having a "meal," many babies will practice cluster feeding—taking in small doses of milk at a time, also called bunch feeding.

Cluster-feeding behavior is also particularly common at 4 months, as part of the four-month sleep shift (see Chapter 6).

Some babies will stay up for hours, nursing and fussing, nursing and fussing, sometimes for hours on end. Evening cluster feeding and fussing is particularly difficult for a parent because it usually starts at a time of day when your blood sugar is low, and you're likely to be tired and cranky, too. The cluster-fuss has a way of striking just as parents are getting ready to sit down to relax together after a long day. The chaos and crying can feel like complete insanity, especially if one parent is trying to take care of the baby without a second adult in the house. And it's rough on a parent's confidence when nothing seems to help the baby.

If you're breastfeeding, you may worry that something's wrong with your milk or your milk supply. Bottle-feeding moms will wonder if they ought to switch to soy or hypoallergenic formula. But unless your baby is having weight-gain problems, is projectile vomiting, or appears to be in pain, cluster-fussing in the evening is not a signal that anything is wrong with your baby's digestion or diet.

But look on the bright side: Cluster feeding and fussing at about the same time every night may be the first sign that your baby is falling into some sort of a schedule! Getting cranky and hungry at the same point every night may mark your baby's first attempts to build up your milk supply and stoke up for a longer phase of sleep.

By 3 months, the average time babies spend crying drops dramatically, to less than an hour a day.[1] In the meantime, all of that crying can be very difficult for parents to take. About 20 percent of the time,[2] intense crying does sometimes cross the line into the "Colic Zone." (For more information on colic, see page 79.)

While you will not be able to do anything to keep your baby from crying, there is evidence that carrying your baby and keeping him in close proximity—not just

Tips for Coping with a Cluster-Fusser

There are many things you can do to get through the six-week crying peak. Here are a few suggestions:

- **Avoid weaning.** Giving your breastfed baby formula won't cure the evening meltdown—both breastfed and bottle-fed babies have fussy periods in the evenings. Formula supplementation will cue your body to produce less milk, and that will only make your baby more demanding and unhappy.

- **Maintain brand loyalty.** If you're bottle feeding, changing your brand or type of formula is unlikely to help.

- **Don't add cereal** to your baby's bottle with the hope it will make him sleep better, unless your pediatrician specifically recommends that you do so as a treatment for reflux.

- **Use motion to soothe.** Put baby in the "colic carry," soft carrier, over your shoulder, in a sling, in a vibrating baby seat, or an automatic baby swing.

- **Share the load.** Let other family members have turns eating and walking the baby at dinnertime.

- **Plan meals in advance.** If you're the designated cook in your family, plan the evening meal in the morning, or better yet, plan your week's meals in advance and cook extra to generate leftovers.

- **Eat at home.** Don't make plans to go out to dinner, unless it's to the home of someone who's going to make you dinner and walk the baby around while you eat!

- **Stoke up.** Have a high-protein snack in mid-afternoon to ward off hungry desperation at dinnertime.

- **Learn new feeding skills.** If baby can be soothed by no one but you, instead of skipping meals, master how to eat with one hand after your partner or an older child has cut up your food for you.

- **Keep some perspective.** Have faith that the episodes will only be a memory a month from now.

during a crying episode, but all day long—could cut in half the average duration of a crying fit, from two hours to one.[3] Researchers theorize that this is because mothers in close and constant proximity to their infant are better able to anticipate and respond to their baby's cues.

WHY IT'S IMPORTANT TO ALWAYS RESPOND

All babies cry sometimes, especially between the ages of 6 and 8 weeks. But letting a baby cry for extended periods without

Babies Crave Closeness

New babies need a lot of carrying around, and that can get tiresome for you. A soft front carrier is a must! Studies show that the more physical closeness you give your baby now, the more secure and independent he'll be later.

offering soothing or comfort can be harmful to a baby's development.

When left alone to cry, babies' brains become deprived of oxygen and flooded with stress hormones. Research appears to show that extreme exposure to stress hormones at a young age can cause lifelong health and behavioral problems. Animal tests and studies of children who were abused and neglected as babies have shown that the brain's exposure to these hormones causes nerve connections to fail to develop and for existing connections to disintegrate, which affects learning and memory.[4]

Scientific evidence shows that babies who cry excessively at a young age also cry more when they're older and are more at risk of acting out in unsociable ways later in life. One study found that babies who cried excessively and had feeding problems were 10 times more likely to have hyperactivity or conduct problems at 8 to 10 years of age.[5] Animal tests have also found that long-term exposure to stress hormones inhibits growth and has been associated with suppression

Do a Little Sleuthing

If your baby seems sleepless, it helps to keep a sleep/wake journal for a few days to get a bead on his actual sleeping patterns and hours. If you discover he's sleeping less than 13 hours over a 24-hour period, and at the same time seems irritable and agitated, here are some things to consider:

• Is he really not sleeping around the clock? Or, does he sleep, but in scattered periods of time? Colic can make it seem like your baby is getting less sleep than he actually is.

• If you're breastfeeding, take a look at the medications, stimulants, or nicotine that your baby may be ingesting with your milk. Ask your health-care provider for help in changing your medications or smoking habits.

• You may have a baby with a difficult temperament or neurological sensitivities that cause him to be overwhelmed by noises, lights, handling, or motion that prevent him from totally relaxing for sleep. (For tips on handling sensitive babies, see Chapter 5.)

Report This Type of Crying to Your Baby's Doctor

Here are some signals that your baby's crying may mean that he's having a physical problem, and your doctor needs to be notified:

- **Constant and shrill.** Your baby cries constantly for more than 3 hours and/or the cries are unusually shrill or intense.

- **Weak and whiny.** Your baby's cries are uncharacteristically weak along with other signs of illness, such as dry lips and fever.

- **Inconsolable.** Your crying baby cannot be comforted.

- **Symptoms of illness.** Your baby seems to be in pain or acts sick, has a rectal temperature over 100.5°F, and is vomiting or has diarrhea.

If you are afraid you might hurt your baby, or you feel so emotionally incapacitated that you cannot care for your baby, call your doctor or your baby's doctor right away.

---

of the immune system.[6] We will probably never be able to determine a "safe" amount of crying and exposure to stress hormones for human infants.

Responding to a baby's cry also gives him his first lessons in causality—that his actions have an effect. Habitually not responding to your baby's cries teaches him he's helpless to influence his environment or that he just has to cry louder and longer to have his needs met. The more responsive a mother is to her baby, the less time he will spend crying, the more securely attached he will become, and the more readily he will develop trust.

So even though it may seem like walking and soothing your crying or colicky baby is of little help, and even though the crying can be toe-curlingly difficult to take, frustrating, and even maddening,

it's still important that someone respond to the baby when he cries.

As your baby matures, you will learn the difference between a tired, complaining cry that means that in a few minutes your baby will settle on his own, and a stressed-out or alarmed cry that requires immediate response. Responding every time now helps establish that level of communication and trust, which is the key ingredient for helping him learn to fall asleep on his own.

However, that doesn't mean that mom always needs to be the one to respond. Let dad, grandma, or anyone else you can press into service take a turn carrying the baby around and soothing him, too. The crying will be (slightly) less upsetting to them, and your baby will learn that there are other people besides mom who are worthy of his trust.

Sudden Infant Death Syndrome (SIDS)

Sudden infant death syndrome, or SIDS, is the third leading cause of baby deaths in the United States. At last report, the deaths of approximately 2,200 babies a year were attributed to SIDS; nearly half of all deaths of babies younger than a year old are attributed to it. Standards set by the World Health Organization and the Centers for Disease Control and Prevention require that SIDS be given as the diagnosis when an infant younger than a year old dies suddenly and unexpectedly, when no clear cause of death can be found after a thorough investigation that includes an autopsy, examination of the death scene, and review of the baby's clinical history.

Scripps Howard News Service reporters conducted an unprecedented survey of more than 40,000 baby deaths between 1992 and 2004. Their 2007 report found that many deaths that may have previously been ascribed to SIDS might actually have been accidental suffocations.[7] For instance, when the Florida Medical Examiners Commission adopted new standards for infant death investigations in 1999, they required an official investigation of the site where babies died. As a result, 256 infants who previously could have been reported as SIDS victims actually died of suffocation from improper bedding, constricting clothing, or being smothered while sleeping with adults or siblings. A more recent study found that when 11 coroners used rigorous, federally recommended best practices when examining the deaths of babies, 72 percent of the 354 infant fatalities in their communities were deemed accidental suffocations instead of SIDS.

Nevertheless, unexplained and sudden infant death does happen, though it may be less common than some statistics may appear to show.

Let's explore what is and isn't known about SIDS and what parents and caregivers can do to help prevent it. If you're the type of parent who feels less frightened when you know more, you'll want to read this entire section. On the other hand, if having too much detail only makes things scarier to you, we suggest that you skip over most of the text and go directly to the quick bullets on page 73 on preventing SIDS, then move on to the next chapter.

FACTS ABOUT SIDS

While most conditions or diseases usually are diagnosed by the presence of specific symptoms, a baby's death from SIDS is not usually diagnosed until all other possible causes of death have been ruled out. That is done through a medical review of the baby's medical history and his environment. So SIDS is really a catchall label for unexplained, sudden deaths of otherwise healthy babies.

Estimating the Risk

Number of U.S. births in 2000: 4,058,814
Number of SIDS deaths in 2000: 2,523

Though SIDS most commonly occurs in babies who are sleeping in a room by themselves—the rate is disproportionately high in child-care settings—SIDS can strike no matter where a baby is sleeping. There have been cases where a baby died while sleeping on the lap of a wide-awake parent.

The American Academy of Pediatrics and Centers for Disease Control recommend that all babies be placed on their backs for sleep. The Back to Sleep campaign, spearheaded by the U.S. Consumer Product Safety Commission in the mid-1990s, is thought to have played a part in the 38 percent drop in SIDS deaths between 1992 and 1996. However, in spite of the well-publicized role of back sleeping in reducing the risk of SIDS deaths, an estimated 13 percent of all U.S. babies are still being placed facedown for sleep,[8] usually by day-care providers or relatives who are presumably unaware of the AAP/CDC recommendation.

FACTORS THAT MAY CONTRIBUTE TO SIDS

The following list is based on postmortem research. So far, no single risk factor or combination of factors can predict which babies will or will not die from SIDS. In the future, we will probably discover that SIDS is attributable to a combination of genetic and environmental factors.

Baby's age. Most babies who die from SIDS do so before they reach 6 months of age. In full-term infants, the incidence of SIDS rises from zero at birth, peaks at 2 to 4 months, and declines to nearly zero by 1 year. The average age of death in full-term babies occurs at 14.5 weeks, and 90 percent of all SIDS deaths occur before 6 months of age.

Prematurity. Prematurity can cause an increased risk for SIDS. Extremely premature babies, those born before 35 weeks' gestation, are thought to have 50 times the SIDS risk of full-term babies. They are also at risk of SIDS for a longer range of time than full-term babies, with the greatest risk of death occurring between 4 and 6 months of age. The rates of prematurity continue to grow in the United States, increasing by 35 percent between 1981 and 2009. More than half a million babies are born prematurely, or before 37 weeks of pregnancy, in the United States each year. That translates into about one in every eight births. In about four out of every ten cases, the reasons for a baby arriving too soon are unknown. Having twins or multiples due to

Ten Things You Can Do to Help Protect Your Baby from SIDS

Following all these tips can't SIDS-proof your baby, nor should it be implied that a parent whose baby has died from SIDS could have prevented the tragedy. What we offer here are some practical steps you can take to help reduce your baby's SIDS risk:

1. **Get good prenatal care.** Do what you can to prevent premature birth during pregnancy by keeping all your prenatal health-care appointments and by following good health and nutrition practices. Getting quality prenatal nutrition and health care can help you ward off health problems that may affect your baby too, as moms who have good prenatal care are less likely to have premature babies. Also, it's important to be well informed about signs of premature labor and get care immediately if you have contractions or your water breaks before 37 weeks' gestation.

2. **Avoid cigarettes and drugs.** Don't smoke during or after pregnancy, and do not allow people to smoke in your home. Don't use cocaine or heroin or other opiates, such as OxyContin, during pregnancy.

3. **Talk to caregivers.** Make sure that everyone who cares for your baby knows about putting your baby down in the *on-the-back* position for sleep. To protect your baby from suffocation, make sure all your baby's caregivers know your rules about avoiding soft bedding, and about tucking in loose sheets and blankets.

4. **Space your pregnancies.** Studies have found a higher risk of SIDS for babies conceived within 6 months after a prior pregnancy.[9]

5. **Put baby on his back for sleep.** Put your baby faceup for sleep on a firm surface, rather than facedown.

6. **Make sure that your baby's nursery is well ventilated.** A 2008 study found that sleeping in a room with a fan lowers a baby's risk of SIDS by an incredible 72 percent.[10]

7. **Keep fluff out of the bedroom.** Keep quilts, puffy bedding, stuffed animals, and other soft materials out of your baby's sleeping area. Tuck sheets in so they cannot cover your baby's head or face.

8. **Breastfeed.** Breastfeed your baby exclusively for as long as you can—at least during the 2-to-4-month high-risk period.

9. **Sleep nearby.** Keep your baby close to you at night, particularly during the vulnerable 2-to-4-month stage of development.

10. **Don't "sleep train" too early.** To encourage deeper or longer sleep periods, wait until your baby is *at least* 6 months old (if at all).

Typical SIDS Risk

The sooner a baby is born, the longer his risk for SIDS. The following list shows gestation and the length of the SIDS risk:

Full-term babies: 14 weeks after birth
Premature babies (28-32 weeks): 15 weeks after birth
Very premature babies (22-27 weeks): 20 weeks after birth[10]

reproduction technologies, and the better survival rates of babies who in decades past might not have lived, may be other reasons why more babies are premature and, therefore, more at risk for SIDS.

Low birthweight. Also at high risk are babies born weighing less than 3.3 pounds who have experienced growth retardation during pregnancy or during infancy.

Low birthweight is defined as less than 5 pounds 8 ounces, and the lower a baby's birthweight, the higher the risk for SIDS. For babies who were less than about 3.5 pounds at birth, the risk is about four times greater than if they weighed more than 5.5 pounds at birth.

Gender. Sixty-one percent of SIDS victims are boys, 39 percent are girls.

Stomach-down sleeping. Putting a baby down to sleep on his stomach or side, rather than on his back, increases his risk of dying from SIDS, which could be related to putting pressure on his jaw, narrowing his airway, or hampering his breathing. It also increases his risk of re-breathing his own exhaled air, which could cause suffocation.

Day care. About one in five SIDS deaths occurs when a parent is not caring for an infant. This may be because some day care centers, grandparents, or other babysitters are not aware of the Back to Sleep campaign, and place babies in a prone position because it facilitates longer, deeper sleep. The deeper sleep that this position may bring is more convenient for a care provider, but it is more dangerous to the baby. Sometimes caregivers also place multiple infants together in one crib, which also appears to heighten the risk.[12] Make sure your infant's care providers are aware of the back-sleeping recommendation and follow it, and that infants are not placed in cribs together.

Exposure to tobacco. The risk of SIDS in a normal birthweight baby is tripled if mom smoked during pregnancy and if the baby continues to be exposed to tobacco smoke after birth. The risk increases with the number of cigarettes a mom smokes. The baby is also at risk if other adults in a household smoke, even if they don't smoke indoors.

Formula feeding. Research has consistently shown a link between formula feeding and SIDS. Formula feeding appears to increase the risk from three to eight times. Studies in England and New Zealand have found that formula-fed babies had triple the risk of SIDS; a Japanese study has suggested a five-fold risk,[13] and a German study has suggested that formula feeding exposes babies to eight times more risk than the babies of non-smokers.[14] The more formula in an infant's diet, the higher the risk. Breastfeeding your baby exclusively (not supplementing his diet with baby formula) for the first 6 months confers the most protection.

Exposure to illegal drugs. A mother's use of cocaine or heroin during pregnancy results in a twofold to fifteenfold increase in the risk of dying from SIDS.[15]

Teen pregnancy. Babies whose mothers are under the age of 20 are more at risk.

Poor ventilation. Many cases of SIDS have been linked to situations in which a baby re-breathed his own exhaled carbon dioxide—because of restricted airflow in the sleeping area. To avoid this, don't put your baby down on a waterbed, a beanbag chair, or couch cushion, and keep the following items out of your baby's bed and away from his face: a soft sleep surface such as an old, too-soft mattress, fluffy bedding such as comforters and sheepskins, regular or polystyrene-bean pillows, crib bumpers, and plush toys. Consider using a fan in your baby's room for constant airflow.

Overheating. Keeping your baby's room too warm and overdressing him for sleep, especially when he has a fever, increases the risk of SIDS.

Babies should be kept warm but should not be overdressed for sleep. The temperature in a baby's room should feel comfortable to a lightly clothed adult. Overheating may induce deeper sleep, which makes it harder for a baby to rouse himself should air restrictions occur. In warmer months, either a "onesie" or footed sleeper is sufficient as long as your baby isn't sleeping directly under an air-conditioning vent. In the winter, a zippered sleep sac can help keep a crib- or bassinet-sleeping baby warm.

Under normal conditions, your baby doesn't need a hat or blankets. Make sure that the crib has nothing in it but your baby.

WARNING: Don't Try to Train a Young Baby to Sleep!

Avoid any "sleep training" program if your baby is younger than 6 months old, especially if it involves allowing him to cry for extended periods of time. Overtiring your baby will affect his ability to wake up during a near-SIDS episode.

If your baby is sleeping in an adult bed, be sure to take into account the extra body heat of the adults when you dress your baby for bed. Because of the extra smothering hazard that heavy blankets can pose in an adult bed, some baby sleep experts suggest keeping blankets completely out of bed and having baby and the family sleep in warm pajamas without any kind of covering. This might be a good option if your bed is on the smaller side and you fear that you won't be able to keep blankets off of your baby's face.

If you do use blankets in bed, use them to cover yourself but keep them away from your baby. Don't swaddle him. His arms and legs should be free so he can swat away any blankets or bedding that accidentally cover him in the night. Keep pillows away from your baby and use a mesh bed rail to keep him from rolling off of the bed.

Separate sleeping quarters. Babies who sleep alone in a separate room from their parents have a five to ten times greater risk of SIDS than babies who sleep near their parents.

Babies who sleep in bed with parents rouse more frequently and appear to synchronize their breathing with their parents'. They are also more likely to breastfeed, which also reduces the risk.

Having your baby sleep in a bassinet or a co-sleeper in your room for the first 6 months of life may also confer a degree of protection.

Flu season. One study found that SIDS is three and a half times more common in winter than summer.[16] Heavily wrapping up a baby and placing him facedown for sleep can increase his risk of SIDS. Also, more recent studies in the United States have found some SIDS babies with higher-than-normal levels of immune system cells and substances, indicating that they may have been fighting an infection.

Ethnic origin. African-American, Native American, and Alaska Native infants are two to three times more likely than Caucasian infants to die of SIDS. Asian, Pacific Islander, and Hispanic infants are the least likely.

Certain pacifier use. The risk of SIDS appears to be higher for babies who habitually use a pacifier, but then aren't given one on a particular night.[17] This may be evidence that babies become dependent, using the pacifier as a breathing and arousal regulation tool. However, babies who reject pacifiers should not be forced to take one. (For more on this, see Chapter 4.)

Couches and armchairs. A disproportionate number of SIDS deaths have occurred when a parent was sleeping with a baby on a couch or armchair.

Sleep deprivation. Being able to rouse from deep sleep appears to be an important defense for babies against potentially dangerous sleep situations. Sleep deprivation is a risk factor, and recent changes in normal life routines have shown to be more common among SIDS

Baby Breathing and Motion Monitors

Studies have shown that home monitors that sound an alarm when babies stop breathing for short periods of time are not effective in reducing SIDS. In fact, the American Academy of Pediatrics does not recommend their use. Sleep apnea is very common in infants, and almost all newborns breathe unevenly at times, but only a tiny percentage of these infants will actually have SIDS-like episodes. While these monitors cause a lot of parental worry with their false alarms, they simply aren't effective enough to be trusted, and babies have died while hooked up to them. In those cases, it was already too late to save the baby once the monitor sounded.

victims, compared with other infants in a control group.[18]

Deep sleep in the early morning. Babies who wake less frequently during the night have been shown to be more susceptible to SIDS. In studies, SIDS victims exhibit fewer complete arousals by the end of the night, and most SIDS cases appear to happen toward the end of the night. Unlike adults, babies under stress appear to sleep more deeply.

Health factors. There is evidence suggesting that some SIDS babies are born with abnormalities in the serotonin receptors in their brains, particularly in the arcuate nucleus (or medulla), which is a portion of the brain involved in the control of breathing and waking during sleep. Babies born with defects in other portions of the brain or body may also be more prone to a sudden death. These abnormalities may be inherited or may result from prenatal exposure to a toxic substance or lack of a vital compound in the prenatal environment, such as sufficient oxygen.

There has also been other evidence implicating certain genetic factors in SIDS deaths. One study found that 9.5 percent of SIDS victims carried a gene variant for long QT syndrome, which is linked to a specific type of heart arrhythmia. Other studies have found that SIDS victims had variants in genes that affect immune response.[19]

AFP. A Scottish study published in the *New England Journal of Medicine* in 2004 surveyed the results of alpha-fetoprotein (AFP) blood tests, also known as the triple screen, quad screen, or penta screen, that were collected from a large group of pregnant women at 4 to 6 months of pregnancy.

The survey was done to establish whether there was a connection between elevated levels of this protein (made by the liver and fetal tissues during pregnancy) and the risk of SIDS deaths in babies. Typically the test is used to predict the risk of stillbirth or Down syndrome, and it can also detect liver abnormalities during fetal development.

Researchers compared the SIDS risk in babies of women with both the highest and lowest levels of alpha-fetoprotein. They found that the risk was nearly three times greater for babies born to women with the highest levels of the protein. Though the overall risk of SIDS was very low—2.7 SIDS deaths per 10,000 births among those with the lowest levels of the protein and 7.5 SIDS deaths per 10,000 births among women with the highest levels—a connection seems to have been made.

High levels of alpha-fetoprotein also appeared to show a common risk factor with stillbirth, which may be linked to physical problems that impair physical growth and development during pregnancy.

As we find out more about SIDS, the evidence appears to show that it is likely to be caused by genetic predisposition and environmental factors. Just as some adults might be predisposed to heart disease but can reduce their risk through diet and exercise, certain babies may be predisposed to SIDS, but with certain measures may be less likely to die from it.

Notes on Storing Breastmilk

After the first 4 weeks, when your milk supply is well established and your baby is nursing comfortably and effectively, you can start hand expressing or pumping extra bottles of milk for later use. Here's what you need to know about storing your milk:

- **Refrigerating.** Breastmilk can be stored at room temperature (less than 77°F) for 4 to 8 hours, or at the back of the refrigerator for 3 to 8 days.

- **Freezing.** Breastmilk can be stored in the freezer compartment of your refrigerator for up to 2 weeks. If your refrigerator has a separate freezer section, milk can be stored safely for 3 to 4 months. It will last for 6 months or longer if you have a deep freeze that can hold the temperature at a constant 0°F.

- **Storing.** When you're gathering milk to be stored, make sure that your hands are clean, and, if you use a breast pump, that the components and bottles have been washed in hot, soapy water and allowed to air dry. Milk can be stored in a plastic or glass bottle with the top sealed and screwed on tight, or you can purchase freezer bags designed specifically for milk storage. Fresh breastmilk can be added to frozen milk as long as there is less fresh than frozen. Breastmilk expands when frozen, so be careful not to fill containers right up to the top. Date the bottles or bags by writing on masking tape with a marker or ballpoint pen.

- **Warming or defrosting.** Don't use a microwave to warm or defrost breastmilk. This can kill important nutrients and leave hot pockets that could burn your baby's mouth. Instead, defrost the milk gradually in a bowl of warm water.

In 2009, the federal Centers for Disease Control and Prevention launched a revolutionary surveillance program to study deaths that were once attributed solely to SIDS.

The health agency is conducting a pilot study for a National Sudden Unexpected Infant Death and Pregnancy Loss Project, also known as IMPACT, that will enter information on all unexpected infant deaths using the Web-based Case Reporting System operated by the National Center for Child Death Review. Information will include results of detailed infant autopsies, pathology and toxicology reports, reports from the death scene investigation and the children's medical records, which may finally help to shed light on the true causes of many unexplained infant deaths.

Colic: The Waking Nightmare

Most (if not all) babies have cranky, upset periods from time to time, including episodes of extended crying for no apparent reason, especially between 6 and 8 weeks of age. If your baby's cry ever suddenly changes into a high-pitched cry and you see him holding his breath in between wails, call your pediatrician as soon as possible. The "emergency" cry may be an early-warning sign that something is wrong.

If, after examining your baby, the pediatrician doesn't find anything physically wrong, yet the high-pitched crying continues for days and weeks, that's colic. The official definition of colic is when an otherwise healthy baby between the age of 3 weeks and 3 months cries for more than 3 days a week. (The non-clinical definition of colic is: "If you have to *ask* if your baby has colic, he doesn't.") Unlike the cluster-fuss, colicky crying seems to be non-stop and occurs around the clock, although it may also be more intense in the early evening.

No one knows exactly what causes colic. In fact, *colic* is just an umbrella term, like *headache*, which has multiple causes. Colic's body signals are identical to those that indicate baby pain, but some recent researchers believe not all baby crying is caused by pain.

The torment of colic is worsened by the fact that doctors and other health-care providers have no universally accepted explanation or cure, and can't offer parents much help.

Usually, babies who have colic are otherwise healthy: They feed well, gain weight, and grow like any other baby. Although some theories about what causes colic seem to hold more weight than others, the cause may differ depending on the baby. Figuring out an answer for your baby (if there is one) is usually a process of elimination—ruling out everything that could possibly be wrong. For most parents, the answer is to get all the support and rest they can muster until their baby simply grows out of it, which is almost always by 6 months of age.

Colic not only seems to cause suffering for the baby, it also causes parents to feel guilt and uncertainty. "Is the crying caused by something I did?" "Is there something I could be doing that I'm not?" Sometimes parents stumble across a magical cure for the screaming—the baby is teething or he has gas, for instance—but more often than not, nothing seems to help.

Being isolated with a fussy baby can be tough. You might find that you avoid leaving the house with your baby because you dread the accusing stares that his screaming attacks draw from strangers. You may be hesitant to invite guests over or leave your baby with anyone else because you don't want to leave your distressed baby or subject others to the all-too-familiar torment you're undergoing.

You're also likely to get really, *really* bad advice from relatives, friends, and strangers on the street. People who have never been mothers won't get it at all, either. "So, babies cry. Just put in some earplugs and go in another room!" "Maybe he just needs to express his feelings!"

The truth is: No one who hasn't lived through the colic experience can understand what happens to a mom when she hears the cry of her own baby. Your blood pressure goes up, you get knots in your stomach and an adrenaline rush, your breasts engorge, and you basically go insane trying to do *anything* to make it better. In fact, your colicky baby's screams give you the same hormonal rush that would give you the strength to lift a car if your baby were trapped under a tire.

The exact cause of colic isn't known. It could be a baby's reaction to something in his formula or breastmilk. It could be an inner ear infection or the onset of an illness or a hernia. Or, it just could be immaturity—the baby's stomach, intestines, and metabolic systems need time to learn how to function together.

It's estimated that more than 700,000 babies a year suffer from colic-level crying bouts.

WHAT WE KNOW ABOUT COLIC

1. **Colic may be caused by gut flora,** that is, the microorganisms that live in the intestines and help break down food, prevent allergies, and help the body resist illness. In the womb, a baby's intestinal tract is sterile, but soon after birth, about 500 different types of microorganisms move in. Multiple studies have shown that colicky babies have different gut flora patterns[21] than non-colicky ones. One study found two types of organisms only in colicky babies, and that the colicky infants lacked *Lactobacillus acidophilus,*[19] a bacterium known to help defend the body against potentially harmful bacteria in the digestive tract.

If your baby has colic, ask your pediatrician if he or she would recommend administering helpful gut bacteria using a probiotic, a special formulation of friendly gut bacteria.[20] Some pediatricians may recommend

Don't Blame the Cow!

Even though doctors often blame baby crying on cow's-milk allergies and other digestive disturbances, they are now thought to be responsible for baby colic only in about one out of every 100 babies.[21]

giving regular doses of simethicone (Mylicon® drops is one brand name) with every feeding. Unfortunately, research suggests that this approach is ineffective.

2. **It is rarely caused or aggravated by an allergy to cow's milk.** Only about 1 or 2 percent of cases can be traced to an actual allergy to cow's-milk proteins, which are used to make most baby formulas. Infants who are breastfed have a lower risk of developing a milk allergy than infants who are formula-fed, but milk proteins do also pass through into mother's milk.

More likely, it is gas. All babies have gas, but if your baby has colic and his stomach also feels hard, or he's pulling up his knees, or you hear bubbling sounds in his guts, one cause could be excess gas, or "trapped wind," as the British call it. Granted, it can be hard to tell if a baby's stomach is hard while he's tensed up and crying—nor is it easy to hear subtle stomach noises over wailing—but try to detect these signs when he has an intake of breath.

Excess baby gas is most frequently caused by a baby's sensitivity to lactose, the sugars that are found in cow's milk and also in human breastmilk, especially if mom consumes a lot of dairy products.

But if your baby has cow's-milk allergies, his body will react to the presence of proteins by sending white blood cells to fight what it interprets as unwanted invaders. The chemicals released during the battle will cause your baby's stomach and intestines to become red, swollen, and sometimes ulcerated. If that's the case, your baby's colic is caused by serious pain.

In addition to colic and irritability, a baby who is allergic

WARNING: Don't Shake Your Baby!

It is very important that you not take out your frustration with the crying by shaking your baby. Even brief violent shaking can severely injure his head and neck and cause lifelong neurological damage or even death. If you feel compelled to shake or violently handle your baby, put him down in his crib or on his back on the floor and get yourself out of earshot until the urge subsides. Call a professional if the feeling doesn't subside.

Eliminating Dietary Causes of Colic

Eliminate cow's milk. If your baby is breastfed, try eliminating cow's milk in your own diet—including cheese, yogurt, ice cream, butter, and so on—for at least 2 weeks to see if it has any effect. (Remember to make up any calcium you'll be missing with fortified juice or nut milk and/or calcium citrate supplements.)

Try soy-based formulas. If your baby is bottle-fed, ask your pediatrician before you switch to soy formula. The doctor may advise switching to soy formula for at least 2 weeks to see if the crying abates, but current research appears to show that babies who react to cow's-milk sugars and proteins are likely to react to soy, too. Soy also appears to have estrogenic (hormonal) properties that could affect your baby. A better, though much more expensive, solution is to switch to a special (but very costly) hypoallergenic formula that breaks down cow's-milk proteins to make them more digestible, such as the Nutramigen® or EleCare® brands. If you haven't stopped breastfeeding for long, you may also be able to re-establish your milk supply by nursing and/or pumping breastmilk to replace formula feedings. (A certified lactation consultant can advise you.)

Avoid certain vegetables. Vegetables can also cause breastfed babies bouts of gas and discomfort. In particular, vegetables in the cabbage (aka cruciferous) family—which also includes broccoli, cauliflower, turnips, mustard greens, radishes, horseradish, and watercress—are common culprits. If that is the case, then you'll notice that your baby will consistently have fits of bawling after the first or second feeding, usually 5 or 6 hours after you have eaten the offending vegetable. Some babies are also sensitive to high-acidity foods eaten by their mothers, such as citrus fruits, tomatoes, and strawberries. But, as mentioned previously, all babies have some gas. If your baby's crying is consistent and persistent, a fruit or vegetable is unlikely to be the culprit, unless you consistently eat the same fruits or vegetables on a near-daily basis.

to cow's-milk protein may also refuse to eat, gag on his food, or develop skin rashes such as bumps or hives. In severe cases he may vomit and/or wheeze after feeding. Symptoms may come on soon after eating, or they may be slower—with the onset taking 7 to 10 days to appear.

And here's more bad news—about 80 percent of babies who are sensitive to cow's milk are also sensitive to soy formulas, too, which some doctors still are prescribing as an antidote for colic.

We suggest you do your homework about feeding soy-milk-based formulas to babies, since some recent reports suggest that soy may have hormone-like effects on the human body. If indeed your baby is reacting to cow's milk, the next step will likely be a hypoallergenic formula with specially formulated proteins and sugars, which, though costly, may solve the problem.

3. **It isn't your parenting style.** Researchers have studied differences in crying patterns between babies who have "proximal care" parents (also known as "attachment" parents), who are in close physical contact with their babies about 80 percent of the time, co-sleep, and respond to every cry and those whose close physical contact amounts to 40 percent of the time. The rate of colic was the same in both groups.

Another study compared mothers' sensitivity and baby crying and found that many moms of colicky babies were even *more* sensitive and responsive than mothers of non-fussers. So colic is neither your fault, nor the fault of your parenting style.

4. **Colic doesn't harm.** Unlike crying related to neglect, plenty of healthy, sensitive, well-adjusted, and smart people in the world were colicky babies. Although some babies may be colicky due to neurological issues, one study found that colicky babies were much more likely to turn out to be easygoing toddlers, while so-called good babies in the early months had a greater probability of becoming hell-raising toddlers down the road. So there may be justice in the world, after all.

5. **Excessive criers may have different sleep cycles.** A Finnish study found that in excessively crying infants, the proportion of rapid eye movement (REM) sleep was higher during the 3-hour period from the beginning of the first long sleep in the evening and lower during the preceding 3-hour period compared with the control group. The researchers theorized that criers may be characterized by a disturbance that affects rapid eye movement and non-rapid-eye-movement sleep-stage proportion during evening hours.[22] Unfortunately the study didn't answer whether it's the sleep disturbances that cause

"One night at 3 in the morning, after the baby had been crying steadily for hours on end and we were afraid our whole apartment building could hear her and would be down the next morning to force us to move out, we all sat down and cried together—me, my husband, and my baby."

colic or the colic that causes the sleep problems.

Another theory is that colic is aided by an infant's lack of melatonin, the hormone that helps regulate sleep. An infant's pineal gland typically doesn't begin to produce melatonin until 12 weeks of age, which happens to be when most colic disappears. (For more on melatonin, see page 100.)

6. There may be a gastroesophageal connection. New studies at the Colic Clinic at Brown University demonstrate that nearly half of babies with colic have mild gastroesophageal reflux (GER), which is caused by milk backing up into the barrier, the sphincter-like muscle between the esophagus and the stomach.

Most infants spit up milk from time to time. A baby's esophagus pushes and squeezes breastmilk or formula down for digestion and, in the early months, the operation of the baby's "swallowing tube" is very primitive and uncoordinated at best. Squeezing and pushing

actions don't operate together very well. The small flap at the top of the baby's stomach designed to hold milk down might not operate very well, allowing milk to flow both downward and upward at the same time.

For some babies, stomach acid, not just milk, comes up during drinking and digestion, irritating the throat and nasal passages. When that happens, the baby will experience a severe burning sensation both during and after feeding that is as uncomfortable as trying to drink orange juice when you have a sore throat.

Here are some of the symptoms of GER: Your baby will cry, arch his back, and pull back from the nipple in protest when he starts to drink. He will spit up a lot and maybe even vomit. He may have frequent, hard hiccup attacks, cough, and seem positively uncomfortable when you try to lay him down on his back.

It helps to put your baby in a semi-upright position in an infant seat after feeding,

Five Things to Remember About Colic

1. It is not your fault.

2. It is not your baby's fault.

3. Colic crying doesn't appear to harm babies.

4. Excessive crying may be caused by intestinal issues, a food allergy, or a sleep disorder.

5. Colic *will* eventually go away—by six months of age, if not sooner.

Your Screaming-Baby Emergency Plan

You may feel powerless when your baby shows signs of colic, but here are some things you can try:

Find the cause.

- Is your baby hungry? Try feeding him or burping him if he stops drinking midway.

- Is he tired? When was the last time he slept for more than twenty minutes? If he's had nothing but catnaps all morning, and it's now afternoon, fatigue may be the problem. Rocking, nursing, or walking may encourage him to doze off.

- Is something under your baby's clothes or in his diaper that's poking or entangling him?

- Does he have a fever? Is he drooling excessively, which could mean he's cutting a tooth?

- Does his stomach feel bloated, meaning he might have constipation or gas?

Try comforting strategies.
(Note: Whatever strategies you use should be continued long enough to bore your baby.)

- Walk your baby into a new environment: Go outside if you're inside, and vice versa.

- Provide rhythmic motion with swoops, jiggles, dips, rocking, or a baby swing (but do not shake your baby).

- Use pressure plus rocking, such as moving your baby back and forth, belly down, on an exercise ball.

- Use vibration, such as a vibrating baby seat or a ride in the car.

- Temporarily swaddle your baby so his body is restrained, or simply rest him on your chest enfolded in a blanket, and hold him firmly so his legs and arms are restrained.

- Try the "colic hold."

- Experiment with droning sounds from a vacuum cleaner or white noise from an FM radio station that's off the air.

Take a breather.

- Recognize that at certain stages, such as at about 6 weeks and during growth spurts, some babies simply cannot be soothed. The only answer may be to just endure and realize that this, too, will pass.

(continued on next page)

- Pump milk. Invest in a breast pump, pump some milk, and at least every other day, arrange for dad, grandma, a friend, or a neighbor to help care for your baby to help you clear your head, baby-free.

- Get out of the house. Shop for groceries, socialize, go to a religious service, a concert, a movie, have lunch with a friend, take a jog, whatever. Just get yourself out of the house so you can recharge your batteries for the next round. If you don't have someone to watch your baby, try to leave the house at least once a day even if it means carrying him, taking him out in his stroller, or driving your car while he's crying. You won't feel so trapped, and the vibrations from the car or stroller may even help calm the crying.

Get the support you need.

- Get relief. If you find yourself losing patience or getting angry with your baby, ask someone else to take over so you can have time to rebalance yourself.

- Soak up the sunshine. Exposure to sunlight while you're outdoors will boost your vitamin D levels, which could boost your mood, and may help regulate your baby's sleep cycle, which is especially important because it may be a link between colic and sleep issues. (For more on sunlight and sleep cycle regulation, see page 100.)

- Seek help. If you feel like you're sinking into postpartum depression—that is, you don't want to get out of bed, you cry a lot, and/or you have recurrent grim thoughts—ask your obstetrician or family doctor for help. You need to feel balanced yourself to help your baby feel better.

or carry him in a soft carrier, to help the milk stay down. A hammock-like baby sleeper that places your baby's head higher than his stomach may help your baby sleep better at night as well. (See our discussion of baby sleep aids starting on page 62.)

Your pediatrician may suggest medications or advise you to add rice cereal to your baby's bottle to help soothe his throat and thicken his food, in order to make it easier for his esophagus to hold milk down. Reflux generally gets better after a baby's third month. Ideally, by 6 months, when he can sit up, this particular cause of baby crying will have gone away on its own.

7. **Colic will go away.** There is currently no generally accepted medical treatment for colic, and the approach taken by medical professionals varies substantially depending on the doctor. Many pediatricians believe that the condition is untreatable, and is best left to run its course, usually by 3 to 6 months of age.

Q: I have a 3-week-old son. How do I get him on a sleeping

schedule through the night? I rarely get sleep and am exhausted all the time! Any advice would be greatly appreciated!

A: We're sure this is not what you want to hear, but trying to get a baby on a sleep schedule before 3 to 4 months of age isn't going to be very successful! You can't convince, cajole, or force a baby to adopt and adapt to a schedule before he is developmentally able. Though a baby at 3 weeks will sleep for about 13 to 16 hours a day, he has a tiny stomach and needs to be fed *at least* every 4 hours (and sometimes as often as every 90 minutes). It isn't until he reaches the age of 5 to 25 weeks that he will become biologically capable of settling into a pattern of sleeping mostly at night, with one or two night feedings and regular naps during the day. And it is only at about 1 month of age that you will begin to see your baby begin to sleep more hours at night than during the day.

The truth is, there is no such thing as a bad sleep habit at this stage. Observe your baby's cues, and take advantage of his portability and flexibility, too. It's a myth that you need to get your baby on a strict schedule from day one "to teach him independence." How about letting him sleep in your (baby-safe) bed or a bassinet or a co-sleeper in your room? That way, you don't have to wake up quite as fully to attend to him. (For more on safe bed sharing, see page 33.)

Q: My son is 7 weeks old and I am having an extremely

difficult time getting him on a schedule and getting him into his crib. Is there anything I can do to help him, or, do I continue to wing it? I have been told by different people to put him in his crib and to walk away, leaving him to cry. If this is true, how long do I leave him there? Is there anything else I can do?

A: It can be downright dangerous to a young baby's health if you attempt to force him to "cry it out" at such a young age. Rather than soothing themselves, newborns will work themselves into long-lasting, wide-awake distress if left alone while they're awake in a crib. Also, at this age, your baby still needs to get at least 30 percent of his calories overnight. And younger babies in particular do not understand what psychologists call "object permanence." In other words, if you leave your baby alone to cry in his crib, he is not developmentally able to realize

> *"If enduring mind-numbing bouts of colic, having your nipples chewed off at 3 a.m., and cleaning up a stinky pile of poop stuck to your baby's bum isn't love, there's no such thing."*

that you are only a few paces away in the hall. All your baby knows is that you, the key to his very survival, have left him. A baby who is left to cry alone will eventually stop crying, not because he's learned to comfort himself, but because he's exhausted.

A baby's need to be close to his mother is why so many parents choose to bedshare with their baby or have him sleep in a bassinet on mom's side of the bed for the first months and then transition to sleeping in a crib in the nursery after he is more mature. In the meantime, don't feel guilty about winging it. Soon your baby's brain will have matured to the point that you'll begin to see a schedule emerge on its own. (See our rules for safe bed sharing, beginning on page 43.)

What you can do to set the stage for a good schedule, though, is to start trying to become aware of when your baby is naturally tired. Usually, a young baby will be ready for his first nap of the day about 90 minutes after he wakes up in the morning. Use this timing to your advantage so you can plan ahead where you would like the baby to have his morning nap every day.

This might be in a crib in his room, or you may prefer having a portable crib somewhere else in your house. Some babies just don't like to lie still in a crib or bassinet and prefer to nap in a swing or a bouncy seat, and as long as your baby is strapped in safely and you keep watch over him, there's nothing wrong with that for now. Some younger babies will also make it clear that they prefer napping on top of mom, and will only fall

> *"My baby screamed around the clock, and I felt horrible about it. It felt like he was blaming me for being a rotten mother. Fortunately, his crying stopped a few months later, and we could finally bond with each other."*

asleep if they're in contact with her. If that description fits your baby, then wearing your baby in a carrier or sling can help (at least until your baby gets so big that your muscles start to get strained).

You can feed him until he falls asleep and then put him down or rock him. If he seems sleepy but then rouses when you try to put him down, pick him up and walk or rock him until he drops off again. Some moms also plan errands that involve a lot of driving to coincide with baby's naps so he can sleep in the car.

Your baby's morning nap may be quite short, or it might last for several hours, depending on how his sleep went the night before. Then, another 2½ hours after he wakes up from his morning nap, you will usually see that he's ready for another. Some babies have days where they skip an afternoon or evening nap, especially if there's a change in their environment or daily routine.

Q: Am I creating a bad habit by letting my baby nurse to sleep?

A: Your baby's nursing to sleep is a very normal and developmentally appropriate thing to do. It is totally normal for babies to nurse to sleep and to wake up more than once at night and nurse to sleep again. By focusing on feeding, your baby can tune out external signals. He can also "stoke up" to prepare for sleeping for a longer stretch.

Falling asleep without nursing is a developmental milestone that your baby will reach when he is ready. As your baby matures he will become more capable of falling asleep without nursing, and you can begin to practice putting him down while he's awake. If you find it annoying to nurse him to sleep, try breaking the suction of your nipple and then substituting a finger or a pacifier once your baby's had enough time to feed and is starting to drift off.

Q: My 2-month-old is still up every 2 to 4 hours. I've started her on formula with no difference. She's eating like a horse. What else can I do?

A: Not much. You're bound to be exhausted yourself, so don't operate heavy machinery and stay away from sharp knives while you're sleep-deprived. Your baby is actually sleeping about as much (or as little) as most 2-month-olds do. Unfortunately for exhausted parents, a baby's ability to sleep through the night is determined by the maturity of her brain and the capacity of her stomach. It's true that formula takes longer to digest than breastmilk, but not to the degree that a baby with 2 hours' worth of stomach capacity, switched to formula, would suddenly start sleeping through the night. As she grows, your baby will gradually start to sleep for longer stretches. Help her along by making night feedings dim and quiet. Some experts recommend also waking your baby to feed before you go to bed, improving your chances of having a longer stretch of sleep yourself.

Q: Is it wise to let my baby suck on a pacifier to sleep? Is it okay if my baby doesn't like a pacifier? Do pacifiers help prevent SIDS?

A: Pacifiers have both their benefits and their risks. Hundreds of thousands of pacifiers have been recalled because they presented a choking hazard for babies. And many dentists warn parents that pacifier overuse can lead to dental deformities, such as overbite, if they're used after teeth have begun to come in. In addition, babies who become addicted to pacifiers may awaken in the night when they lose them in their cribs. However, some researchers believe that pacifiers may help to protect some babies from SIDS.

The American Academy of Pediatrics recommends "that pacifiers be offered to infants as a potential method to reduce the risk of SIDS. The pacifier should be offered to the infant when being placed for all sleep episodes, including daytime naps and nighttime sleeps . . . based on the consistency of findings and the likelihood that the beneficial effects will outweigh any potential negative effects. In consideration of potential adverse effects, we recommend pacifier use for infants up to 1 year of age, which includes the peak ages for SIDS risk and the period in which the infant's need for sucking is highest. For breastfed infants, pacifiers should be introduced after breastfeeding has been well established."

The AAP adds: "The pacifier should not be used as a substitute for nursing or feeding, nor should it be coated with sugar, honey, or other sweet substances. Once the infant falls asleep, the pacifier should not be reintroduced if it falls out of the mouth, nor should infants who refuse a pacifier be forced to take one."

Dealing with Exhaustion

As your baby enters the 6-week peak, especially if he sleeps in another room, you may find yourself hitting your own peak of fatigue. Not only is his crying at its worst, but by this point, your partner may have returned to work, and grandparents and in-laws have gone back to their regular schedules, leaving you alone, for the most part, to cope with the fatigue.

There's actually a name for the exhaustion parents of babies feel: postpartum fatigue (PPF). And it can affect every aspect of your life, from your health to how well you function to interactions with the baby and how quickly you heal from giving birth.

People who have never had babies or don't remember the newborn experience may chirp, "No one has ever died of sleep deprivation!" But believe it or not, they're wrong.

Not sleeping for more than 11 days can actually cause death, and short-term sleep deprivation can lead to dangerous situations. Adults need 8 to 9 hours of sleep for every 24-hour period, though a few people seem to be fine with as few as 7 hours of sleep. Less rest than that, though, and sleep deprivation begins to have a powerful effect on mood and performance. On days without enough sleep, you feel as though you're swimming through syrup. You get befuddled and frustrated by the simplest tasks. If you don't shut down your brain periodically, your brain will start to shut itself down for you.

One study published in a British scientific journal found that people who drove after being awake for 17 to 19 hours have slower reaction times than test subjects with a .05 blood alcohol level.[23] (A .05 blood alcohol level is approximately the equivalent of two drinks, or a level that would impair the driving of a 140-pound woman.) Researchers estimate that between 16 and 60 percent of road accidents are sleep-deprivation related.

Being sleep-deprived can also cause people to gain weight, which could be one of the reasons that extra baby weight can be so difficult to lose, and could be part of the reason fathers also gain weight postpartum. Sleep deprivation can result in your body producing less of a hormone called **leptin** that cues the sensation of being full and increases metabolism and production of the hormone **ghrelin**, which drives sensations of hunger. Sleep deprivation also appears to hinder the body's ability to regulate and metabolize glucose, which can lead to type 2 diabetes, high blood pressure, muscle aches, and clinical depression.

After 48 hours of sleep deprivation, you may experience mood swings and hallucinations, such as hearing voices or mistaking inanimate objects for people or animals. (Sleep deprivation has been used by various religious mystics to induce visions!)

Sleep duration counts, and sleep quality also counts. One sleep study that used wristband monitoring to keep tabs on how much new parents were sleeping found that in the first months moms lost an average of 41.2 minutes of nighttime sleep (and fathers lost an average of 15.8 minutes).[24] This doesn't sound like a whole lot, and if parents were getting their sleep in solid stretches and were able to make it up, it probably wouldn't be a big deal—just enough to cause some occasional crankiness and clumsiness. But new parents face not just sleep deprivation, but being awakened over and over before they have the chance to fall into restorative REM sleep, which takes about 90 minutes to set in.

What this can mean for new parents is a lot of lost keys, moments when you blank on people's names or the steps of tasks that you used to do routinely before the baby was born. You may find yourself getting in the car to drive to the grocery store, and then realizing on the way that you're actually en route to your former job. Your partner may ask you what you'd like for dinner, or ask you to make some other simple decision, and you'll find having to pick between any number of choices takes up more of your brainpower than it ought to.

MOMSOMNIA

What we call "momsomnia" can make sleep deprivation worse. That's when you finally get the chance to sleep, but can't because you know that that baby—or the phone, or the doorbell—is just going to wake you up again as soon as you get comfortable. Anxiety about how much sleep you're not getting can actually make it hard to fall asleep, too!

Sleep is one of those rare things in life where the harder you try, the more likely you are to fail. It can also be hard to sleep in the middle of the day if you're not used to it. If you can't sleep when you get the chance, try not to get frustrated, and just lie down and relax. Being still and quiet is restorative also.

It's also important to acknowledge that sleep deprivation affects moms more than dads. Most fathers (73 percent, according to one 2004 study)[25] return to work a week after the baby is born, and working dads tend to pitch in on the night shift a lot less. Realistically, whether dad is working or not, if you're among the 80 percent of mothers who breastfeed during baby's first month, there will be only so much dad can do, anyway.

The Big Ps: PPF and PPD

An estimated 10 to 43 percent of moms develop post-partum depression after giving birth (PPD). Postpartum fatigue (PPF) is now being recognized as a problem for moms too, and there may be a link between PPD and PPF. Although moms often think that things will get better once things "settle down," serious PPF often doesn't improve after delivery and could hang on as long as 6 weeks or for more than a year. Two recent studies have found a connection between PPF at 7 and 14 days after delivery and PPD at day 28.[26, 27]

MORE TIRED THAN YOU SHOULD BE?

Unless you're sharing a bed with your baby, you're going to be awakened a lot, getting up a lot, and you're going to be really tired. But there are other factors that can make new-parent fatigue even worse: post-partum depression, anemia, post-partum thyroiditis, and certain medications. If you feel tired to the bone even after you've been able to catch up on sleep, talk to your doctor. A simple blood test should be able to reveal if you have thyroiditis or anemia. Let your doctor know about any medications you're taking, including herbal supplements and over-the-counter drugs. Allergy medications in particular can cause excessive fatigue.

Tell your doctor if you also have any symptoms of depression, such as recurrent negative thoughts, thoughts of hurting yourself or others, crying a lot, or feeling hopeless or guilty for a large part of the day. Depression can sap your energy and will, and help is available.

ELEVEN TIPS FOR OVERCOMING SLEEP LOSS

1. **Support, support, support.** You can deal with short-term sleep deprivation if you have a chance to catch up on some of the sleep you've been missing. If you have a partner who works late hours, consider having a high-school student or neighborhood retiree come over during the day to hold the baby or take him on a stroller ride while you rest.

2. **When you go off-duty, be really off-duty.** When your partner comes home and is ready to take over watching the baby, *do* hand over the baby and go have a rest in a dark, quiet room, far away from baby noise. *Don't* follow your partner around the house telling him everything he's doing wrong, or try to tackle household chores.

3. **Bedshare.** Bed sharing doesn't work for every family, as we mentioned in Chapter 3. But

when bed sharing does work, it usually means less sleep disturbance for adults, at least until the baby is old enough to thrash and kick.

4. Forget the phone for a while. Get Caller ID and turn off the ringer on your home phones. Set your cell phone to vibrate. Turn everything back on and check your messages when you wake up, in case someone besides a telemarketer really is trying to get in touch with you.

5. Get messy. This is no time for household perfection. Let the housework go and make your and your baby's welfare your number-one priority.

6. Avoid caffeine. Caffeine can give you the horrible sensation of being physically tired but unable to sleep. Depending on your diet, hormones, and intake, caffeine can stay in your system for 2 to 6 hours (and some people report that the effects last longer than that). And, if you're breastfeeding, very small amounts of caffeine can also pass through your breastmilk, which some moms believe make the baby irritable and hard to settle.

7. Avoid sedatives. They will make you even more tired when you have to get up before they have worn off.

8. Get blackout shades. These are window shades designed to block light from coming into a room, usually lined with Mylar or some other heavy material. If your baby

(like most) wakes up at the first light of the morning, install some in the nursery.

9. Change your expectations. You may have hoped things would return to normal a few weeks after birth, but this isn't always the case for every mom or for every pregnancy. It can take 1 or 2 *years* to get your core body energy back, especially if delivery was complicated and you lost a lot of blood. A lot depends on the support you get, your nutrition, your life demands and stress, and your child's sleeping patterns.

> *"Life just feels like a blur. I can't focus on anything, I just ramble around, and I feel guilty because I just don't have the energy to finish even the simplest tasks."*

10. Insist on "self" time. It's inhumane to expect yourself to be "on" 24/7 day after day without a break. Enlist the help of your partner, family, and friends to make space for meeting your own needs for rest and restoration.

11. This will pass. By 4 to 6 months, your baby will probably be sleeping for 5- or 6-hour stretches. And by her first

Sleep Deprivation Don'ts

When you have a new baby, a certain amount of sleep deprivation is unavoidable, especially in the first 3 to 4 months. So it's important to factor that reality into any plans you might make. When you're sleep-deprived:

- **Skip driving.** Don't drive a car if you can avoid it.

- **Avoid pointy things.** Don't operate machinery that could hurt you, such as drills, mowers, or saws, and don't try to slice firm foods, like carrots or bagels, with a sharp knife.

- **Don't blame.** Try not to blame family members for your frustration or say things you'll regret later.

- **Forget diets.** Don't bother trying to lose weight.

- **Be careful with alcohol.** Sleep deprivation will further impair your motor skills.

- **Parent-proof your house.** Be sure there are clear pathways around the house, and if at all possible, get rid of any furniture that has pointy corners.

- **Invest in Post-it® notes.** Memory lapses are normal when you're sleep-deprived, and leaving notes for yourself can be a big help.

- **Replenish supplies.** Keep a running grocery list on the refrigerator, and note pads by the telephone and the front door to write down any supplies you need to replenish. Toss the lists in your diaper bag before you leave the house.

- **Say no to social commitments.** You do need to get out sometimes for fresh air and have conversations with grown-ups, but realize before you RSVP to any party that by the time the occasion arrives you may be feeling too wiped out to have a good time.

- **Get help!** If you're often exhausted, enlist the help of your partner, a neighbor, or a relative to take the baby on regular walks so you can catch up on your sleep. During the first few weeks, lactation consultants advise against giving baby a bottle of pumped breastmilk lest he develop "nipple confusion." But after about a month, once your baby gets the hang of breastfeeding, pumping extra milk for a caregiver will buy you extra sleeping time.

birthday, odds are you'll get to put the baby down to sleep and have a few hours of grown-up time before your own bedtime. Whatever will you do with yourself?

> *"I think that you and your husband should agree that anything you say to each other while you're both sleep-deprived doesn't count."*

GOOD MORNING, SLEEPY AMERICA!

We live in a sleep-deprived society. According to the National Sleep Foundation, fewer than half of all Americans over 18 say they get a good night's sleep every night or almost every night. By some estimates the American sleep business is worth about $20 billon,[28] when you include clinics, medical devices, mattresses, gadgets, and herbal supplements. In 2006, Americans spent $3.7 billion on 40 million prescriptions for sleep-inducing drugs.

POWER NAPPING

Is it possible to function on just 2 hours of sleep a day? Some people believe so—that a system of quick naps (known as a polyphasic sleep schedule) can train your body to cycle through the stages of sleep more quickly.

In situations where sleep deprivation is inevitable, sleep researcher and long-distance boat racer Claudio Stampi advocates what he calls the Überman's Sleep Schedule—a regimen of six naps of 20 to 25 minutes each, 4 hours apart, for a total of 2 hours every 24-hour period.

Artist and engineer Buckminster Fuller (known for inventing the

> *"In the head of the interrogated prisoner, a haze begins to form. His spirit is wearied to death, his legs are unsteady, and he has one sole desire: to sleep. . . . Anyone who has experienced this desire knows that not even hunger and thirst are comparable with it."*
>
> —Former Israeli Prime Minister Menachem Begin, *describing his sleep-deprivation torture at the hands of the Soviet KGB*

geodesic dome) claimed to have napped for a half hour every 6 hours for 2 years of his life, which he called the Dymaxion sleep schedule.

Leonardo da Vinci, aviator Steve Fossett, and record producer P. Diddy have all claimed to be adherents of the polyphasic sleep lifestyle. Supporters claim that after a 10-to-14-day adjustment period, tiredness wanes.

Skeptics point out that there are no published, peer-reviewed medical studies to prove that the human body adjusts to napping, and nappers who self-report their sleep schedules have a tendency to underestimate how much sleep they get. Also, there are very few test subjects available, because not many people who attempt to adopt the schedule can make it through the initial adjustment period without oversleeping or giving up.

Plus, this is a monophasic world we live in. Most people's jobs and lifestyles are not conducive to frequent napping, and people who have tried the polyphasic schedule report feeling bored and lonely at night. And sleep scientists claim that while the body might be able to tolerate a nap schedule for a while, eventually the symptoms of sleep deprivation, like memory loss, slowed reflexes, and a compromised immune system, could eventually become an issue.

Still, if you have a baby in the house, you're going to be engaging in polyphasic sleep whether you plan to or not!

Could it be possible to stave off new-mom fatigue by adopting a polyphasic schedule in the weeks before the baby's born? We don't know, because even if a research institution designed such a study, we have a feeling not too many women would volunteer to be subjects.

Three to
Four Months

Developing a Daily Routine

For the first 3 months, newborns are more alike than they are different—they sleep a lot, eat a lot, and want to be glommed onto mom at all times. Their basic four states are feeding, dozing, fussing, and staring into space. But then, as your baby reaches the 3-month mark, she leaves the "fourth trimester" of extended fetus-ness, and graduates into a bona fide little person who smiles, tracks things with her eyes, and lights up when mom or dad walks into the room.

Your baby now spends more time in a calm-alert state, and other daily rhythms become more consolidated, too. She becomes able to go longer without feedings and to sleep more soundly for semi-regular periods. This gives you and other caregivers more freedom—at least during the time your baby is sleeping and napping. But predictable naps also mean that if they arrive, and baby isn't given the opportunity to sleep, a meltdown can ensue.

A routine of napping at regular times is also important because, unlike an adult, the deepest sleep for a baby comes after a mere 10 to 20 minutes. This means frustrating mini-naps, where your baby gets too tired and drifts off for 15 minutes, then wakes up seemingly fully refreshed.

The mini-naps play out something like this: You decide to get in the car to run some errands with your baby, and you're so sleep-deprived that just the act of getting the diaper bag together and strapping the baby in the car seat exhausts you to the point of almost falling asleep at red lights. On the way home, your baby is lulled to sleep by the monotonous drone of the car's engine, and you start to fantasize about how great it's going to feel to have your head on a pillow once you get home. You pull into the driveway, turn off the car engine, gingerly carry the car seat into the house, and the minute you step in the door those little eyes blink wide open. Her catnap has fully refreshed her, and she's wide awake and ready to play! You rock her, you nurse her, you try to send sleepy vibes her way with all your power, but she's wide awake for another 2 hours, then takes an extra-long nap in the afternoon to make up for it.

Until now, you may not have had good associations with the word *schedule*. You probably hated being on a schedule as a kid—all those times you had to get out of bed when you didn't want to, and all the times a parent made you go to bed and lie there anyway, even when you weren't tired.

But at the same time, most people's best memories are of cherished routines: eating with the family, playing together, the nightly bath, and getting tucked into bed. The truth is, babies and children (and adults) do best with a certain level of daily predictability and knowing what's going to happen next. No matter the age, everyone benefits from the proper amount of eating, sleeping, waking up, cleaning up, sunshine, and exercise.

Also, if your baby becomes used to routines, it makes it easier for other caregivers to step in, because you'll be able to give them clear instructions about what your baby expects them to do and when to do it.

What's Happening in Your Three-Month-Old Baby's Brain

As your baby matures, her brain and metabolism are going through an enormous amount of change. Her sleep hormones are shifting, and you may now begin to see her sleep patterns clustering toward more sleep at night than during the day.

HELLO, SLEEP HORMONES!

Twelve weeks (or 50 weeks after conception, if your baby was premature) marks a new developmental stage for a baby: the beginning of melatonin production in the brain. Melatonin is a hormone produced by the brain's tiny pineal gland located in the center. Its daily fluctuations are of key importance in the chemical process that regulates body temperature and drowsiness. During peak times at night, your 3-month-old is now producing five to six times more of it than she was producing at 6 weeks.

Secretion of melatonin is lowest during the day. Melatonin

is light-sensitive, and production of the hormone is lowest when a person's face and hands are exposed to the bright light of the morning. Then, production rises in the evening, peaks in the middle of the night, and then gradually falls during the second half of the night, with some normal variations in timing according to an individual's chronotype. (For more on this, see page 113.) Research has found that babies who are exposed to light in the early afternoon sleep well at night.[1]

Though melatonin supplements are available over the counter in drugstores, the use of melatonin by babies or children is not recommended, because there simply haven't been enough studies to test its safety, and it's clearly a very powerful hormone.

The best way to encourage your baby's melatonin production is to schedule daily outdoor time and exposure to natural sunlight, especially in the morning.

VITAMIN D: ANOTHER REASON TO GET OUTSIDE

Exposure to sunlight is especially important for breastfed babies, who need it to manufacture adequate amounts of vitamin D. Skin makes vitamin D when exposed to ultraviolet B (UVB) radiation from the sun without sunscreen, or it can be supplied through vitamins. For the first 8 to 12 weeks of life, your baby will have stores of vitamin D remaining from her time in the womb. After that, though, particularly if you are exclusively breastfeeding and baby is darker-skinned, your baby will need to get sunlight on a regular basis to manufacture adequate vitamin D. Formulas are fortified with extra vitamin D, but not much vitamin D that is ingested by a mother is passed through into her breastmilk.

How much sun your baby will need in order to manufacture adequate vitamin D on her own also depends on the latitude where you live, the season, and how lightly the weather permits you to dress your baby. If a light-skinned infant is dressed but not wearing a hat, she will need about 2 total hours of sun exposure per week; if she is only wearing a diaper, a half hour of sun will do.[2] Infants with a medium skin tone need an estimated average of 168 minutes a week of sun exposure while dressed without a hat, and very dark-skinned exclusively breastfed infants may need an estimated 3 to 12 hours of sun exposure weekly to produce adequate vitamin D supplementation.[3]

So for biological reasons (and for your own sanity), it's a good time to get out of the house and to add controlled blocks of sun time to your schedule when your baby is about 3 months old.

Vitamin D is stored in the body, so if the weather is bad—or you can't get out of the house for some other reason—on a particular day, your baby will still be able to make enough vitamin D to make up for missing a day's exposure to sunshine. Melatonin is produced on a daily basis, though, so if it's too cold to go out or it's cloudy, your baby can also get adequate light exposure by sitting next to a window.

To optimize the effects of melatonin but minimize the risk of skin damage or overheating, it's best to take your walks or have outdoor time in the morning (after breakfast, say), and then again in the afternoon. Avoid taking your baby out in the sun during the hours when the sun's radiation is the most intense, usually 10 a.m. to 2 p.m. in colder months, and

Baby's Skin Tone	Suggested Weekly Sunshine Time, Diaper Only (U.S. contiguous states)	Suggested Weekly Sunshine Time, Fully Clothed, No Hat	Recommended Average Per Day (rounded to the minute)
Fair	30 minutes	120 minutes	4-17 minutes
Medium	42 minutes	168 minutes	6-24 minutes
Dark	160 minutes	12 hours	23-103 minutes

10 a.m. to 4 p.m. in the summertime. If you're out in the middle of the day or exposed to sunlight longer than the recommended daily range, shield your baby from the sun with UV-blocking clothing or sunscreen.

Feeding and Sleep: The Big Differences Between Breast and Bottle

Between 12 and 16 weeks, according to studies, the sleeping schedules of breastfed and bottle-fed babies continue to diverge. Bottle-fed babies sleep about a half hour more every 24 hours, and they become capable of sleeping for much longer stretches than their breastfed peers. Unlike babies that have been formula-fed all along, breastfed infants are not neurologically wired for 9-to-12-hour sleep stretches.

A 1986 study from Harvard, "Sleep/Wake Patterns of Breast-Fed Infants in the First Two Years of Life," was among the first to examine how diet and sleeping arrangements influenced the change of infant sleep patterns over time. The results were not subtle: By 7 months, the formula-fed infants averaged five feedings every 24 hours, while breastfed infants nursed more than twice as many times, averaging 10½ feedings over 24 hours (they also slept in shorter stints).

By 4 months, formula-fed babies were sleeping for as many as 8 full hours at night, while breastfed babies' maximum sleep stretches were significantly shorter, at just under 5 hours. And at 7 months, breastfed babies were sleeping in even shorter stints than they did soon after birth—not a single breastfed baby in the study slept for longer than 4 hours in a row.

When it came to total number of sleep hours in a 24-hour period, the breastfed babies in the study also slept fewer total hours on average: half an hour less at 7 months of age, and 1 hour and 42 minutes less at 10 months.

Coping Strategy

If your baby is waking up more than once or twice at night after 6 weeks of age, try increasing your feedings during the day to at least once every 3 hours. At night, put her down *before* she's in a limp sleep, even if you have to wake her up a little. At night, try other soothing strategies besides feeding to help her get back to sleep.

Average Sleep Duration

Age	Sleep for Breastfed Babies	Sleep for Formula-Fed Babies	Additional Sleep Time for Formula-Fed Babies
7 months	12.5 hours	13.0 hours	90 minutes
10 months	11.8 hours	13.5 hours	102 minutes
13 months	11.8 hours	14.2 hours	2 hours 24 minutes

Maximum Sleep Duration

Age	Sleep for Breastfed Babies	Sleep for Formula-Fed Babies	Additional Sleep Duration for Formula-Fed Babies
7 months	4.0 hours	6.8 hours	2 hours 48 minutes
10 months	3.8 hours	7.5 hours	3 hours 42 minutes
13 months	3.4 hours	14.2 hours	10 hours 48 minutes

HOW SLEEP DIFFERS

This chart shows average sleep differences between breastfed and bottle-fed babies over a 24-hour period.[4]

It appears that formula feeding changes both a baby's metabolic process and her basic circadian rhythms. For sleep-deprived parents, that may actually sound like a pretty compelling argument to speed out to the closest warehouse-size shopping club for a barrel of the stuff. But here's the paradox: While formula-fed babies sleep more, their parents actually sleep *less*.

According to a study that used sleep diaries of mothers with wrist monitors that recorded their activity, mothers of formula-fed babies actually got 45 minutes *less* sleep every night compared to exclusively breastfeeding moms. The moms of formula-fed babies reported *more* nighttime disturbances. How could it possibly be that breastfed babies sleep about 1½ hours less yet their moms sleep an average of 45 minutes *more* than bottle-feeding moms?

The answer in two words: *bottles* and *poop.*

Formula creates more waste: not just dirty bottles, rings, and nipples, but also more dirty diapers and laundry. Breastfeeding a baby does take longer—at 3 months it takes about an hour longer for a mom to breastfeed than bottle-feed every day. But formula feeding creates extra work.

Parents must spend time at night matching rings and nipples, mixing up bottles of formula, soaking dirty bottles, hand-washing nipples, loading up the dishwasher, and scrubbing off left-on crusted-up formula deposits.

And formula-fed babies poop a lot more often—about one stool every 24 hours after 1 month of age, as opposed to one stool every couple of days (or as infrequently as once a week) for a breastfed 3-month-old. So formula-feeding parents must spend more time out of every day changing poopy diapers and administering emergency bottom baths in the sink.

They will also have more laundry to do, because on the other end of the baby, formula spit-up leaves stains but breastmilk spit-up doesn't. All those little bits of time add up.

Also, while it seems like having another person around to take over the duties of feeding the baby would equal more sleep for mom, the reality is that most moms don't use the extra time to rest, but instead catch up on household tasks.

The other reason breastfeeding moms tend to get more sleep is that most of them (about 70 percent of the ones whose babies are 3 months old, according to the study) practice bed sharing for at least

---

Your Twelve-Week-Old at a Glance

Average total hours of sleep:
Sleep in a 24-hour period: 13
Night sleep: 8.5
Daytime naps: 4½ hours' worth of ½-hour to 2-hour naps

Average weight in pounds:[5]
All boys: 13¼
Breastfed boys: 14
All girls: 12
Breastfed girls: 13

part of the night, which allows for sleeping and baby feeding to happen concurrently. (See bed-sharing safety tips in Chapter 3.)

And, of course, human breastmilk has numerous, lifelong health benefits for babies, including lower rates of childhood obesity, cancer, respiratory infections, and heart disease. Human milk has a perfect nutritional balance and a calorie content customized to a baby's needs. Researchers believe that the amino acids in formula are metabolized into glucose and stimulate a baby's body to produce more insulin, which, over a period of time, could lead to a buildup of fatty tissue.[6] Breastfeeding may also introduce the habit of eating smaller portions of higher-quality food more frequently, which is an excellent strategy for weight control and for regulating metabolism and controlling hunger for babies, children, and adults.

Breastfed babies also get an extra 30 to 100 more minutes to exercise every day and to learn from their environments.

Breastfeeding is beneficial to a mother's health, too. Moms who breastfeed have lower rates of certain breast and ovarian cancers. And it gives you a calorie-burning boost, so if you're trying to lose weight, you'll see quicker results from your efforts.

To receive the maximum benefits from breastmilk, it appears that a baby needs to be exclusively fed human milk for at least the first 6 months of life.

However, if you can't breastfeed all the time—you're working full time and are unable to pump milk at work, for instance—you and your baby can still gain health benefits from breastfeeding in the time you have together. This can be tricky to achieve, however, if you don't pump at work. Your milk supply will diminish almost daily, and the process of weaning will begin very quickly, since human milk supply depends upon a baby's frequent demand to nurse. If your body goes from ten feedings a day to five, your body will quickly slow down to only making enough for five feedings.

WHAT ABOUT SOLIDS?

At about 3 to 4 months, most babies go through a growth spurt. They seem to be hungry all the time, and their evening cluster-fussing and feeding may begin (or resurge). However, this is not a sign that you should put rice cereal in your baby's bottle or begin to feed her solids. The American Academy of Pediatrics, along with the Centers for Disease Control and the World Health Organization, recommend that you offer nothing but breastmilk and/or formula until your baby is at least 6 months old.

Feeding your baby only breastmilk or formula for the first 6 months will ensure that she gets enough nutrients. An infant's gastrointestinal tract will not be mature enough to properly digest and utilize solid foods until around 6 to 8 months old.

What's more, studies have shown that adding cereal to a bottle doesn't work—researchers have found no difference in the sleep patterns of babies who received solids before bedtime compared to babies who were not given solids.

In fact, giving solids to your baby in an effort to help her sleep for longer periods may backfire—literally. The gas and stomach pains she may experience will keep her—and probably you—awake.

TUMMY TIME PRACTICE

Another way to help regulate your baby's sleep schedule and improve the quality of her sleep is to help her get some exercise every day. You can do this by carrying or wearing your baby and by providing opportunities for tummy time.

At first, while your baby is a newborn, she'll probably hate any form of tummy time that doesn't involve being held in your arms or lying on your chest or your partner's. But by 12 weeks, you can begin to add new elements to her tummy time workout, and you may find that she actually enjoys it.

Here are a few things to consider:

- **Chest pillow play.** Your baby may be more comfortable belly-down when her chest is supported so that her arms are free to move in front of her. You can either purchase an activity center, which usually consists of a mat, a wedge-shaped pillow to prop the baby on, and some toys at a baby-product store, or you can create your own tummy time experience for your baby by putting a towel on the floor and placing another

rolled-up towel or firm pillow under her torso. But never leave baby unattended on the pillow: She could fall off or get her vulnerable neck compressed if she slides backward. If your baby falls asleep in the tummy-down position, don't leave her in that position whether flat on the floor or propped up. Instead, gently roll her over or place her on her back to continue sleeping.

- **Fun toy choices.** Special baby toys are nice to motivate your baby to stay interested in being belly-down, or you can also choose familiar objects, such as spoons, baby-safe teething keys, or crackly material that makes sounds when you scrunch it, like tissue paper or Mylar®.

- **Smooth floor play.** A non-carpeted floor such as one made of wood, ceramic tile, or linoleum may not look too comfortable to you. But a hard surface is actually better for encouraging pushing up and pre-crawling, because it will help your baby to feel her movements and get traction for trying to move forward or scrunching backward.

- **Lap play.** Place your baby facedown across your thighs or with her diaper pressed against your belly, making sure that her arms and head are comfortably supported by your legs, and gently move your legs up and down to change her positions. Be careful not to compress her delicate throat.

Nap Routines

Newborns are so portable, and their sleeping schedules so unpredictable, that trying to enforce some kind of sleep schedule is futile. But once your baby hits the 3-month mark, natural day and night patterns will begin to emerge. And, while it was once not very difficult to carry your baby in a sling or a soft carrier, by 3 months she will start to get seriously heavy, and it's not so easy to "wear" her all day and most of the night. Once this happens, everyone can benefit from your baby's regular nap times and bedtimes in a crib or other baby-only bed.

As your baby matures between months 3 and 4, you will start to see the regular sleep episodes begin to emerge. This is the perfect opportunity to start building some predictability into your baby's days, which you can then expand into more predictable nights. That is not to say that at 12 weeks your baby will suddenly start napping at 10, 2, and 5 o'clock, but you will begin to notice these tendencies if you track your baby's sleep times over the course of a week. If you're not sure when your baby's natural nap times are, keep a sleep diary, writing down what times—and where—your baby is napping.

It's easier to start building a daily routine with daytime naps than it is with nighttime sleep, because during the day parents will be (relatively) well rested, it isn't dark outside, and at this age, babies' nap times become pretty predictable. Most babies are ready for a nap about 2 hours after waking up from a previous stretch of sleep, and they tend to have longer awake periods in the evenings.

You may also begin to notice that your baby is starting to wake up at about the same time every morning, and she'll start to look ready for the first nap of the day at the same time every day.

Timing of naps is important, because there is such a thing as an overtired baby who cries because she's tired and then is kept awake by her own crying.

If you've been winging it until now when it comes to naps—baby has been napping mostly in her car seat, swing, or wherever she happens to be when she falls asleep—this is the perfect time to let her practice going to sleep by herself in a suitable baby nap spot, without sleep props or being fed until she falls asleep.

So, if your baby wakes up at 7 a.m., a simple nap-time ritual at 9 or 10 a.m.—a feeding, rocking, and put-down while she's still awake in a proper crib (as opposed to a stroller or bouncy seat)—can help her learn to go to sleep by herself. After you've gotten your nap-time ritual and schedule down, you can then expand on this routine to create a nighttime ritual.

It's common for a baby of this age to take three naps: one midmorning, about 2 hours after she wakes up from her last sleep of the night, then a second in the early afternoon, about 2 to 3 hours after she woke up from her first nap. Some babies then take a third, early-evening doze.

At the same time you're working toward a predictable schedule, don't get too caught up in the supposed-to's. It's common for a baby to have a nap at a reliable time for a few days, and then, for seemingly no reason, to diverge from her routine. Or, a baby might lie down for a morning nap as usual, but then sleep for only a short time. Since it's impossible to force a baby (or anyone) to go to sleep or stay asleep if she's wide awake, the best a parent can do is to create the *opportunity* for napping to take place on a regular basis, and then fill the rest of the time with plenty of activity.

Some sleep-book writers are of the opinion that you should set baby nap times in stone and put the baby down for them, and if the baby cries in protest, leave her there screaming for the whole nap time, as long as an hour. In our personal experience, not only is this harrowing for baby and parents, it simply doesn't work. It just makes a drowsy baby learn to wake herself up completely when she realizes she's about to be put down somewhere she doesn't want to be.

Sure, create opportunities for naps, but if your baby just wakes herself up more when you try to put her down, and the Perfect Put-Down (see page 110) simply doesn't work, try some active play for 10 or 15 minutes, like tummy time or peek-a-boo, before you try to put her down again.

If your baby's nap times are predictably unpredictable, here are some things to try:

- **Check your schedule.** If you're fortunate enough to be a stay-at-home, bed-sharing mom, it's very tempting to sleep in as long as you can get away with in the mornings, or to stay up late because you don't feel tired at 7 or 8 p.m., when your baby is ready to go to bed. But if you want your baby to have a predictable napping and sleeping schedule, both of you will need to go to bed and get up at the same time every day.

- **Watch your stimulant intake.** If you're breastfeeding, keep in mind that some medications may cause wakefulness in your baby. If you wake up and have four cups of coffee followed by a few puffs from your asthma inhaler, your baby will probably have a tough time settling down for her morning snooze. (See Common Medications That May Affect Your Baby's Sleep on page 21.)

- **Watch for signs of tiredness.** There is such a thing as a baby getting too tired to nap, and once she crosses the line into real fussiness, putting her down may become more difficult. If your baby usually wakes up at 7 a.m. and naps at 10 a.m., but starts to get fussy, rubs her eyes, yawns, and/or looks spaced out at 9 a.m., respond to those "I'm sleepy" cues and put her down for a nap while she's sleepy.

WHERE SHOULD BABY NAP?

If you're bed sharing at night with your baby, naps are a good opportunity to give your baby a

Changing Nap Needs

Baby's Age	Number of Naps	Total Hours of Nap Time
4 months	3	4-6
6 months	2	3-4
9 months	2	2.5-4
12 months	1-2	2-3
2 years	1	1-2
3 years	1	1-1.5

How regular a baby's naps and nighttime schedule are depends on individual characteristics, her particular stage of development, and also how predictably she gets sunlight and exercise.

chance to fall asleep somewhere else. It's unsafe to leave a baby unattended in an adult bed, and by this time, you will have recovered enough from childbirth not to need to sleep when your baby sleeps every day, unless your complications were extreme. So if you're bed sharing or co-sleeping, the first nap of the day is a particularly good time to give your baby the opportunity to sleep where you hope she'll eventually sleep—such as in a crib in her own room.

Schedule First, Location Second

Before you try to change where your baby is sleeping, spend some time becoming attuned to when she is sleeping.

- **Babies thrive on routine.** They feel the most settled and

secure when they know what's coming next. A consistent bedtime is a very basic way to add predictability and structure to the day.

- **Stick to your plan.** Without a schedule, most babies don't get enough sleep. You'll probably notice that no matter what time you put your baby to bed she'll wake up at the same time the next morning! Not getting enough sleep has been proven harmful to a baby's attention span, health outcomes, and quality of life.

- **Be kind to you.** Adults need routines—and sleep—too! After spending a full day with your baby, it can be a great relief to know that you'll be off-duty at some point (even if only for a few hours—or a few minutes—before you fall asleep yourself).

So, make a regularly scheduled nap time a priority. Don't try to squeeze naps in between other activities, or plan to be driving or strolling her when it's close to nap time (you do not want her dozing off in her stroller or car seat for 5 minutes in place of a proper nap). If you know she always naps at 9 a.m. but seems wide awake one day, put her down anyway and give her a chance to nap. You may be surprised to find that she falls asleep, even though her eyes were wide open just moments before.

Q: Is it actually possible to put a 3-month-old down drowsy but awake? A lot of sleep books recommend that I do this, but my baby just gets himself worked up. He is still figuring out how to use his hands, so he gets frustrated trying to suck on them. He still has quite a Moro startle reflex, and this frustrates him, too, when he's just about to fall asleep and he startles himself awake. He fusses and screams and cries. I've tried putting my arms around him in the crib and leaning over so he feels like I'm holding him. He just wants to be held. So I end up picking him up and rocking him and waiting 20 minutes until he's in his "deep sleep." Sometimes, he still wakes up when I put him in the crib. Any advice?

A: In our opinion, it's simply too early to start "sleep training," or sleep coaching, or anything else that involves having a distressed baby cry himself to sleep. During babyhood, huge developmental changes happen in a short period of time. There's a big difference between 3-, 4-, 5-, and 6-month-olds!

For now, think of putting him down drowsy but awake as something to practice. It will become more possible as you and your baby get to know each other, and you begin to learn just the right point of sleepiness to put him down. The day will come when you find that point, when he complains for a few seconds or a few minutes but then, to your shock, will doze off on his own. The first few times will seem like a fluke, and the next five times you try to put him down he may wake up and cry right away, but then it will happen again—you'll feed him, he'll nod off, you'll put him down, he might squirm a bit, and then he'll fall asleep.

In the meantime, practice the perfect put-down:

1. Put one hand under his head and the other under his bottom.

2. Lower him gently so that his feet go in first, then his bottom, and his head touches the mattress last. Go slowly to avoid triggering his startle reflex.

3. Gently slide your hand out from under the back of his head.

4. After you put him down, slide your lower hand over his belly, which will help reassure him and make the temperature difference less startling.

5. If he wakes up anyway, listen to his cries and give him a chance

Vocalizations

At the 3-month stage, a baby's noises will start to take on new dimensions: grunts, squeals, the whiny cry, the angry cry, and that old chestnut, "eh, eh, eh!"

Her new vocalizations can give you clues to her mood and energy level, and you will start to notice that certain sounds go with specific times of day.

Baby's new sounds will provide you with a whole new set of clues to help you tell how she's feeling.

This stage in your baby's development is the perfect time to reinforce crib sleeping . . . but many babies resist being put down to sleep.

to settle. You will probably find that falling asleep on his own will happen sooner if you *don't* leave him to cry once he starts getting worked up. Instead, as soon as you can tell he's not going to go to sleep, pick him up and soothe him. When he starts dropping off again, try again. If you have the stamina to repeat this process several times and are consistent, eventually he will start to get the message.

It will help if you are vigilant about making sure that nap time is always the same time every day. Don't try to fit naps in-between other activities, or let nap time be in a car seat or stroller. Until he's napping regularly, make it a priority to be at home and have him nap in his crib.

Q: My son is 3½ months old. During the days he has never liked to sleep in his crib and I've managed to either make do with holding him or putting him in his swing. I agree with the mentality that you can't spoil a newborn, so I've pretty much done what I need to do to make him happy. This week has been quite difficult, though, as he has decided that he wants to be held to sleep at night now too. I need to sleep, I have a 3-year-old as well who demands my attention during the day and I am just so tired. I don't want him to just "cry it out," but I am getting confused and feel I need more options. Any ideas?

A: We agree that you can't spoil a baby. But, it's simply not possible to hold a baby every minute of the day and night, especially after they hit the 10-pound mark. He wants to sleep in your arms, and who wouldn't? It's warm and comfortable, smells nice, and if you're nursing he can wake up periodically to sip on a milkshake. Who wouldn't want that? But even the most devoted and self-sacrificing parents have to do things like, say, go to the bathroom or make a sandwich or open the mail!

First, let's start with naps. Holding him for his naps is lovely, until you have to go to the bathroom, or answer the phone, or your leg falls asleep. What would work better for both of you is to figure out the best place for him to take his naps, and to start getting him used to that location. There's nothing inherently wrong with letting him nap in his swing, but do keep in mind the potential pitfalls: At some point, usually around a year of age, he will outgrow the swing's weight limit. If he goes to a babysitter's house or to day care, his swing won't be there. And, should there be a power outage or you run out of batteries one day, you'll have to stand there swinging him.

As long as you are okay with accommodating your baby, whatever his sleep preferences are, there's no problem. But if your baby will only sleep while he's attached to you, nursing and dozing on and off for hours and waking up the minute you move, or if your baby can only sleep in a car or swing, then it may be time to get him used to sleeping by himself somewhere that's optimal, like his crib.

Between 90 minutes and 3 hours after he first wakes up in the morning, you will probably start to notice the telltale signs of tiredness: rubbing his eyes, yawning, or making sleepy, vaguely dissatisfied sounds. As soon as you see one of these signs, or if he's been up for at least 2½ hours, nurse him, rock him, or do whatever you usually do before he falls asleep.

Then, when he's almost asleep, put him down. You want him to be almost asleep, but not completely asleep, because you want him to know what's happening, and you want him to learn that it's okay to fall asleep somewhere besides on top of you. If he's out cold he won't learn this, and also, when he wakes up he will be distressed to find himself somewhere unfamiliar. He may begin to fight going to sleep as a result.

How you put him down to sleep is important, because if you put his head down before his body, you'll set off his startle reflex, and he'll be fully awakened and start crying. But a baby's head is heavier than his body, so achieving a good put-down can be a challenge! Stand up and walk to the crib. Check your own relaxation level, because your baby takes cues from you. If you're tense, take a deep breath, relax your shoulders, and calm yourself before you start to put him down. Envision you and your baby surrounded by a bubble of calm, relaxing, soothing energy. Next, slowly and gently lower him down, making sure that his feet or his bottom touch the crib first. Then ease his body down, one vertebra at a time, and place his head down last. Then keep your hand on his stomach. After you see him relax, slowly, slowly, take your hand away.

If he cries a bit, give him a minute before you pick him up, and listen to his cries. Are they loud cries of distress, or is it a tired and cranky cry? Tired and cranky may mean that he will settle himself, so give him a few minutes. If he's wide awake and becoming increasingly upset, though, pick him up and soothe him, then put him back down again when he's almost asleep. Keep rocking and soothing him until you can finally put him down and he falls asleep. The goal here is for your baby to practice learning how to fall asleep without feeding and without having to be on top of a parent.

If your baby wakes up and cries after sleeping for less than 2 hours all night, he's probably not waking up because he's hungry (no matter how you've fed him—breast or bottle). He may be crying because he's lonely, uncomfortable, or because he woke up and can't figure out how to get back to sleep again. So before you offer a bottle or a breast, try something else, like rocking, crying, or walking around with your baby.

For nighttime, we suggest giving your husband a chance to try the soothing routine, too. Nurse your baby, then hand him off to your husband to do the put-down, or let your husband do the pickup at night if your baby wakes up. There's a practical reason for getting dad involved in the process, too: Because your baby associates being fed whenever you're near him, just seeing you may cue him to get hungry and want to feed, even if hunger wasn't the reason he woke up in the first place!

Putting your baby down for a nap in the crib may take a couple tries the first time, and even then, his nap may be pretty short. It may take several days or as long as a whole week before he takes to this new routine. He may always complain a little bit when you stop feeding him and put him down to sleep. But it's important that you give the routine a chance to work and stick with it, or you risk confusing him even more, shifting the message from "it's time to go to sleep in the crib" to "it's time to get up and cry, so I can have my nap on mom's lap."

Charting Your Baby's Day/Night Patterns

At this stage in your baby's life, her sleep/wake patterns begin to gel into more predictable day/night rhythms. Getting a visual picture of when your baby is most likely to be asleep or awake can help you to prepare for each day and also feel more assured that, even though it may not seem like it, your baby is, in fact, getting sleep, having times when she's alert and ready to engage with you, and eating more or less regularly (although teething pain, illnesses, or upsets in daily routines can temporarily affect the pattern).

Babies have sluggish/alert patterns according to the time of day, just as their parents do. As you may have noticed, adults differ and may be morning or evening types. Do you wake up with energy, or do you do your best work late at night and prefer to go to bed late? Your typical daily energy pattern is called a chronotype.

While most people are neither "larks" nor "owls" and have distinct morning and evening patterns of alertness, about half the population has a distinct chronotype, with activity patterns that favor either morning or night. And, in rare cases, someone's "lark" or "owl" chronotype is so strong that it becomes difficult to lead a normal life.

Some babies have distinct chronotypes, too. In the 1940s a Swiss pediatrician named Fritz Stirnimann studied the sleep patterns of newborns and

The Nap-Time Put-Down

1. Make sure your baby is ready for a nap: At 3 months, she is ready if it's been at least 3 hours since she woke up from her last sleep, or you see signs of tiredness. If it's only been 90 minutes, but she's yawning, seems fussy, or looks glazed, take that as a sign that she is ready for a nap. Make a note of what time it was when she began to seem tired, so you know when to start her nap-time ritual the next day.

2. Lower the shades and dim the lights in your baby's room.

3. Feed your baby if she is due for a feeding.

4. Hold and rock her until you see her eyelids begin to droop.

5. Slowly lower your baby's body into the crib, so that the change in temperature and the lowering motion won't startle her.

6. To avoid triggering the startle reflex, put your baby down so her feet touch the crib first, then her bottom, and then her head last of all. This can be complicated if your baby arches her back. If that's the case, put her down on her side, then roll her onto her back.

7. Keep your hand on baby's belly, and then gently raise your hand.

8. Some parents repeat key words every time they put their baby down to sleep, such as "time for baby night night! Mommy loves you!" or, more simply, "time to go to sleep!" It doesn't matter what you say, just be sure to say the same thing in the same way every sleep time. Babies and children (and many adults) thrive on consistent routines, and "magic words" are a good element to add, because other caregivers can use your words.

9. Some parents also use white noise, a fan, a special CD, or other type of sound cue to help signal that it's time to sleep (for more on this, see page 62).

10. If your baby wakes up in less than a few minutes after you've put her down, give her a minute or two to settle down on her own before you pick her up. If it's obvious she's not going to settle on her own, repeat the process from step 4—but don't let her fall all the way asleep. If you're consistent about making sure your baby always sleeps in her crib (or as often as possible, anyway), and that you put her down every time she's drowsy, she will adjust to sleeping on her own.

compared them to the chronotypes of their mothers during pregnancy. He found, remarkably, that newborns' sleep patterns mimicked those of their pregnant moms with early risers and night owls having babies who tended to follow very similar day-night proclivities.

Stirnimann's conclusion was that babies adjust their rhythms to their mothers' even before they're born.[7] But it is possible to give birth to a baby who has an entirely different and distinct chronotype from yours, which will be more apparent when your baby's sleep rooster. The luckiest situation, of course, is when a baby has two parents with opposite chronotypes who can care for her during their optimal hours so the other can rest!

Charting your baby's sleeping, eating, and playing patterns can help you figure out what your baby's natural tendencies are and spot patterns of predictability. You don't need to do elaborate charting to get a bead on your baby's sleep habits—you can just take notes. Here's an example of what a simple chart looks like.

6 a.m.	7 a.m.	8 a.m. ✓	9 a.m. T ☀	10 a.m. T ☀	11 a.m. ✓
Noon	1 p.m. T	2 p.m.	3 p.m. ✓	4 p.m. ☀	5 p.m.
6 p.m. ✓	7 p.m. T	8 p.m.	9 p.m.	10 p.m. ✓	11 p.m.
Midnight	1 a.m.	2 a.m.	3 a.m.	4 a.m.	5 a.m. ✓

cycles start to become more regular at about 3 months.

If you're a night owl, you may have a baby who's programmed to stay up with you and sleeps relatively late in the morning. On the other hand, your baby may be an early-morning riser, while you are a late sleeper. In that case, you'll need to rouse yourself to respond at dawn to your crowing

Put a check in the box every time your baby has fed for at least 5 minutes during that hour, provided it is at least 10 minutes after the end of a previous feeding. Use a sunshine symbol to designate outdoor time, and a "T" for each 3-to-5-minute block of tummy time.

If your baby is in day care or has a sitter, ask your care provider to do the charting, as well.

6 a.m.	7 a.m.	8 a.m.	9 a.m.	10 a.m.	11 a.m.
	✓			✓	
Noon	1 p.m.	2 p.m.	3 p.m.	4 p.m.	5 p.m.
	✓				✓
6 p.m.	7 p.m.	8 p.m.	9 p.m.	10 p.m.	11 p.m.
	✓				
Midnight	1 a.m.	2 a.m.	3 a.m.	4 a.m.	5 a.m.
			✓		

Shade a portion of the box when your baby takes a nap—however much of that hour she slept.

If your baby is bottle-fed, you will have fewer, bigger shaded areas; if you're breastfeeding, there will be more feedings and shorter sleep stints.

To help your baby develop a schedule, mark down when she sleeps and eats over the course of a day. If you want to, also indicate tummy time and outdoor time. Over the course of a few days of keeping track, you will start to see natural patterns emerge.

The Nighttime Put-Down

What time should a baby go to bed at night?

Babies do best with early bedtimes, sometimes as early as 6:30 p.m.! Some first-time parents may think that if they keep their baby up, it will be easier to put her down for sleep at night and she will sleep better. This may work sometimes for grown-ups, but it isn't true for babies. Early bedtimes actually help babies have longer, higher-quality sleep, and to be more cheerful in the morning. An overtired baby will get a second wind, which is when cortisol kicks in. An overtired baby seems energized—her limbs flail, and she squirms and arches her back when you try to hold her—but she's unhappy. If you can't calm her down, then the second wind will move into a full-blown meltdown.

To find your baby's perfect bedtime—usually between 6:30 and 7:30 p.m. for "larks" and between 7 and 8 p.m. for "owls"—start watching for signs of tiredness. Make a note of the time when you first start to notice these signs. Then start your bedtime ritual the next night about 40 minutes to an hour before the time you first started to notice signs of fatigue. This will help keep your baby from getting a second wind!

Signs of Tiredness, in Ascending Order

➤ Looking glazed or spacy

➤ Rubbing her face or eyes; yawning

➤ Lowered eyelids

➤ Starting to get fussy (the "active-alert" stage)

➤ Seems unhappy no matter what you do

➤ Full-blown meltdown

Some parents may be reluctant to adopt an early bedtime if one parent is working and is just getting home for the day at 6 p.m. or later. If you haven't seen the baby all day, you want to interact with her, of course! But instead of keeping baby up, most parents find it works best if the working parent takes over some or all of the bedtime ritual, and wakes up early with the baby.

Baby's early bedtime can also complicate bed sharing, because most adults are not ready to go to bed as early as the baby does (not every night, anyway). If you are bed sharing, it's a good idea to let your baby sleep for the first stretch of the night in her crib, then bring her into bed after she wakes up for her first or second nighttime feeding.

DROWSY BUT AWAKE?

At first glance, two of the steps in the "nighttime put-down" schedule may look as if they should be reversed. Why, in our bedtime routine, does step 8 (rock in a rocking chair, sing a song) come

after step 7 (nurse or bottle-feed)? If baby is tired, feeding is a surefire way to put her to sleep! But that's actually the point. You don't want nursing or feeding to be what puts baby to sleep, for a couple of reasons.

First and most important, you want your baby to practice learning to go to sleep on her own, without needing any props to get her there. If your baby nurses or feeds to sleep every night, instead of going to sleep on her own, she'll need to suck on something (a bottle, a pacifier, mom) to fall back to sleep when she wakes up in the night. If this is the case, you'll be getting up every couple of hours for many months to come and you'll have to nurse or feed your baby back to sleep or replace her pacifier if she loses it.

Second, falling to sleep while feeding will be bad for her teeth when she gets them. The sugars from the milk will pool around her teeth and erode the enamel.

And finally, bathing baby, dimming the lights, singing, using "magic words," and rocking give your baby clear cues that bedtime has arrived. This reassures her that you're not just putting her somewhere and accidentally leaving her. Also, letting her feed until she's almost to the point of sleep, then waking her up a little, also lets you, the parent, be sure that she really is tired enough to go to sleep before you put her down. If she cries a little bit after you put her down, you can be sure that she's crying because she's exhausted and frustrated that she can't get comfortable and doesn't know how to get to sleep on her own, not because she's hungry or simply not tired.

If you put your baby to bed drowsy, but she still wakes up frequently at night wanting to nurse for comfort but without the vigorous sucking of hunger, try putting her down when she's a little bit more awake next time.

If you put your baby down in a drowsy but awake state, one of three things is going to happen:

1. She closes her eyes, turns her head, and goes to sleep. Bingo! Home run!

2. She wakes up and cries a quiet, tired, or complaining cry. If this is the case, give her a chance to settle. Listen to her crying for a minute. Is it winding down or winding up? If it's winding down, leave her be, she will probably drift off within minutes.

Tips for the Nighttime Put-Down

1. Try to take a walk or spend time outside in the early evening (after 4 p.m.), so that baby will get the benefits of melatonin's effect on her circadian rhythms.

2. Begin your bedtime ritual about a half hour to an hour before signs of baby's tiredness typically appear.

3. Lower lights in the house and turn off the television. Create a dim and calm atmosphere.

4. Lower shades in baby's room, especially in summertime and if it's still light outside.

5. Bathe or spot-clean the baby. Until she starts solids, she may not need a full-body bath every night.

6. Dress baby for nighttime in a clean diaper and an outfit that will keep her at a comfortable temperature without a blanket.

7. Nurse or bottle-feed.

8. Rock baby in a rocking chair, sing a song, or tell a story.

9. Practice the put-down.

3. She wakes up fully and has a shrill, alarmed cry that's getting louder. If this is the case, pick her up, rock her, or walk her around. (We're against letting a baby cry to sleep until she's older—and some parents are never okay with letting a baby cry. More on those options in the next chapter.) Don't feed her if you know she isn't hungry. Try a little walking or rocking. When she settles down, put her back in her crib.

Some babies show self-soothing abilities almost immediately—the easy-going, extremely flexible babies who, after the newborn stage, grow into very regular guys in their eating and sleeping patterns. If your baby seems to be one of these, don't brag too loudly, because a new developmental phase can kick in, usually in month 4, and your so-predictable baby will suddenly change. Acquiring a new skill, cutting teeth, or an illness can also change a "predictable" baby's schedule.

Some babies rouse and cry at the slightest provocation; or, on the opposite end of the scale, a baby may be extremely deadpan and so non-reactive that nothing seems to draw her out.

And, unfortunately, parents don't have much choice about how well their own temperaments are going to synch with their babies'. The meshing of parents and their babies can make a huge difference when it comes to how successful they feel about their roles as parents.

Sometimes a laid-back mom will discover that she's paired with a highly reactive, extremely sensitive baby who forces her to watch her Ps and Qs. A mom who's a dedicated control freak or a neatnik almost inevitably seems to get the extremely irregular and uncontrollable baby who randomly wakes up day and night throughout the first year.

If your baby is high-demand, you're likely to find yourself parenting *in extremis*, a situation that calls for utmost patience and self-care to match the around-the-clock requirements that you're experiencing. In that case, you're more likely to spend your days wandering around like a zombie and find it hard simply to function.

It helps, sometimes, too, to say out loud what you're observing about your baby. If her eyes are bright and open wide; her head is turned toward you; her shoulders are relaxed, lowered, and folded forward; her movements are smooth or she's staring at you and being perfectly still; and her skin tone is even, rather than red or mottled, then most likely she's signaling that she's comfortable and aware of your presence.

If, on the other hand, she's tense; fussy; arches her back; looks pop-eyed; peers up to the ceiling or anywhere but your face; turns her head to the side when you're trying to engage her; or she's hiccupping, coughing, sneezing, or spitting up—then she's saying she's not comfortable.

That may mean slowing down, softening your voice, turning down the lights, muting the noise, checking on the temperature, and trying not to over-handle your baby. One sensitivity trick is to imitate the signals you're getting from your baby. This will help you become more baby-aware, and it could also help her feel more comfortable and less threatened and overwhelmed by the world's cacophony.

Tips for Handling Your Unique Baby

Here are some of the characteristics of the most challenging babies and here are some of our handling tips that may help. (Note: You may find that your baby is a combination of more than one of these baby types.)

Highly active. While other babies just lie there looking winsome, your very wiry and active baby continually cycles her arms and legs. The baby is very hard to settle, resists change, and jolts awake the minute you try to lay her down in the crib. No amount of patting, soothing, or ignoring will persuade her to stay there without lusty protests.

Handling strategies: Let your baby experience brief periods outside with sunlight to help her adjust her day-night rhythms. Massage and gentle arm and leg movements may help her calm down. Swaddling her snugly from the waist down, briefly sitting her in a vibrating infant seat, or teaching her how to suck on her fist may help her learn to soothe herself and slow down.

Highly sensitive. Your baby appears to be upset by being touched or handled and is simply overwhelmed by too much stimulation. She becomes restless and strains away from you when you try to hold her. Every move appears to be jarring to her, as though she has trouble managing the bright, loud world in which she finds herself. When she gets into a cycle of crying, she's like a horse racing to the barn: She just keeps getting more and more upset.

Handling strategies: Try moving slowly and deliberately. Keep noise levels low and soften your voice. Swaddling her in a blanket to buffer her skin from sensations and restraining her movements may help. Respond quickly to her signals to intervene before she really loses it. Feathery touches and "finger talking" can be unpleasant to this type of baby, so don't distract her by touching or talking to her when she's trying to feed. Deeper touches, such as massage that milks her limbs may work. For the most sensitive babies, nursing while enfolded in a pillow may be more soothing (but don't let her sleep that way—she could suffocate). Use rocking for soothing, but if that doesn't help, sit her in a motionless infant seat with the toy bar removed so she can "cocoon" and have space to compose herself. Keep her crib area low-key and don't attach a mobile or activity center there. Record the monotonous sounds of a droning fan, air purifier, vacuum cleaner, or clothes dryer; or use the white noise from an off-air radio station to help mask intrusive sounds that would normally awaken or startle her.

"Don't fence me in." Your baby resists being confined even for

Crying It Out: Not Until Six Months

"Crying it out" is when parents put their baby down for the night and don't pick her up again until morning, no matter how much she cries. (Don't ask us what "it" is that a baby should be crying out.) Another variation on "crying it out" is to check in on your baby at progressively longer intervals of crying (also known as Ferberizing or **controlled crying**). We think letting a baby cry herself to sleep should be considered a strategy of last resort—when no other go-to-sleep method has worked and parents have reached the extreme end of the rope—and should not be attempted until a baby is at least 6 months old (if not 8 or 9 months of age). Here's why:

1. There is evidence that extended crying is harmful to a baby's brain (see page 145), and may cause behavioral problems later.

2. Your baby may begin to become fearful of bedtime and resist sleep even more.

3. Listening to a baby's cries is difficult for parents, and may even be physically painful for nursing mothers.

4. The crying is upsetting to other children.

5. If your baby is younger than 6 months old, she is still in the prime danger zone for SIDS. Crying to sleep is exhausting to a baby, and being over-tired is thought to be a contributing factor in SIDS.

---

1 minute. She arches her back and screams the minute you try to fold her into her car seat. She hates having shirts pulled down over her head and feels imprisoned in a front carrier, baby swing, or jumper.

Handling strategies: Give your baby lots of space for gazing around while she lies on her back. Offer her a variety of textures to explore with her body. Bring her car seat inside and let her sit in it when she's fed and happy. Play with her using a soft toy, but use constant supervision so the seat doesn't topple over and injure her. Use only the softest T-shirts—with smooth seams and no tags—and

clothing that won't evoke her fear of suffocation and entrapment. Make the back seat of your car more tolerable by installing a soft activity play bar, and let her hear soft music.

"Please carry me." This baby only wants to be where you are day and night—on your *person*, that is. When you hold her, she molds her body around you. She stubbornly fights being put down for sleep, or doing *anything* that separates her from your loving arms and body.

Handling strategies: When your baby is alert, give her time to briefly explore separation by

Every Baby Is Unique

Every baby has distinct and unique patterns of personality and temperament. Moms tell us that, almost from day one: Each of their new babies is completely different from their other children. Among other things, babies differ in how active they are; how easily distressed they get; how they react to unexpected stimulation, including touches, sights, and sounds; how being confined or restrained affects them—some love it, some hate it; how shy they are or how quick they are to warm up to others; and how intensely they pay attention to things outside themselves.

placing her in an infant seat while you stay close by. Lay her on a blanket on the floor while you sit next to her with your hand on her back or chest, or try placing one hand at the top of her head and use your other hand to support the soles of her feet, so she can feel what it's like to be separate, but in your comforting presence.

"Shush! You're too loud." This baby is "ear sensitive" and startles to noises that you have learned to ignore, like the whistle of a passing train, or the garbage truck outside the window. Her hearing may be strangely selective: She may not respond if you call her name from nearby, yet appear to pause and listen to the cat leaping on the windowsill in the next room. Rhythms and noises that she doesn't like will cause her to become restless or fussy.

Handling strategies: Speak in a low, soft monotone, and try repeating simple sounds when you comfort her, such as "shusssh . . . shusssh," or "bahhhh . . . bahhh." Consider temporarily shielding nursery windows from loud noises or bright light with thick drapes or blackout shades. Keep the television turned off or the volume low. Droning and

Things That Help Sleepless Parents

- Getting more rest.
- Reassurance that the baby's okay and nothing's wrong.
- Sharing feelings and frustrations with other parents.
- Learning more about how babies sleep (or don't).
- Getting a handle on baby crying and colic.
- Keeping a journal of baby's sleep patterns.
- Discovering baby-soothing techniques that work.

Share Your Worries

At any point if you suspect that something is wrong with your baby or she simply isn't responding as you think she should, don't hesitate to share your concerns with your baby's doctor. The doctor can reassure you that your baby's development is normal or help you find an infant specialist to evaluate your baby or examine her for other possible problems.

monotonous sounds may work for this baby as for the highly sensitive baby. Try exposing her to gentle, low-key music, such as recordings of baby lullabies or heartbeat sounds.

"Just leave me alone." Your baby is so low-key, she seems almost to be lazy. No matter how much you talk to her or try to get her to react to things, she seems to draw back into her shell, becoming increasingly more passive and uninterested. Unlike babies who become alert and interested when they've finished feeding but aren't ready for sleep, this type of baby may not welcome eye contact, may not turn toward you when you approach her or respond when you pick her up or put her to your shoulder. Her body may seem floppy rather than firm. And some of that uninterest and floppiness could be her way of defending herself from becoming overwhelmed.

Handling strategies: Instead of working hard to calm this baby down as you would a highly active baby, you may need to work harder to have her engage with you and the world around her. If sound, touch, or movement don't awaken her senses, there may be other methods for getting her attention. Things she sees, animated expressions, and brisk movements may help her. She may prefer voices in the mid-range, rather than those that seem too low or too high. Later the task will be to help her liven up, whether it's with silly faces, brightly colored toys or pictures moved in front of her, or a noisy rattle. Other ways to stimulate her will be vigorous movement, playing with her toes or fingers, or simple games like moving a flashlight beam around in her darkened room.

The Easily Startled Baby

About one in ten babies is born with a tendency to be fearful. These babies startle more easily and react intensely to anything out of the ordinary. They have a slightly faster heart rate than other babies, even when they're asleep. Parents may find they have to be very gentle in moving, rocking, or relating to these babies, and they may need to control noises, glare, and other things that could cause their baby to overreact.

Four to Six Months

The Four-Month Sleep Shift

Just when you've gotten used to a little bit of predictability in your baby's routine—he wakes up at around the same time in the morning, seems ready for his first nap of the day at about the same time, and may be sleeping for predictable stretches at night— here comes a new developmental milestone: the four-month sleep shift, also known as the four-month sleep regression, or the four-month wakeful period.

Babies who have been sleeping for 5- or 6-hour stretches at night may start waking up much more often, like after just a few hours, or in the middle of the night, or very early in the morning. Babies who have been taking predictable morning naps may suddenly become wide awake and bright-eyed when nap time arrives and stay awake for daytime stretches that last hours longer than they were ever previously capable of before.

Parents may wonder if they should start enforcing some sort of strict napping and bedtime schedule but will find that this is easier said than done, because the issue is biological, not behavioral.

A baby's new alertness actually coincides with the start of a new stage of neurological development, in which his brain ramps up the production of certain hormones. Four-month-olds also become keenly aware of their environment and are more capable of holding themselves up and looking around.

This new awareness means fewer, shorter feedings during the day (because sounds and activity are so distracting) and a harder time blocking out stimulus at night, paired with a growth spurt and the need to fuel brain development and physical activity by extra nursing binges.

While waking up four times every night may not feel like progress, if you log your infant's sleep patterns over the course of weeks, you will notice a tendency toward longer sleeping clusters at night.

WHEN WILL BABY NAP?

Early to bed, early to rise!

Most 4-month-olds will tend toward waking up very early (5 a.m. to 7 a.m.), going to bed early

---

Hint!

If someone else watches your baby during the day, ask him or her to make a note of when and for how long your baby naps. This can serve as your baby sleep "weather report" for the afternoon and evening. If he hasn't slept much, you'll know to keep your baby's afternoon activities low-key.

(6 p.m. to 8 p.m.), and taking two naps (morning and afternoon). In the morning, expect to see signs of tiredness (see page 117) start to show up about 2 to 3 hours after the last wakeup in the morning, then 4 to 5 hours again after the morning nap.

SHOULD WE STILL FEED AT NIGHT?

If your baby is hungry, he's hungry.

There are sleep books out there—very popular ones, whose "training methods" are followed by millions of parents—that tell you not to pick up your 4-month-old baby or feed him for at least 12 hours in a row overnight, and that he should nap at predetermined times, no matter what. Some rare babies do pull 6-, 8-, or even 12-hour stretches of sleep at this age, but because breastmilk is rapidly digested, for most breastfed babies this expectation is unrealistic. Pay attention to your baby's cues. If he wakes up and seems ravenous at night, he's trying to tell you that he needs a nighttime feed for nourishment.

Though it is probably true that if you leave your baby to cry in his crib for 12 hours in a row, he will fall asleep out of exhaustion—and may eventually learn to give up calling for you and lie there quietly, hungry or not—the risk of physical and psychological damage brought on by this "method" seems much greater than any potential benefit.

At this age, your baby is growing at a tremendous rate. Some babies will have doubled their birthweight by now, and will double their weights again by their first birthday. At 3 and 4 months, a baby's brain is undergoing major development, making new brain cells, and forming new connections between them. This is not a good time to deny a baby the nourishment and nutrients that are so vital for growth.

Like the six-week crying peak, the four-month sleep shift is a normal phase to get through, and it will pass on its own, usually within a month, more or less. In the meantime:

Feed your baby in a quiet room during the day. At this highly distractible stage, you may find that he doesn't eat as much during the day, because any noise or activity will make him stop feeding and look around. He may even stop feeding just because he wants to look up at you and smile! Bottle-fed babies won't be as affected by this problem—they can feed from a bottle and check out the scene at the same time—but breastfed babies often start to eat less during the day, and more at night, because daytime has become so interesting, and it's their way of stoking up for sleeping longer times at night.

Don't assume your baby isn't hungry. Even if your baby was previously sleeping 6 straight hours 2 weeks ago but is now waking up every 3, that doesn't mean he is not hungry now. Don't worry about getting your baby into a bad habit of feeding at night. This phase will pass, and by 6 months (or sooner) most babies will begin to sleep in longer stretches without feeding on their own. In the meantime, make sure he gets good-size feedings in the daylight hours, so he'll be less likely to need long feedings at night. A baby's growth rate during the first year is tremendous, so it's not surprising that he may seem insatiable sometimes, even if he's started solids or is formula-fed.

Nevertheless, don't rush to start solids. When your baby can pick up a spoon or a finger food and place it in his mouth by himself (which typically happens between 6 and 9 months of age), he is developmentally ready to start solids. Studies have shown that adding solids to a baby's diet does not appear to help him go to sleep any earlier or stay asleep any longer,[1] and starting solids before 6 months may increase his risk of anemia, food allergies, and even obesity later in life. Until your baby is an active toddler, any food he eats will mostly just take up space in his gut, make him gassy, and then pass right through him without bestowing much in the way of nutrition. Early solids and formula also stretch a baby's stomach more than a breastmilk-only diet.

So, don't start solids too soon, and after you do start them, don't reduce your baby's milk or formula intake relative to how much solid food he eats.

Babies have striking differences in sleep patterns. At 4 months of age, formula-fed babies sleep from a half hour to more than 2 hours of total sleep longer than breastfed babies. On average, breastfed babies typically sleep for fewer hours at a stretch overnight—about 3 to 5 hours at the longest point—in contrast to the 6- to 8-hour stretches that formula-fed babies may be able to pull off at this age.

If your breastfed baby usually sleeps in bouts that are shorter than 3 to 5 hours at night but he has slept for longer periods in the past, you can try to hold out between feedings for as long as you know he can go, in the hope of extending his sleep stretches. But most moms find it quite difficult to withhold a feeding from a crying baby for 20 or 40 minutes in the middle of the night—the baby

Sleeping and Eating by the Numbers

An average of 13.3 hours in a 24-hour period with feedings no longer than every 3-5 hours apart for breastfed infants.
An average of 13.8 hours in a 24-hour period with feedings no longer than every 6.5-8 hours apart for formula-fed infants.

AVERAGE DAILY BREASTMILK INTAKE FOR A FOUR-MONTH-OLD:
Eleven 8-minute feedings[2]

AVERAGE DAILY FORMULA INTAKE:
Between 26½ and 41½ ounces for girls
Between 30 and 43½ ounces for boys

just gets more awake and angry, mom gets more awake too, and the baby will often make up for the time by taking longer to feed and calm down once he finally does get to a nipple. Or, if your baby is extra-smart, he may learn to start crying a half hour sooner, with the expectation that it will take mom that much longer to respond.

But, at 4 months, formula- and breastmilk-fed infants both need close to the same *amount* of sleep—about 13½ hours—in a 24-hour period. Remember if you are reading a "sleep training" book that says your baby should be sleeping for longer than 6 hours at a time, that "should" could apply only to exclusively bottle-fed babies.

Think of your baby's sleep in terms of a 24-hour cycle: The average breastfed baby (and remember, no baby is ever average!) will spend a total of about 3½ hours of out of every 24 feeding.

If you are physically separated from your baby during the day and he's getting pumped milk or formula during that time, it's going to be your baby's natural inclination to want to feed and be close to you at night. Most bed-sharing, breastfeeding babies will want to feed about every 2 hours, and it's not unusual for larger

babies to want to cluster-feed several times an hour overnight in close sleeping quarters.

Breastfeeding and bed sharing tend to go together, especially for babies between 4 and 6 months, who will need to stoke up and cluster-feed for a couple of hours between sunset and sunup, particularly if mom has been away from home for most of the day. A breastfeeding mom who's not pumping milk or supplementing with formula has two options between 2 and 6 a.m.: try to stay awake while feeding sitting up in a chair, or bring the baby into the grown-up bed. About 75 percent of exclusively breastfeeding moms share an adult bed with their babies for more than an hour a day.[3] If you're going to do this, make sure that you are able to provide a safe sleeping environment for your baby (see Chapter 3). If you feed your baby overnight in a chair, be careful not to fall asleep in your feeding chair with baby on your lap! It isn't safe, though sometimes it's hard to help it. Ask your partner to check on you if you don't return from baby duty in a half hour.

Also, if nighttime waking(s) are starting to exhaust you, consider working out a compromise with your baby, such as putting him to sleep in his crib earlier in the evening, and then bringing him into your safety-maximized adult bed later. It may not be the ideal arrangement in the long run, but if it helps extend breastfeeding or staves off chronic sleep deprivation for you, then the benefit to overall health will outweigh the difficulty of having to transition your baby back to his crib later.

Wake-Up Calls

One survey of both breast- and formula-feeding parents found that from 4 to 12 months, 12.7 percent of babies wake up three or more times every night.[4]

Feed in dim light with quick, calm nighttime visits. Rely on night-lights, not overhead lighting. If you're bottle-feeding, keep a bottle with pre-measured formula and some water in your baby's room, so you can pour, shake, and pop the bottle into your baby's mouth before he is fully roused. Avoid eye contact with him, which will wake him up even more.

Finally, don't put a clock in the nursery, and if you have one in the bedroom, turn it toward the wall. It doesn't help to sit there counting how many hours you *haven't* been sleeping.

Q: I have a beautiful 4-month-old little girl. She is breastfed, and since about 8 weeks she has been getting up once a night to feed. About a week ago she started sleeping through the night. Well, for the last couple of nights she's been up again at 3 a.m. I'm not sure what is going on with me but I'm totally exhausted. I don't know if it is the fact that this is my first baby and I'm not used to it or what, but I've never been so tired in my whole life! Should I try and let her cry it out when she wakes up at 3 a.m. or is she too young? I've been so tired lately, I've been bringing her into bed with us and I know this is the worst habit to get into. She is with a nanny during the day and takes three bottles, 6 ounces of milk in each (which is a lot for a 4-month-old), and then I typically breastfeed her three to four times daily, sometimes more. I guess if she is going to continue to wake up I need a plan to not be so tired! Any advice would be greatly appreciated!

A: If your baby wakes up crying at 3 a.m. and seems to be hungry—and she seriously feeds, instead of just sucking a bit and dropping off to sleep—then she probably *is* hungry, and denying her nourishment isn't going to help her learn to sleep any better. But if she's up two or three times a night, hunger is unlikely to be the issue.

When a baby's diet contains both breastmilk and formula, it can be difficult to figure out exactly how much or how often a baby needs to feed, because the calorie content and baby's intake of breastmilk will vary. With formula feeding, you raise the

Is Something Wrong with My Baby?

Parents often worry that a baby's sleeplessness will affect his development. A long-term study of 142 babies with sleep problems at 4 to 6 months and 10 to 12 months of age found that sleep difficulties decreased with age for babies who were at low risk for developmental problems, but increased over the first year for babies at high risk. High-risk and low-risk babies both had nearly identical sleep-wake patterns, and their development of body skills was not affected by their sleeping problems.[5]

Did You Know?

The components of breastmilk will vary over the course of the day. "Night milk" has higher levels of carbohydrates and less protein, and it contains the amino acid tryptophan, a natural tranquilizer.[6]

number of ounces the baby gets as she gains weight. With breastfeeding, the baby gets about the same amount of milk at every feeding, but the calorie density of the milk itself goes up as the baby grows.

Here's a question: Are you able to successfully put her down in her crib at bedtime "drowsy but awake"? (See Chapter 5, page 116, the Nighttime Put-Down.) If so, you know she's capable of putting herself to sleep without your assistance, so when she wakes up and cries, it's not because she doesn't know how to go to sleep without you. Instead, she's asking you for help with something else. The way to get the most sleep in that situation is to figure out what your baby needs and take care of it as quickly and unobtrusively as possible. Go into her room, don't turn on the overhead lights, offer her a nipple and let her feed, and when she's through or her sucking slows down to 5- to 10-second intervals, put her down before she falls asleep completely.

And, yes, if you're sure you want her sleeping in a crib, for everyone's sake, it's best to be consistent. It's even more confusing to her if sometimes she gets to go into the big bed, and sometimes she doesn't—that sends her mixed messages and turns nighttime into the lottery!

You may want to consider pumping milk, so that your partner can share in the joys of the 3 a.m. feeding. Or swap out some of the formula feedings during the day with the pumped milk and provide the formula at night.

Is bringing your baby into bed with you the *worst* thing you can do? Don't be so hard on yourself! There are costs and benefits to every kind of sleep arrangement.

Bringing your baby into bed at 3 a.m. certainly could encourage more nighttime awakenings and disruptions if she becomes accustomed to waking up and crying and going into the warm, snuggly, big bed. You will have to make your bed baby-safe, and if she's a thrasher or a wiggler, you may be sleeping more lightly than you would if she were in the crib. (See safety tips for bed sharing in Chapter 3, page 43.)

But for your baby, the benefit of sleeping in bed with you is the opportunity to breastfeed more; from a nutritional perspective, the higher the ratio of breastmilk in her diet, the better. She's getting disease-fighting antibodies, custom-made brain-building fatty acids, and a plethora of health benefits.

And the benefit to you, of course, is more sleep. Sometimes moms sleep more lightly if they expect to hear their baby. So once the baby's in bed with them, they can relax more, knowing they won't have to get out of bed again.

If you bring your baby into bed with you on a regular basis, consider that she'll have to re-learn how to sleep in her own bed at some point. This may not be as hard as you fear and may only take a night or two, or it may be difficult. It depends on how old your baby is when you put her back into her own bed, how consistent you are in getting her to sleep there in the future, and her individual temperament.

Remember that for the first year of a baby's life, the whole family will be in the process of constantly tweaking schedules and re-learning how to do everything together—eating, drinking, sleeping, staying clean—usually one-handed and backward while holding the baby. And once you get the hang of it and get into the groove a little bit, the nanny will

quit, or you'll get fired, or the baby will get sick, or the car will break down, and you'll have to re-learn everything all over again.

The point is, while it's good to have set routines and schedules that you can stick to, it won't always be possible, and sometimes you'll find that other things—sleep, health, sanity—have to take precedence. It's okay to decide that what you've been doing isn't working out.

Being sleep-deprived is not a state that anyone can reasonably be expected to maintain for very long. Going to bed earlier and taking naps can certainly help pay off your sleep debt, but not everyone's schedule will allow for that.

Q: My 5-month-old has been sleeping in bed with us since birth. We've tried putting him in his bassinet and his crib to sleep at various times, but if we put him down when he's awake, he starts crying immediately,

---

Are You More Tired Than You Should Be?

Consider that there may be other factors contributing to your fatigue—most commonly anemia, post-partum thyroiditis, post-partum depression, and/or certain medications you may be taking. If you're going to bed at a reasonable hour (9 or 10 p.m., say), being awakened once at night may be unpleasant but shouldn't be completely debilitating under normal circumstances.

Your doctor should test the levels of iron and thyroid hormones in your blood and ask questions about your moods to determine if you're at risk for depression. Also be prepared to tell your doctor about any medications you're taking (which drugs, the dosage, and how often you take them), including any over-the-counter medications. Allergy medicines, particularly Diphenhydramine hydrochloride (Benadryl®) and cetirizine hydrochloride (Zyrtec®), are common culprits when it comes to prolonged fatigue.

if we put him down when he's asleep, he wakes up and starts crying as soon as he realizes where he is. So in the interests of getting sleep, he always ends up back in the bed, and that's been okay . . . until recently. Lately he's been waking up every 2 hours or so, kicking and squirming until he finds a nipple, then nursing for just a few minutes before he goes back to sleep. If I turn over to face the other way, he kicks my back. I feel like a human pacifier. I'd like him to sleep in his crib and nurse just once or twice a night, but I don't know how to get there.

A: Your sleeping arrangements aren't working, and it's time to re-evaluate.

It sounds like your baby hasn't learned how to go to sleep by himself. He's nursing at night not because he's really hungry, but because he's waking up as he moves out of one sleep cycle to the next, and he doesn't know how else to put himself back to sleep. If it's starting to affect your ability to function, it's time for him to learn how to sleep on his own!

First, when and where does your baby nap during the day? Do you put him down in his crib at specific times, or are you winging it with a buffet of car seats, strollers, swings, and slings?

If you've been letting him fall asleep during the day whenever and wherever, then it's time to pin down regular times and places for his daytime naps. Somewhere between 90 minutes to 3 hours after he wakes up in the morning, he'll be ready for a nap. (Read more about putting baby down for naps in Chapter 2.) About 2 to 3 hours after he wakes up from that nap, watch for signs that he's ready for another.

There may be some complaining cries as you put him down in his crib to fall asleep by himself for those first naps while he's still awake. But he's now old enough that you will probably be able to tell the difference between the cry that means he's hungry, the one that means he's sleepy (but can't figure out how to settle himself down all the way), and a cry that means "I'm wide awake! Get me out of here!"

If you're not comfortable with hearing any crying, or your baby just gets wide awake and furious, then pick him up and soothe him until he seems drowsy again. Then put him back down before he's completely asleep. If you wait until he's completely asleep, he may wake up alarmed after only a very short time because he doesn't know where he is.

You can stay in the room with him if you sense your presence is soothing. But if it makes him more wide awake and enraged, you may want to step out to give him a chance to settle.

If you are consistent about insisting that your baby does his sleeping in the crib—falling asleep there, and not on top of you or with the use of vibration or motion or pacifiers—he will eventually adjust, and being put down in his crib will become a cue for him that it's time to go to sleep.

Once your baby is able to put himself to sleep in his crib at regular intervals for naps during the day, nighttime will be a much easier transition. Set a date for when you plan to start having your baby sleep in his crib overnight, and make sure no one has to get up early the next morning! Your baby may wake up multiple times at first, as he gets used to putting himself back to sleep at night—without being able to roll over and "snack" any more—and as long as he is breastfed, he will still probably wake up a few times to be fed at night. But that's better than eight or ten times a night, right?

Six to Nine
Months

7

Your Baby's New Sleep Patterns

By now, your baby has had 6 months of practice going to sleep, and you will be able to recognize definite patterns of more sleep at night and morning and afternoon naps, even if she doesn't go to sleep or stay asleep at exactly the same times every day. She may also fall into a nap-time or bedtime pattern that lasts for a few days or weeks and then shifts, especially if she begins cutting a tooth or reaches a new developmental milestone.

Like an adult, she'll wake up briefly between sleep cycles, and she may or may not be able to put herself back to sleep without your assistance. If she wakes up between sleep cycles and finds things have changed—a parent was there and now isn't, she fell asleep in your arms and now she's in a crib—she'll likely wake up fully and call for help.

If your baby is still resisting sleep and is waking up crying over and over in the night and only barely catnaps in spite of your best efforts to tire her out, it's only natural to want to find some kind of "cure" so you can at last have a full night's sleep. It's hard to sustain the tension between your desire to be there for your baby day and night, and your own physical needs for adequate rest to be able to function well in the daytime.

Basically, you have two options when it comes to your baby's sleeping patterns: You can keep doing what you've been doing and wait, or you can intervene in the hope of getting her to sleep by herself and in longer stretches.

Is It Time for a Change?

Does your baby need "sleep training"? That's the big question and the one only you can answer, based on your own needs and your baby's.

When you see patterns begin to emerge in your baby's schedule, it's time to start to:

- Provide the opportunity for naps at the same time and place every day.

- Maintain a consistent bedtime routine.

- Maintain a consistent bedtime.

- Practice putting the baby down when she is drowsy but still awake.

But what if none of this is working for you and your baby? You've been providing consistent opportunities for naps, but your baby won't go to sleep on her own unless she's right on top of you. Instead she fusses and cries hysterically until you pick her up, then eventually falls asleep in her high chair.

You have your bedtime routine of bathing and changing and rocking and songs and you follow it faithfully, but after weeks of trying to put your drowsy-but-awake baby down to sleep in her crib, she goes ballistic every time.

You pick her up, soothe her, put her back down, she cries, you pick her up . . . and eventually, after repeating this routine three or four times, she falls asleep for a little while, but only long enough to wake up sufficiently refreshed to begin crying again.

Or, maybe you've been bed sharing all along, and now it's just not working for you—your baby thrashes around, your partner is becoming resentful, and, instead of sleeping better yourself because your baby is near, you're sleeping less and less.

Here are some questions you may want to ask yourself:

Is it time to employ a new sleep strategy?

Does my baby need sleep training?

How long is it okay to let a baby cry?

Before we offer you various sleep-training techniques, we want to make it very clear that these are three very big questions that *science does not have a clear answer for*, and that parents must use their own judgments to answer.

If your current sleep strategy is working for you and your family, then there's no reason to change it. If you're bed sharing or co-sleeping and your pediatrician or your grandma doesn't approve, so what? They don't have to sleep with you!

But if whatever you're doing *isn't* working for you, your partner, and, possibly, your baby, too, then you may wish to try some type of intervention.

These may be the issues when it comes to continuing bed sharing at this stage:

- Your baby's movements and sounds are keeping you up at night.

- You're breastfeeding, and your baby wants to "snack" all night long by feeding for a couple of minutes every hour, then twiddles your nipples like radio knobs.

- Your baby is so active at night that you worry she'll get hurt falling out of bed or become entangled in pillows and blankets.

- Either you or your partner no longer enjoys bed sharing with the baby, and/or it's causing distance in your relationship.

- You know you don't want to bed share for an extended period, and want to transition before your baby is mobile enough to vault out of the crib.

Typical sleeping problems:

- Your baby is sleeping in a bassinet in your room, but she's outgrowing it.

- Your baby's sleeping noises are keeping you up at night.

If your baby is sleeping in her own crib, these may be issues for you now:

- Your baby is up every couple of hours at night, then takes long naps all day.

- Your baby seems to be doing most of her feeding at night.

- It takes hours to get your baby to go to sleep in her crib every night.

- You're awakened so many times at night that it's becoming difficult for you to function during the day.

- You're back to work, so other people schedule your child(ren)'s daytime.

What Is Sleep Training? Does It Really Work?

Sleep training is any kind of behavioral intervention used by parents to alter their babies' sleep habits. It has two goals: to help baby fall asleep by herself at bedtime and to put herself back to sleep without your help if she wakes up in the night.

As far as sleep-training methods go, research appears to show that there is only one factor that seems to work across the board: consistency. Researchers at the journal *Sleep*, the official publication of the Associated Professional Sleep Societies, reviewed 52 studies of sleep strategies for children ages 2 to 11 months conducted from 1970 through 2005.[1] Sleep-training strategies were divided into five distinct categories:

1. **Extinction,** also known as "crying it out," when parents put the child to bed and didn't respond to the baby again until morning, unless the baby was ill or in danger (though in some cases parents stayed in the room with the baby).

2. **Graduated extinction,** sometimes called Ferberizing, after Dr. Richard Ferber, the proponent of this method. The method is similar to extinction, but parents go in to soothe the child on a fixed schedule of progressively longer intervals, like every 3 minutes, then 5 minutes, then every 10 minutes.

3. **Positive routines and a faded bedtime,** in which a set bedtime routine, wake-up time, and naps are established; then, the baby is taken out of the crib for a certain amount of time if she has problems sleeping. Sleep training is initiated with a later-than-usual bedtime while maintaining an early, consistent wake-up time with the baby being tired initially. Then, bedtime is moved up earlier in 15-minute increments until it becomes early enough for baby to get a good night's sleep.

4. **Scheduled awakenings** have parents record the baby's nighttime wake schedule for a while, followed by waking the baby up during the night 10 to 15 minutes before she would predictably wake up. In that way, parents gain control over the baby's night waking by gradually increasing the times between their planned awakenings as a way of nudging the baby toward longer and longer sleep periods.

5. Parent education and prevention teaches parents of babies younger than 6 months of age the importance of bedtime routines, a consistent schedule, and gives them the recommendation that their babies be put down to sleep in a "drowsy but awake" state to help encourage independent sleeping.

Research showed that *any* one of the above strategies could be effective in altering babies' sleep patterns. The most important finding was that it wasn't the specific *strategy* that got results, but the fact that parents applied their approach *consistently*.

And parents using a strategy— any strategy—reported more confidence in their parenting skills, reduced stress, and higher marital satisfaction. One study found a 45 percent decrease in maternal depression.

So what's your sleep strategy?

Of the strategies, the grimly named "extinction" (aka putting the baby down and leaving her and ignoring any crying) was found to be the quickest to get the baby into a routine of falling asleep at a set time each night in less than 10 minutes and reducing night wakings. But this technique turned out to be the most stressful for parents because it was the most difficult for them to consistently apply.

Equally effective was parental education, which emphasized prevention of sleep problems and the importance of putting the baby down "drowsy but awake."

Graduated extinction also worked. It took longer for babies to settle themselves than with all-out extinction, but after 3 weeks, the "graduated" babies were slightly better at sleeping through the night than those on the more radical extinction program.

Both positive routines and scheduled awakenings still boasted an effectiveness rate of higher than 80 percent.

Basically *all* the sleep strategies work. The important thing is that you and your partner agree on your plan and apply it at the same time every night. Sounds simple, right? But as you may soon discover, things aren't as simple as they appear.

PLANNING AHEAD TO CHANGE YOUR BABY'S SLEEP PATTERNS

If you plan to implement any kind of sleep-training program, no matter what method you choose, it's important for a family to agree on the plan ahead of time.

To make any sleep-training method work, it's vital that you stick with it for long enough to effectively change your baby's habits.

The last thing you want to do is try a method for a day or two and give up before the new routine has a chance to become a habit. Inconsistency can create sleep problems where there weren't any before. Erratically responding and then not responding basically puts your baby on what psychologists call an "intermittent reinforcement schedule," which will make your baby fight sleep and cry longer and harder because she does not know what to expect.

If you've been "intermittently reinforcing" your baby, that is, trying to let her cry it out one night, then bringing her into bed the next, expect any sleep method that you choose and apply after that to take much longer to work. Instead of trying the method for at least a week, it may take 2 weeks, or as long as a month, before your baby is going to bed easily.

Regardless of the sleep-training method you choose, it's important to set a date to begin—preferably a night before a weekend or holiday when no one has to get up early the next morning.

Next, you and your partner should agree on how long you plan to try a given method, and what your Plan B will be, and what modifications you will make if, after a given amount of time, your first choice isn't working.

Both parents need to be in total agreement, since no sleep-training method will work if, for example, dad decides baby should be put down and left all night, and then mom sneaks in and picks the baby up.

So, whatever method you select, you need to make up your collective mind now to be consistent and to consistently stick with the plan for at least a week to give your baby time to adapt.

EXTINCTION METHOD

Extinction, also known as "crying it out" (or CIO, on the Internet), is seemingly about as straightforward as it gets. You pick a bedtime for your baby, you go through your routine of bathing, feeding, and so on, and then you put the baby down and don't pick her up again until "it's time," unless there is an obvious safety concern.

How long it is between bedtime and the time you're "allowed" to pick up the baby depends on whose sleep-training book you're reading.

Before you begin, it's important to be aware that every single pro-extinction sleep book that we've encountered in our research has been based on the sleep patterns of formula-fed infants.

Dr. Richard Ferber, author of the landmark 1985 book *Solve Your Child's Sleep Problems*, and thought to be the inventor of "graduated extinction," asserts that "most healthy full-term infants are sleeping through the night (which really means that they are going back to sleep on their own after normal nighttime wakings) by 3 or 4 months of age."

This authoritative statement simply doesn't hold true for breastfeeding babies, who are rarely able to sleep longer than 5 hours in a row, even after they've started solids. So, demanding that your breastfed baby sleep for 12 hours in a stretch is simply not a fair or reasonable goal.

Extinction puts the responsibility on the baby to put herself to sleep. As the theory goes—feeding, rocking, and snuggling to sleep—keep a baby from learning how to fall asleep without the parents' help. So, if your baby wakes up at night, as she transitions from one sleep cycle to the next (as all babies and adults do), then she hasn't learned the skills of how to go back to sleep again without expecting your assistance. So the theory is that making her do it on her own is how she will learn to make the transition.

Some parents have a parent stay in the room with the baby, but often this makes the whole process harder on everyone. It's upsetting for the parent, but probably even more upsetting for the baby, who is (hopefully) used to getting a response to her cries, and will become increasingly enraged and upset if she can see you but you aren't responding and picking her up for reasons she is not able to grasp.

To make sure your baby is okay, you may want to use a video baby monitor that allows you to switch off the sound and still be able to visually confirm that your baby is not in any physical danger. In some cases the baby may become so distressed that she vomits—in which case parents are advised by advocates of this method to quickly clean up the child and crib and return her to the crib as soon as possible. Otherwise, parents are to stay out of the room until it's feeding time or morning.

Positives: Of all sleep-training methods, this has been shown to work the fastest, and usually after three nights, a baby can be expected to fall asleep more quickly and to stay asleep for longer periods.

Negatives: In our opinion, this method should not be used for an infant younger than six months of age. Extended crying could cause your baby to become overtired, which has been shown to negatively affect a baby's body's responsiveness to breathing difficulties.

Some babies become so distressed that they throw up, and if vomiting occurs during distressed crying, your baby could inhale the vomit, leading to choking and possibly to pneumonia. And at that stage it can be tough to know for sure if your baby is crying because she's unable to calm herself without your help, or for another reason altogether, such as hunger, a dirty diaper, or an oncoming illness.

Not answering your baby's cries can be extremely distressing to your baby, but it can also be distressing for you, your other children, and neighbors as well, particularly during the first few nights.

There's no way to predict in advance how much crying time to expect before a baby gets into the habit of falling asleep on her own.

Some babies take to it relatively well, crying for only 15 to 30 minutes the first night and less each successive night, until they barely whimper when put down for bed without waking up again for 4 or 5 hours (or longer). Then they will feed and fall back to sleep with no protests. Some parents report that they expected a battle on their hands, only to find that their baby went to sleep relatively quickly and stayed asleep, and seemed to actually sleep better alone, and that all the worry was for nothing.

But other babies have much more severe reactions to this method and are capable of screaming for hours on end for many days in a row, working themselves into extreme stress to the point of vomiting or popping a vein in their temples. After a week or longer, some babies may still be crying for hours at night, eventually falling asleep out of sheer exhaustion, then waking up after only a short stint of sleep only to start crying again. Unfortunately, we suspect that these are also more likely to be the same babies that also sleep more lightly, making bed sharing and co-sleeping difficult, too.

If it turns out that your baby falls into the "crying for hours" category, then you are likely to find yourself in a Catch-22, or a situation presenting two equally undesirable alternatives. If you are forced to abandon the plan, and return to bed sharing or feeding your baby into a deep sleep, all of the crying was for naught and you may find yourself feeling like a failure or feeling resentment toward your seemingly uncooperative baby. Or, you could continue to stick with the plan anyway, only to find that the situation still does not improve, and the nightly crying for months on end is making you feel like you live in a Halloween hell house.

And, even if you succeed at getting your baby to go to sleep at bedtime, there is no guarantee that she will stay asleep. Though some experts assert that a baby should be able to sleep all night without a feeding by 5 months, breastmilk digests quickly, so the definition of *all night* for a breastfed baby is 5 hours, not 8 or 12. Until your baby's stomach has matured to the point that she can properly absorb calories from solids, she will still need to feed every 3 to 5 hours.

The "Crying-It-Out" Controversy

Family-bed proponents and attachment-parenting advocates oppose any sleep plan that involves a baby crying, citing research that appears to show extended crying has an impact on baby development. When left alone to cry without intervention, crying babies' brains are deprived of oxygen, and their bodies are flooded with stress hormones. There is also evidence to show that chronic stress-hormone exposure at a young age can contribute to lifelong health and behavioral problems.

Both animal and human studies of severely neglected babies have shown that the brain's exposure to stress hormones results in nerve connections failing to develop, and for existing connections to disintegrate, affecting learning and memory.[2] Researchers believe that there is a connection between early separation anxiety and heightened risk for adult panic disorders.[3]

There is also solid scientific evidence that babies who cry excessively at a young age also cry more when they're older, develop poorer language skills, and act out later in life.[4] But it's unclear whether babies' crying for long periods without comfort caused the problems, or that the constant crying and being inconsolable were just one symptom of organic disorders manifesting themselves at a very early age.

And how long is an "extended period"? Obviously there is a

difference between letting a baby cry for, say, half an hour a night for a week as you try to change her sleep habits, and the kind of around-the-clock child neglect that infant research is based on. Still, no one really knows what a "safe" amount of exposure to stress hormones is.

And, if crying it out is the method that studies show works the fastest, then, paradoxically, it may be the method that promises the least amount of total tears, especially when compared to the non-method of picking the baby up at every cry.

So, crying it out carries theoretical risk. Your baby may respond quickly to this method with very little crying overall, or she may not. Some babies respond quickly to consistency and begin to settle down with minimal fuss after about three nights, but some babies will cry for a while almost every night at bedtime, well into toddlerhood.

But, on the other hand, there is also the theoretical risk of long-term effects of sleep deprivation as a result of a child not learning to fall asleep by herself without props or assistance. Going to sleep by herself is something she will have to learn eventually. You can't do it for her, as much as you might want to. And while staying asleep will become easier as she grows, learning to go to sleep will get progressively more difficult as she matures. At some point—tonight, next month, or next year—you will have to learn to ignore a certain amount of your child's resistance to bedtime, because constantly going

into her room to soothe her will only reinforce her anxiety.

By the time your child is a toddler, if she still doesn't know how to soothe herself, her blossoming imagination and mobility will make bedtime a long, difficult battle every night at the expense of everyone's rest, including hers. If you give her lots of attention every time she complains that she can't sleep or if she says there's a monster in the closet, this will actually suggest to her that there *really might be* a monster in the closet or that she *really can't* go to sleep without help.

There are parents, including certain celebrities, who bed share for an extended period and don't have bedtimes for their kids, letting them fall asleep where they lie or having them tag along when the adults go to bed. Though parents who follow the "whatever" method (our name for it) may do so lovingly, the reality is that children need as much as 5 hours' more sleep than adults do, and leaving a baby, toddler, or small child in an adult bed unattended is simply not safe. While "whatever" may work beautifully with a portable, cat-napping newborn, it's a quick route to sleep deprivation and unsafe situations all around for toddlers and older children.

So, "crying it out" may be bad for the brain, but so is sleep deprivation. There's no doubt it causes a baby distress, but a toddler or older child learning to sleep alone for the first time will be anxious and distressed, too. Unless you are dedicated to bed sharing for an extended period of time, with all that it involves (such as childproofing your bedroom and going to bed at 8 p.m. every night), there's a lot to be said for establishing independent sleep before your child is a toddler.

Tips for Using the Extinction Method

Rather than putting your baby in her crib when she's completely awake, we suggest feeding and rocking her almost to sleep, and then waking her up just a bit to put her to bed. Usually, getting up and putting her down in the crib will be enough to wake her up, but if not, singing a song or stroking her back should do it.

It's important that she is awake when she gets put down in the crib, otherwise she won't learn to do the going-to-sleep part herself, and she may be stunned and unhappy to find that she is out of your arms and in the crib when she wakes up between sleep cycles.

Also, if she almost drops off in your arms you can reassure yourself that she's fed, she's tired, and that you've done all you can do to meet her physical needs. There is some comfort in knowing that any crying that follows is not because she's hungry or isn't tired.

Then, remind yourself, as you listen to the crying, that sooner or later, your baby is going to have to learn how to put herself to sleep on her own. She can learn this skill relatively easily when she's young, but it will become progressively more difficult as separation anxiety sets in and she becomes more mobile.

A lot of parents who try this method will sit outside of their baby's door, listening to the crying and chewing their fingernails. Guilt can make you feel like you need to be right there, suffering with your baby. But listening and feeling bad don't help the baby.

If you use this method, remind yourself that you have decided that the benefits justify the potential risks, and that it is not fair to anyone to change your mind before you give the method a chance to work. If it's been a solid week or more and you're not seeing any less

Authors Who Endorse the Extinction Method

Marc Weissbluth, *Healthy Sleep Habits, Happy Child*: "When you put a time limit on how much protest crying at night you can tolerate or accept before going to the baby, you teach the baby to cry to that time limit."

Jennifer Waldburger and Jill Spivack, *The Sleepeasy Solution*: "The long-term effects of sleep deprivation are far worse than a few days of your child's frustration in learning a new skill or accepting a new limit."

crying or any more sleeping, *then* it's time to rethink.

GRADUATED EXTINCTION

Graduated extinction is also known as "progressive waiting" or "Ferberizing," after Dr. Richard Ferber, the director of the Center for Pediatric Sleep Disorders at Children's Hospital Boston, and author of the landmark 1985 book *Solve Your Child's Sleep Problems*.

Graduated extinction is essentially the same as simple extinction, as described above. Parents develop a bedtime routine and place their baby in her crib while she's awake. The difference is that parents go in to check on and reassure their baby—without picking her up—at increasing intervals; 3 minutes, then 5 minutes, then 10 minutes, up to half an hour.

Positives: Graduated extinction seeks to avoid uncontrolled crying on the baby's part by setting time limits, which can be more reassuring to parents.

Negatives: The underlying assumption of this approach is that going in and checking makes the process easier on both parents and babies. But in practice, it could have the opposite effect—your baby may rouse and become frustrated and angered when she can see her parents and yet they won't respond to her. It's arguable that progressive checking is more for the parent's peace of mind than the baby's.

Tips for Using Graduated Extinction

Ask yourself if your presence is soothing or stimulating to your baby.

If it's "time" to check on your baby and reassure her, and she seems to be quieting down, give her a chance to settle before you show your face. If she's getting more worked up, make sure her diaper's clean, her room is not too hot or cold . . . then run out and wait some more, twice as long as you did the last time.

POSITIVE ROUTINES AND A FADED BEDTIME

Positive routines and a faded bedtime, also called rescheduling, suggests that parents follow a

---

Authors Who Endorse Faded Bedtime

Elizabeth Pantley, *The No-Cry Sleep Solution*:

"The idea is to slowly, respectfully, and carefully change our baby's behavior to match our own needs more closely."

Elements of Bedtime Routines for Six-to Twelve-month-olds

- Bathing
- Tooth brushing or cleaning baby's teeth with gauze
- Singing
- Dimming lights
- Baby massage
- Playing music
- Turning on a fan
- Rocking in a rocking chair
- Reading or telling a story
- Saying good night, using the same words every night

go-to-sleep routine every night, including activities such as taking a bath, changing into pajamas, and reading a story.

The program advocates a late bedtime and waking the baby at the same time every morning. You then move the baby's bedtime earlier by 15-minute increments on successive nights, but if the baby has problems sleeping, you take her out of the crib and soothe her.

Positives: This is the only sleep-training method that doesn't involve the baby crying herself to sleep, so we suggest using this approach as your "Plan A." If you can get your baby to sleep by herself without tears, that's obviously better than any other option.

You've already used this method, minus the "faded bedtime" part, from 3 months onward if you've been following our suggestions.

Negatives: The rescheduling method does not work as quickly as other methods and may not work at all for some babies.

Picking up your baby every time she cries may not allow her to learn to fall asleep without your assistance, which means she may wake up fully and cry every time she transitions between sleep cycles.

Tip for Using Faded Bedtime

Sometimes travel or special occasions can disrupt your bedtime routine or force you to skip steps, rush, or improvise. Still, do your best to start, progress through the steps you've chosen, and end your routine at the same time each night. The predictability will be reassuring to your baby.

Nighttime Routine Derailers

These are the main reasons why sleep-training efforts fail:

- Parental guilt or disagreement
- Inconsistent sleep routines
- Oncoming illness or teething
- Sleeplessness during the acquisition of new motor skills
- Late or early naps affecting nighttime sleep
- Travel, moving, and other changes that interfere with predictable sleep habits

SCHEDULED AWAKENINGS

This is really a single strategy, rather than an entire sleep-training system, that may help with your baby's sleep problems. Think of it more as a helpful tool, rather than a total solution.

Here's how Scheduled Awakenings works: You keep track of your baby's nighttime wake schedule for a while, then you begin to wake her up during the night 10 to 15 minutes *before* she would usually wake up. Once you're used to doing that, then you gradually increase the amount of time between wakings to encourage your baby to sleep for longer stretches.

Positives: Scheduled Awakenings reduces nighttime crying with a pre-emptive wake-up. It can also make nighttimes more predictable and may help stretch out time between nighttime feedings.

Negatives: You'll have to set an alarm to get up for feedings.

Some babies' waking habits are more unpredictable than others, and even predictable babies will have changes in nighttime sleeping habits due to illness, teething, or hitting a developmental milestone.

EXTENDED BED SHARING

Another approach that's worth considering is not to apply any of the above theories, and, if you're bed sharing, to plan on continuing the practice for an extended period of time.

Positives: There is overwhelming evidence that the more touch and physical contact with parents a child gets at a young age, the calmer and less fearful she will be in adulthood. Touch doesn't have to be limited only to daytime hours. Another benefit: You won't have to deal with crying or the downside of any of the plans described above.

Negatives: You may need to get a bigger bed. You will need to figure out where to have your baby sleep

The Best Sleep-Training Advice There Is

First, both parents must agree on using sleep training. Together, choose three different plans, using one or a combination of sleep-training strategies. Agree to stick with your chosen strategy for at least a week to give it time to work, or longer if previously you were applying a method inconsistently.

between her bedtime and yours, because it's not safe to have a baby sleep alone in an adult bed. Keeping your baby up with you until you're ready to go to bed won't allow her to get adequate sleep, since babies need 3 or 4 more hours of sleep than adults do.

Your baby's ever-increasing mobility will create new hazards—you will basically have to make your bedroom as safe as a giant playpen, putting your mattress and box spring on the floor, bolting shelving and dressers, and getting rid of breakables, electrical cables, drapery cords, or anything else that might choke your curious toddler if she wakes up before you do.

Also, some babies find it's more stimulating than relaxing to have parents nearby, and instead of settling themselves will wake up to play or to nurse. Some moms find overnight breastfeeding problematic, due to the "snacking" issue. Because she smells your milk constantly, your baby may want to stay attached to you, flutter-sucking and using your nipple as a pacifier, or she may turn over and want to nurse for just a few moments at a time every few minutes for hours. It's very difficult—some say impossible—to persuade a breastfeeding baby to nurse less overnight as long as you're still sharing a bed. This can make it hard to get a good night's sleep.

Authors Who Endorse Extended Bed Sharing

Linda Folden Palmer, *Baby Matters*:

"Honor babyhood, rejoice in all the special cozy comforts parents are designed to provide, and shower our babies with unrestrained love."

William Sears and Martha Sears, *The Baby Sleep Book*:

"Putting a baby down to sleep alone in a crib and leaving him to cry himself to sleep and go back to sleep when he awakens is both biologically and developmentally wrong."

OTHER IDEAS

Consider compromises that work for you and your unique baby, such as having her go to sleep in her crib for part of the night, then bringing her into bed after her first night waking, or having the baby go to sleep in her crib for part of the night, but responding quickly every time she wakes up.

As your baby becomes better able to digest solids, her first sleep of the night will get progressively longer on its own.

If you're bed sharing reluctantly because of your baby's harsh reaction to sleeping alone at night, start out by consistently putting her in the crib for naps during the day, even if you have to tire her out by pushing her morning nap later and squeezing out the afternoon nap. Then try the crib again in a month for the first stretch of sleep of the night. (Just remember that when you try the crib again you must stick with it long enough to give your baby the chance to adjust to the new routine.)

Q: Is there such a thing as too much sleep for a baby? My little one is almost 7 months old and he sleeps through the night (7:30 p.m. to 7 a.m.). He also takes his morning nap at 10:00 a.m. to noon, then he naps again from 2 p.m. to 4 p.m. It seems like he only wakes up to eat. At 7 months is this good, or should I be encouraging him to do more when he is awake?

A: Babies differ in the amount of sleep they require and when they choose to do it. Your baby's sleep patterns may be somewhat rare for a 7-month-old, but they're still within normal range. Most likely, his need for two naps in the daytime will diminish soon. Baby experts are concerned, though, about babies who are overly sluggish and floppy, or who fail to master basic development skills, such as head raising and rolling over. Babies who are not responsive socially or don't seem eager to interact with their parents by this time are also a concern. Should you have any concerns about your baby's health, share them with his care provider. Consider getting a second opinion from a baby-development expert if you're not seeing progress and your baby's doctor doesn't seem to respond to your concerns.

Q: My adorable, just-turned-6-month-old is still taking several short naps a day instead of the two "biggies" all the sleep books I've read recommend. We pay attention to sleep cues: She falls asleep easily and also sleeps a 12-hour night (6:30 p.m. to 6:30 a.m. with occasional night wakings). But she rarely naps for more than 40 minutes! She usually wakes up refreshed and energetic (and in general she's a very alert and happy baby), but I still have the nagging feeling that something is wrong. Is she really getting the rest she needs? Help!

A: If your baby is happy, refreshed, and energetic, there's no need to worry that your baby isn't getting enough sleep. Watch the baby, not the clock! And, in fact, your baby's sleep does fall within the normal range. Consider yourself very lucky if your baby falls asleep easily and sleeps for a 12-hour night! It's worth noting, though, that some sleep-deprived babies become increasingly more "hyper" rather than tired as the night wears on. If that's the case, then it's time for parents to step in and slow their babies down.

Q: My daughter has gotten into a terrible habit. She won't sleep unless we put her in our bed. I am not totally opposed to co-sleeping, but I prefer that she sleep in her crib. She is 7 months old. She slept beautifully through the night from 3 months to 5 months and then she started teething. Sometimes we could rock her back to sleep, and on some desperate nights we let her sleep in bed. My husband and I both work, so sometimes sleep is the priority. We thought we could sleep-train her once her first tooth came in; however, this has not been successful. She cries immediately after we lay her down. We have a nighttime routine to give her the message that it is time to sleep. If we wait until she is asleep to put her down, she'll either wake up immediately and start to cry or wake up a few hours later crying. I have stopped nursing in the middle of the night so she isn't waking up expecting a snack. This weekend we tried letting her cry it out, going in after 5, 8, and 10 minutes, for just a minute to

soothe her. Each time we went in she cried even harder. After a half hour of crying we finally picked her up. She was so upset that it took a good half hour to calm her down and she started right back up as soon as we laid her down. Last night, she even cried when we put her in our own bed. I'd like her to learn to self-soothe, but I don't know how long to let her cry it out. I knew that it would be rough the first few nights, but I thought the end result would be sleep after an hour of crying, but she just gets worse. I am trying to teach her to self-soothe during the day by spending some time in her crib and in her play area by herself. I try to let her take one nap by herself in the crib but on some days she refuses to sleep unless we hold her. Even worse, in the middle of the night she only wants me, so my husband isn't able to get her to stop crying. Tonight we will try the cry-it-out method again. We have a mobile and a musical aquarium toy to play for her. I will probably pick her up after a half hour (with periodic soothing) to calm her and try to put her back to sleep. Any suggestions?

A: Whatever your sleep strategy—bed sharing, a faded bedtime with routines combined with picking her up or letting her cry it out—what's important is that you and your husband are committed to handling bedtime in the same way every night. Uncertainty and unpredictability—brought on, for example, by letting her sleep in your bed when she cries sometimes, but not other times—can create long crying marathons. If both you and your husband are uncertain—either you don't agree on a bedtime strategy or you're not completely sure you're ready for her to sleep in her crib yet—you're going to create problems.

The first step is for both of you to decide that the crib is where she's going to sleep, and to set a date for when. You may decide, for the sake of your own sleep, to wait a month for her stomach to be mature enough to more completely digest solid food. That will mean longer stretches of sleep for her, and make the crying you will have to endure more worth it. If you decide she needs to be in the crib as soon as possible, you do not need to feel guilty about that decision. You are not hurting her, endangering her, damaging her sense of trust, or causing her any kind of damage by lovingly and consistently putting her down to sleep in a safe and sturdy crib instead of your bed.

Once you decide it's time for the crib, it's important, whatever sleep-intervention method you choose, not to relapse and bring her back into bed. The great thing about babies is that they're adaptable, and most of the time you can change their habits if you can apply the new routine consistently for long enough.

If you've tried routines and the Faded Bedtime method and it hasn't made anything better, then it could be time to try Extinction or the graduated version of it. Although there may be risks

involved in allowing your baby to cry for extended periods, there are also risks involved with ongoing parental sleep deprivation: Babies don't understand that tonight's sleep-deprived mom might be tomorrow's car accident!

She may not like having to adjust to the new routine, but sleeping alone is a skill that she will need to acquire sooner or later. In Western society, people usually sleep in their own beds until they're married or in a live-in relationship (and sometimes not even then). So being able to fall asleep without having a person next to her is a good thing to know how to do. And, she may surprise you by taking to crib sleeping rather quickly now that she's a little bit older and you and your husband have made a pact to be consistent.

So, whatever week you decide on, start on a Friday, go ahead with your soothing routine (feeding, bathing, songs, and so on) and put her down when you see her eyelids start to get heavy but while she's still awake. She may scream, but keep in mind you're not hurting your baby, you're helping her learn a valuable life skill, even if she's disagreeing with you and doesn't care to learn it! Sometimes what's best for your family as a whole isn't what your baby may want at a given time. If her crying is distressed and goes on beyond what you can bear, go in and check for a poopy diaper, spit-up, or other problem. If there is a problem, solve it quickly and go. If there isn't one, reassure her but don't risk sending a mixed message by picking her up.

Nine to Twelve Months

All About Toddler Sleep

Grasping, pulling up, crawling, cruising, and jabbering: From 9 to 12 months, your baby begins to leave babyhood behind to embark on the world of toddlerhood! But with these new developmental milestones come new sleep disturbances. Parents are often alarmed to discover that their baby—who was previously sleeping well—has now started to wake up in the middle of the night again.

Like the Four-Month Sleep Shift, some babies who were previously sleeping through the night will begin to wake up thrashing or crying at some point between about 8 and 10 months. This new sleep disturbance comes at the same time a baby's visual memory starts to become stronger, and it could be that scary dreams come along with that development.

Separation anxiety sets in around this time as well, as your baby begins to understand his own selfhood and that he is a separate person from you, his primary caregiver. At the same time, the concept of object permanence emerges—when children learn that something still exists even when it is not seen or heard.

For the first time, your baby is able to tell the difference between situations that are familiar and unfamiliar and begins to understand that he can be separated from you. At the same time, he isn't able to grasp when you will return, nor does he have a concept of time, and so he can react anxiously whenever you leave him. This reaction is both normal and healthy at this stage of his development.

Separation anxiety may set in as early as 8 months, or even earlier for some highly aware babies, or it may occur as late as 12 months, and other toddlers never seem to go through it at all. When your baby reaches this developmental milestone, he will be clingy, fearful of letting you out of his sight, and adamant about not wanting to sleep alone in his room.

This phase of resistance to separation can be trying for parents. You may have decided that you are going to consistently refuse to pick your baby up overnight, but then find that his crying is simply excruciating for you and the whole family. It tears you up, feeling the need to be there for him but not wanting to ruin the independent sleep skills that you've been working so hard to establish all these months. It can also cause strife if parents and family members disagree on if, when, and how to respond to nighttime crying.

What you decide to do when you reach a tough phase like this is personal. In our opinion, you should not feel guilty if your baby's crying is so wrenching that you or your partner decide you can't take it anymore and you pick him up to soothe him. Do you risk sending him mixed messages? Sure. Are you encouraging more nighttime tantrums in the future? Possibly. But as a parent you also know better than anyone when your child's cries are not just overtiredness or letting off steam but are in the real panic zone, and

Crying Action Plan for Older Babies

- Give him a chance to settle down on his own.

- Listen to the crying. Is your baby over-tired or fussing in his sleep, or is the crying becoming louder, more shrill and alarmed?

- Check on the baby. Is there an obvious problem? If not, try soothing him in the crib.

- Consult with your partner and use your judgment. Is this run-of-the mill crying, or is it time to intervene?

- If you decide to pick him up, keep the lights low.

- Put him back in his crib when he's soothed and drowsy, yet not completely asleep.

you know when it's time to make an exception to the rules.

Q: I have a 12-month-old girl who started sleeping through the night at 2 months. But for the past week or two she has been waking up two or three times a night. I have tried not letting her sleep as much during the day, but that doesn't seem to be helping at all. I'm just not sure what would be causing her to wake up in the middle of the night. Any ideas on how to help her sleep better?

A: Everyone—babies, children, adults—wakes up a little bit a few times every night. But while adults know how to just roll over, close their eyes, and lie still to go back to sleep, your 12-month-old is still figuring out the ways of the world. If your daughter wakes up at night, quickly take care of any problem she might have (dirty diaper, tangled blanket, needs a quick hug, etc.) and then tell her

something like, "It's still nighttime, sweetheart, lie down and close your eyes and be quiet and still, and you'll fall back to sleep." (It's helpful to use the same, simple phrases every night.) Then leave and go back to your own bed, or if you're bed sharing, close your eyes and "play possum" until she goes back to sleep. In other words, try to make your nighttime responses as quick and no-nonsense as possible. Don't turn on the lights and don't pick her up or take her out of the crib. Offer reassurance, but not stimulation.

Q: My son is 10 months old, and after nearly 3 months of almost-ideal sleeping patterns, he has begun to fight sleep again. Last week, he was sleeping from between 7:30 p.m. to around 6:00 a.m. with only the occasional midnight awakening. After our bedtime routine, he breastfed and went into his crib with no problem, falling asleep with a minimum of fuss.

His naps were almost always 2 hours after his morning waking at 5:00 a.m. and about 4 hours after his first nap (so around 8:00 a.m. and 1:30 p.m.).

For the past 4 days, however, even when he falls asleep at the breast, when I put him into his crib, he *screams*. Usually, he just whimpers, even when he's wide awake, when I put him in bed. His naps have similarly deteriorated: He's been fighting me at 8:00 a.m. and waiting to fall asleep at 10:00, then falling asleep again late in the afternoon.

We don't know what sparked the change. He's a very active little man and has been crawling for 3 months, cruising for 1 month, and pushing walker toys for 3 weeks. He has 6 teeth that all came in with very little drama. He's still not waking during the night, but getting him to sleep has become a nightmare. We usually let him cry for about 15 minutes, hoping he'll calm down (as he did before), but when I go check on him, he is standing in his bed, sweating, and with a runny nose from the screaming. I feel so bad that I rock him until he is limp with sleep and I'm able to lay him down.

Please, if you have any suggestions—or even an explanation for this reversion—let me know!

A: It sounds as though your son is suffering from separation anxiety. He's becoming increasingly aware of when you're not around. Part of separation anxiety has to do with

the developing of memory. Between the ages of 6 and 12 months, a baby's memory goes through a rapid phase of development. While a newborn lives completely in the moment, your baby is increasingly able to hold you in his mind while you aren't present. In other words, he's developing the ability to miss you. These same neurological changes may also cause him to have vivid or frightening nightmares.

So, you want to be there for your baby, but at the same time you don't want to risk feeding his anxiety and making him incapable or unwilling to go to sleep without you. It's up to you if you want to rock or pick him up, but keep in mind that he will remember that you do this, and come to expect it. If you stop doing it, he will become even more distressed. A compromise is to go to him and reassure him that you're still there, but don't pick him up, turn on the overhead lights, or talk very much. Talk softly or hum to him and pat his belly so that he can learn what it feels like to go from being upset to calm and relaxed. Relax yourself, with deep breaths and slow, gentle movements. Turning on a familiar CD of baby lullabies may help, too, especially if you've played the same tracks at times when he's drifting off to sleep. You're there for him and supporting him, but not reinforcing his anxiety or creating a new routine that will be difficult to change later.

Once your baby has calmed down and is on the verge of drifting off, whether it's daytime or nighttime, don't give in to the temptation to sneak away while he

According to a poll of primary caregivers by the National Sleep Foundation (NSF), by 9 months some 70 to 80 percent of babies are sleeping a straight 9 to 12 hours every night. But that also means one out of three to one out of four babies still isn't.

isn't looking in the hope of keeping him from becoming distressed. It's important for your baby to see you leave, whether you're leaving him at day care or in his crib for the night. This helps him know that you are trustworthy and that you won't disappear over and over again unexpectedly without preparing him for it. Eventually he'll learn to anticipate your leaving and to learn strategies for letting go.

It's also important not to make your good-byes or good night departures overly drawn out or dramatic because they build up tension and only serve to heighten your baby's stress and anxiety. Keep good-byes short and simple.

HEAD AND CRIB BANGING

It's early in the morning and you're trying to sleep, but you hear banging coming from your baby's room. This could be a sign that your baby is becoming a "crib banger." Sometimes a baby will butt his head against his crib, shake it back and forth, or knock on it rhythmically.

As strange as it may seem, head and crib banging are actually quite common; in fact, it's been estimated that up to 20 percent of babies do it. It may be that the rhythmic motion or repetitive

sound is relaxing, just like being rocked, or your baby may have just discovered the new sensation and finds head and crib banging and the noise they make interesting. In some cases, it may mean that your baby is feeling pain from an earache or from teething, or it could be a part of his acting out when he's frustrated.

As long as your baby isn't injuring himself, there's no need to worry—though this is a good time to take out the wrench and make sure that all the nuts, bolts, and screws on your baby's crib are nice and tight. Make sure, too, that the mattress is positioned on the lowest level, that the crib is well away from the wall, and that the crib's wheels are either in the locked position or set into rubber cups to keep the crib from being "walked" into the wall.

Most kids outgrow the habit by the time they're 3. If your child is head-banging and is at least 14 months old and also not able to point at objects or follow your gaze, that might indicate a neurological issue and you should seek the guidance of your toddler's physician.

PULLING UP

Sometimes a baby at this stage (9 to 12 months) will pull himself up to a standing position using the bars of his crib, only to find that he doesn't know how to get back down once he gets there! You may find him clinging to the bars in serious distress.

If this happens to your baby, you can help by teaching him how it's done. Help him get back down by walking his hands down the bars of the crib so he can learn how to do it for himself. You may even have to help him bend into a sitting position and then lay him down again so he learns the lowering trick for himself.

CLIMBING OUT

Your baby's new mobility skills may also come with the ability to vault out of the crib! This can be quite dangerous, especially if you have uncarpeted floors in your baby's room. You may wish to install something soft under the crib, such as thick, padded carpeting, just in case.

Q: My son is 10 months old and usually takes three naps a day. He goes down for the night at 6:30 p.m. and wakes up for the day at 5:30 a.m. He does wake during the night, babbles a while, and goes back to sleep without our help. He eats three solid meals a day with a 4-to-6-ounce bottle following each meal and a snack in between. He can't stay up for more than 2½ to 3 hours—3 is pushing it. I have tried to move him to two naps without success. I'm getting a little tired of getting up at 5:30 a.m. every day, but our pediatrician has told us that this is the way it is for now. I don't buy it, as *all* of my friends with kids his age are sleeping 12 and 13 hours a night and taking two naps.

A: What other people's kids are doing can be interesting to know, but it doesn't change what's going on in your own child's brain. While some kids drop the second nap at about 6 months, it's also completely normal for a baby to still take three naps at 12 months. Your friends are actually pretty lucky; there are still plenty of 10-month-olds who don't sleep for more than 4 hours in a row. When it comes to getting up early in the morning, we have to agree with your pediatrician that there isn't much to be done to change this aspect of your baby's schedule. The good news, though, is that he's ready for a nap pretty soon after he gets up in the morning, which means that you get to have a nap, too. Resist the urge to put on a huge pot of coffee at 5 a.m. so you can enjoy it! It will also help if you go to bed early yourself—if you go to bed at 9:30, you'll be getting a solid 8 hours.

Twelve Months and Beyond

9

The Challenge of Toddler Sleep

Dealing with toddler sleep problems can be a challenge! Toddlers are mobile, have vivid imaginations, and seem to feel that protesting going to bed at night is a matter of principle. They want to stay up just like grown-ups and be in on all the action that they imagine is going on in their absence. And they have a need to test what their limits are, so trying to make them do something they don't want to, like heading off to a dark room to sleep, can bring out their contrariness.

Even though your toddler may seem to be demanding to be in control, what she's really asking is the opposite: to know who's in control and what her limits are.

Most toddlers make up for lost sleep at night with naps in the daytime. At a year of age, most toddlers will be taking two naps, morning and afternoon, although some may still take three, or even one nap. How much sleep a child needs per night depends on the child. Children who as babies needed a lot of sleep during the first year are also likely to need more sleep as toddlers. Similarly, children who required less sleep as babies will follow the same pattern as they mature.

Fifteen percent of 2-year-olds wake regularly in the night.

There are numerous reasons why toddlers don't sleep at night as we would like them to. They may simply be too wound up and excited about waking life to shut everything down, even though they need the rest for brain development and body restoration. It's important to understand that not even the most skillful and perfect parent can force a child to go to sleep, just as no one can force you to go to sleep. You can prepare your child for the gentle descent into dreamland and make her environment as sleep-worthy as possible, but ultimately, it's your toddler who has to learn to calm her own body and mind.

Toddler sleep pattern:

12½ to 15 hours per night, with 1½ to 3 hours of napping during the day.

Exercise Is Important

Toddlers need rigorous physical activities to help them stretch their growing muscles and to let off steam during the daytime so they're not kept awake by built-up tensions at night. They also need daylight to suppress melatonin production during the day and to manufacture vital vitamin D. Plan for your child to have at least 3 hours of active moving around during the day, especially outdoors in fresh air. If your child attends day care, be sure that the center schedules a lot of physical activity for its children.

If you're a stay-at-home parent, seek out activities where your toddler can play vigorously and you can relax, like a playground with lots of fun equipment for kids and nice comfy benches for parents.

Handling Delaying Tactics

The more your child matures, the craftier and more elaborate her going-to-bed delay tactics can get! You may have thought that once you convinced your child to sleep in her crib, that would mark the end of bedtime drama. Little did you know it was just the beginning! Children just don't like to sleep alone, and you may find that, even as a first-grader, your child still wants to sleep in your bed or have you sleep in hers. Some parents do have a family bed, and this also poses its own challenges, because toddlers need so many more hours of sleep than adults do.

Probably until high school, your child will test the limits of your bedtime routine, wanting to stay up for one more book or TV show, or dragging out bath time, asking for extra songs or stories, telling you not to leave because she's afraid of the dark or being alone. But beware: If you give in to a tactic once, expect it to be used again and again. Remember that no matter what your toddler or child may say, she needs limits, structure, and sufficient sleep to function.

It's okay to sometimes give in to the urge to give your child what she wants. Just don't do it at the expense of her needs or yours.

When you've got a dawdling toddler, nip the stalling techniques in the bud with a pre-emptive strike. Anticipate your toddler's needs and requests and work them into your bedtime routine. If she always asks for a glass of water, make sure you provide one (not too full, as spilling the water is another delay tactic).

If she always wants you to stay, make it part of her bedtime routine to keep her company by sitting in a rocker or a bedside chair, or lying next to her in her bed, but only for a limited amount of time.

If your child stalls in the bath or with tooth brushing, you might set a time limit for all the steps in your routine (an oven timer will help):

6:10—bath
6:30—brush teeth, get water
6:40—read books
6:50—sing a goodnight song
6:55—lights out, stay to keep child company
7:00—leave the room

Then, if your child stalls getting out of the bathtub, you can legitimately say, "You can keep playing for two more minutes, but we won't have time to read together," or, "We won't have time for me to stay and keep you company." This helps your child develop a concept of time and empowers her to make choices, but still draws clear limits. If you use this method, it helps to have an "I just work here" attitude: Bedtime is what it is; all 2-year-olds must go to bed at that time, and that's just the way it is.

Twenty Tips for Toddler Bedtime

Here are some tips to help you get your older child to sleep (or back to sleep).

1. **Do a reality check.** Recognize that even the most effective parent in the world can't force her child to fall asleep, and trying to do so is simply counter-productive. Your job is to simply set up the environment for restfulness so your child can learn to read her own tiredness cues and nod off peacefully without interference. If your child says she can't sleep, a good answer is, "That's fine, you don't have to sleep, but you do need to be quiet and still, and rest your body."

2. **Create basic go-to-bed rules.** Your toddler will thrive on predictability. Even if she's too young to read a clock yet, knowing that her bedtime rituals start at the same time every night can be reassuring.

3. **Remember: Sleep makes for sleep.** Don't be fooled into believing that by postponing your child's bedtime she will sleep later in the morning. It just doesn't work that way.

4. **Be sensitive to tired signs.** Bedtime may need to be earlier than usual if your child is whining, rubbing her eyes, dragging around, or getting irritable. Start the bedtime ritual and the next night, try a bedtime that's 15 minutes earlier than usual.

5. **Remember sometimes "hyper" is a sleepy sign.** Some toddlers may get draggy at bedtime, but others rev up their engines and act out. In that case, you may need to hold your child and help her learn how to calm down by herself.

6. **Tone down pre-sleep stimulation.** Avoid active play, such as wrestling or running games, at least an hour before bedtime, even if it's the only time dad has to be with his child. When your child is over-stimulated, she'll have a hard time slowing down and turning her little engine off. Instead, make after-dinner time a quiet time for shared sleep rituals.

7. **Use a kitchen timer for an impersonal five-minute warning.** Give your child a warning before it's time to start getting ready for bed, and then use a kitchen timer to sound the alarm (instead of you).

8. **Offer win-win options.** Your toddler wants to feel in control of her life. You can help give her that feeling of control by offering her two choices, rather than forcing her to take only the action you want. It's a simple parenting trick, but it works: "Would you rather go to bed right now? Or would you like me to read five pages in a book you choose for 5 minutes and then go to bed?" You're actually

the winner regardless of the option she chooses, but your toddler feels like she's in control because she has choices.

9. **Encourage the use of a security blanket, a very soft square of cloth, or a prized, huggable animal.** Transition objects can help your toddler feel secure at night. Pacifiers, on the other hand, can get lost in the bed, leading to nighttime wakeups. They can also affect how your child's teeth come in and the shape of her jaw, so you should phase them out after her teeth begin to come in.

10. **Don't exaggerate the farewells.** Keeping your toddler company for 5 minutes or so before you leave the room can be a nice luxury, and you'll probably find that she will talk to you about all sorts of things you might not ordinarily hear about in a bid to stay up a little bit later. But plan to stay for a set amount of time.

11. **Turn into the Beddy-Bye Robot.** If you have a toddler who gets out of bed a lot, use sheer repetition to train her to sleep. Here's how it works: Toddler gets out of bed. You put her back into bed. Repeat as many times as needed for a series of nights until the message is delivered—quietly, firmly, and without speaking or anger. It may take 20 or 50 or 100 lay-downs, but you should begin to see a change after the third or fourth night of playing the sleep robot.

12. **Stick with middle-of-the-night waking rules.** You'll also need rules for your toddler if she wakes up during the night and can't seem to fall back to sleep without your intervention. Keep her company if you want to—and are willing to do that every time she wakes—but don't let her get out of the bed. Making exceptions to the rules, such as letting your child climb into bed with you after you put her down, will make things harder for both of you in the future because it makes waking up more rewarding than sleeping.

13. **Keep your space.** If your toddler has night terrors, you may elect to stay in the room with her, but make some rules. For example, you might choose to tell her that you'll only stay in the room for 10 minutes while you quietly read a book to yourself. Emphasize that it's no longer "her" time, but the whole family's time to rest, and that you'll enjoy playing with her in the morning when she wakes up.

14. **Encourage stoking up on fluids mid-afternoon.** Rather than having your child awaken over and over with the plea "I'm thirsty," offer plenty of water starting mid-afternoon so that she is well hydrated before the sun goes down.

15. **Use familiar cues to help.** Pulling down the shades, turning on the same soothing lullabies, ocean sounds, or the

droning white noise created by a fan or air purifier can help mask extraneous noises and voices in the house, but they can also signal that it's sleepy time. If your child is in the potty-training process, make potty sitting a prerequisite to beddy-bye to help prevent wet-bed wake-ups.

16. **Share the load.** If there are other adults in the house, don't become the *only* person who can put your toddler to bed.

17. **Don't be ruled by guilt.** Parents who work long or late hours may find that they give in to a toddler's cries for attention or make allowances for an inconsistent bedtime, because they feel guilty or simply miss their children and want to spend time with them. (A better solution is to spend that time in the morning.) Some parents, especially first-timers, may have difficulty setting limits for their child because they're afraid of hurting her feelings. But the result is almost always an exhausted, grumpy, sleep-deprived child, not to mention exhausted and grumpy parents!

18. **Deal with your own sleeplessness.** Do you find it hard to fall back to sleep once you've been awakened? Does your mind race with thoughts about the next day? Try some relaxation exercises, soothing music, or ocean sounds—or get up and change beds to help turn off your mind so you can get the sleep you need to cope with your toddler in the morning. Then, if possible, go easy on yourself the next day, lying down for mini naps when possible and letting household chores wait for another day.

19. **Work as a team.** One partner can sabotage the other when it comes to establishing bedtime routines. Just as when your toddler was a baby, you and your partner need to be on the same page when it comes to bedtime rules. If your toddler is coming into your bed, you both need to take turns marching her back to her own. If one of you is bearing the brunt of bedtime activities while the other gets to watch television or rest, then there needs to be a more even distribution of duties.

20. **Get siblings involved.** If there's an older sibling, consider their sharing the same room for a while to help tots get used to how "big girls" and "big boys" sleep.

> If your baby is sharing a room with another child, position her crib as close to the door as possible. That way, you may be able to attend to your baby's needs without disturbing your older child.

Coping with Your Early-Morning Riser

Almost all kids are like roosters, awakening at the first signs of daylight. That can be very trying, especially if you've been up several times with your poor sleeper or you've got to head off to work in just a few hours and were hoping to steal every second of shut-eye you could get.

You may need training yourself. Don't lie in bed in the morning waiting for your baby to start making her first noise and then leap up to rescue her from her crib. Instead, give her time to occupy herself and chatter to herself until she is clearly restless and upset. She may surprise you by settling down for a second snooze.

Here are some ideas to help keep your baby asleep for as long as possible in the morning:

Light-blocking shades. Consider installing blackout shades or thick, lined drapes to keep the sunlight from beaming into your toddler's room. Not foolproof, but it could help occasionally.

Playthings. Place a few playthings and a sippy cup of water where your toddler can reach them, so she can keep herself occupied with them when she awakens. Consider putting a play yard in your bedroom with special toys where your child can occupy herself while you get a few more minutes of sleep.

The Changing Nap-Time Scene

Typically, nap times consolidate as your baby reaches toddlerhood, and her first nap of the day will arrive progressively later and later in the morning until there's just one afternoon nap after lunch.

On some days, your toddler may get cranky and need a nap in the late morning and then not want another until later on in the afternoon. It helps to build your toddler's day around her napping patterns, such as having an early lunch if you know she tends to get sleepy around noon.

There will come a time when two naps a day are just too much, but one nap just doesn't do the trick. She may be absorbed in playing and forget about the first nap only to need a later nap, since she doesn't have the energy to make it all the way to bedtime without resting in between. By the end of her second year, she'll probably only need one nap a day, which could come in the late morning or sometime in the afternoon.

Maintaining a nap schedule is important, though, because toddlers are in such a state of constant activity that they can get overtired without realizing it. An overtired toddler is more likely to pitch a fit, cry at some small problem, or lose her coordination and fall. That's when it's time to call a halt to everything, cuddle her, and help her slow down.

When your toddler awakens from her nap, she may not spring up refreshed, but may be sluggish and grumpy for a while. That's a good time to sit and quietly talk with her, read to her, or just to make your presence known.

Containing a Roaming Toddler

Once your toddler gives up her crib, there's always the risk that she'll get in trouble while you're still fast asleep. It usually takes a few days for a toddler to discover her newfound freedom, but once she does, the whole house becomes her playpen if you're asleep and don't hear her get up.

We suggest completely toddler-proofing your child's room, installing electrical outlet covers and window guards, making sure all blind and drapery cords are well out of reach, bolting chests and shelves to the walls so they can't turn over on her, and keeping chairs away from windows so she can't climb up on them and fall out. By doing that, the entire room can become your tot's "crib."

OPTIONS FOR PROTECTING YOUR OUT-OF-THE-CRIB TODDLER

- **Put a safety gate across the door at night.** The best gates are hardware-mounted with screws so that your toddler can't push the gate over, but an effective pressure gate may work

if you tighten it enough. Watch out for gates that have a metal threshold across the bottom that could be a tripping hazard in the night.

- **Install a burglar chain.** Install a burglar chain or hardware high up on the outside of the nursery door that allows the door to be only partially opened so that you can peer in and your toddler can call out, but the door can't be completely opened to allow her free access to roam around the house.

- **Install a door alarm.** Travel catalogs offer security alarms for hotel and motel doors, and inexpensive magnetic, stick-on versions are available in hardware stores. Put it on the outside of the nursery door, not the inside, and make sure it's not something your toddler can set off by playing with it.

- **Install a Dutch-style half door.** At a large home supply store you may be able to find a door that allows the top to be open while the bottom remains shut. Just make sure you have a locking doorknob so it's locked from the outside, not the inside.

- **Keep your hall lights on.** If your child does wake up at night and she starts to roam, this will help keep her from falling or getting lost on the way to your room.

WHEN YOUR CHILD JUST WON'T SLEEP

Although most toddlers settle down to regular sleep routines as they mature, there are others who never take to sleeping and will awaken repeatedly, night after night, no matter what parents do to try to calm them.

If that's the case, then you're likely to be a very, very tired parent! And, you're also likely to try *anything* just to steal some sleep for yourself, including sleeping under the dining room table or gating yourself inside the living room with your toddler so you can grab even 10 minutes of rest.

If you've been sleep-deprived for a very long time, then you badly need support to help you make it through your days and stay civil, not only to your child, but also to your mate. Here are our suggestions for making it through:

- **Get HELP!** If your partner is unavailable or you are winging it on your own, then consider asking relatives, neighbors, or friends, or hiring a teenager to pitch in on specific days that will allow you to: (1) get out of the house for some time alone or (2) have your child entertained outside of the house so you can pull down the shades and simply sleep, uninterrupted, for a few hours. It's important to set up specific days and times when you know help is coming, such as Tuesday and Thursday afternoons between 2 p.m. and 5 p.m.

- **Share night duty.** Insist that your partner alternate nights with you to be in charge. That way, at least one of you will get sufficient sleep every other night.

- **Try light and air "therapy."** Children need vigorous, outdoor play to help them let off steam, stretch their growing muscles, and for their bodies to manufacture vitamin D that plays an important part in body development and immune system responses. Ensure that your child gets plenty of outdoor exercise every day.

- **Seek professional help.** Don't try to deal with your child's chronic sleeplessness alone. Talk with her pediatrician, get help from parenting support groups, and go online to chat with other moms who are facing the same difficulties and who will gladly offer practical advice and understanding.

Monsters and Night Fears

Bad dreams are fairly common among 3- and 4-year-olds because they have such vivid imaginations, and they have trouble telling the difference between thoughts, dreams, and reality. When that happens, your child may wake up with a loud scream or crying, but may fall back to sleep just as quickly.

It can be scary when your child can't be easily awakened from a dream. During a nightmare, you may find your child's eyes open, but she won't actually be conscious that you're there. She may shout in a strange, garbled language that she has no control over. Don't try to force your child to awaken. Instead, remain by her side and try to comfort her and let her know you're there.

It's also not unusual for toddlers to go through a stage when they fear monsters in the closet or tell you that something is in the room and is out to get them. Sometimes the cause of these terrors in the dark can be readily addressed, like the brushing of branches or leaves against the window or shadows caused by passing cars, or perhaps it's odd night sounds, such as bumping furnace ducts, or howling sounds from the wind, but sometimes it's hard to tell exactly what's evoking the fears.

It's best to simply remain calm and reassuring. Simply placing a press-on, battery-run light in a closet may do the trick, or even talking adult-to-monster and firmly telling the culprit to leave may do the trick. And, fortunately, when it comes to terrifying dreams, most kids forget about them almost as soon as their heads hit the pillow again.

SUGGESTIONS FOR HANDLING NIGHT TERRORS

- **Turn on the lights.** This will help your child see that she might have been looking at a shadow, not something "real." Consider a nursery lamp with a 20-watt bulb to give the room more light, or string holiday lights along one wall of the room to give visual reassurance.

- **Reassure.** It's best to do any comforting when your toddler is in her own bed, rather than picking her up or putting her into bed with you. Otherwise, you may end up having a little partner in your bed when there aren't any monsters—and when you're desperate for a little sleep (and privacy) yourself. Let your child know that you are strong, that you can hear her if she needs you, and that you won't let anything harm her. Let her use a flashlight to illuminate the dark places in her room for herself.

- **Listen to her story.** "That sounds scary." Consider small rituals that might help her feel better, like turning on a dim nursery light or sprinkling some baking soda ("monster poison") at the base of the closet for protection. Glow-in-the-dark stars or a night-light that projects the moon or a starry night may help give the room a safer feel, as can CDs or sound machines that produce soothing sounds of birds, rain, or waterfalls. A strong, muscular action figure could be enlisted to stand guard, too.

- **Help her write a "re-dream."** Some Native American tribes believe that bad dreams should be rewritten by the dreamer to the way they would like the dreams to turn out. Help your child revise the bad dream so that she's no longer a victim, but a victor. And a dream catcher hung high over the bed may symbolically help to chase away bad dreams.

Moving from Crib to Bed

Falling out of the crib could be potentially dangerous, and some babies suffer severe head injuries because they have fallen head-first onto hard floors. Typically, this type of accident usually happens between 1½ and 2 years of age.

If you're expecting a new addition to your family who will need the crib, you may need to transition your child sooner than

> *"The most important thing is not to worry. Just because your child wakes up in the night because of monsters or bad dreams doesn't mean that there's something horribly wrong. It's just a minor sleep problem, so treat it that way."*

that. But don't wait until the baby arrives to evict your toddler from her familiar crib or expect her to adapt to a new bed immediately after you've moved to a new residence. In both these situations, it's better to either make the change well in advance or to wait until months afterward so things keep a semblance of familiarity in the midst of change.

Making the move doesn't have to be traumatic at all. Here are some tips for helping the process:

Remove one crib side. Make sure the mattress support is at the lowest position, and then reconfigure your toddler's crib by sliding off one of the drop sides from its tracks so that the crib is open on one side. This will only work if the crib has a metal stabilizer bar attached underneath to hold the two end boards together. If the crib doesn't have that crossbar, the bed will be far too unstable to be safe.

There is one major disadvantage to using the crib this way: Your toddler will have a long way to fall if she accidentally rolls out the open side of the crib. A firm exercise mat or cushion taped along the floor around the open side can provide some protection until your toddler learns how to sleep without rolling out of bed.

Place the crib mattress directly on the floor. Remove the mattress from the crib for use directly on the floor and unscrew the crib's components and re-box them for storage. If you plan to use the crib for another baby or resell it, it should be stored in an area that's not too hot (an attic) or too damp (a humid basement).

> *"One night my daughter tried to go to sleep for about 15 minutes, then got up and told me she couldn't sleep very well. I had sympathy and let her stay up and read a book with me. Well, the next night it was 'I can't sleep very well!' and the night after that, and the night after that, and periodically for about a year I heard the same thing!"*

Either condition will cause the glue holding the bars and end boards together to deteriorate, compromising the crib's safety.

Place the crib mattress (or a larger, twin-size one) on a soft rug against one corner of the room so only two sides are open. Then make your toddler's sleeping nook as enticing as possible using familiar sheets, toys, and other accoutrements that say "home" to her. This way, she will have easy access to the bed with no danger of falling.

Purchase a new bed. You can either buy a toddler bed frame designed to fit a crib-sized mattress or you can invest in a "real"

furniture suite, such as a twin bed, chest, and desk set you can expect to last through childhood. If you go with the second option, remember to be scrupulous about protecting the mattress from urine odors and stains by keeping it covered with a waterproof mattress pad. Needless to say, quilts, blankets, and other accessories should be sturdy enough to withstand multiple washings without fading or shrinking.

Install a zippered mesh dome over the top of a new baby crib to discourage your older child from piling toys inside the crib, covering the baby with a blanket, or trying to climb into the crib herself.

If you buy a new regular-size bed, consider pushing the bed frame flush against one wall of the bedroom and purchasing a side railing to protect your toddler from rolling out the open side during the night. Guard rails for beds usually have elbow-shaped arms designed to fit under the mattress to hold them in place. Just be sure that the bars are close enough together so that your child's body can't slip through them and trap her head.

Bed-wetting

Even if your toddler has mastered self-toileting, there are bound to be nighttime "accidents" (hopefully not in grandma's antique bed)! It has been reported that 5 to 7 million kids continue to wet their beds after toilet training, and one out of five 4-to-12-year-olds are bed wetters, with more boys than girls having the problem. It's during the school years, when social situations make your child worry about being ostracized by others, that it becomes an issue for your child.

It's important to recognize that your child can't help bed-wetting. For some children, it's the result of an immature bladder. Other children may sleep so deeply that they aren't aware of the sense of a full bladder yet.

It's not a good idea to deprive your youngster of fluids to try to keep her dry through the night. Dehydration can exaggerate aches and pains and make night waking more of a problem. And lack of fluids doesn't stop bed-wetting; it only reduces the amount of urine. It *does* make sense, though, to keep your child away from sugary candies and caffeine-laden beverages, and desserts that act as bladder stimulants. It also helps to have a few 3-to-5-minute potty visits prior to bedtime.

When it comes to the arduous chore of changing your child's wet bed over and over in the deep of night, try not to get grouchy or punitive. It works better to either be silent or make it a "team" effort: "Uh oh, *we've* got a wet bed again," rather than loading blame and shame on your child's shoulders when she can't help what's happening. Rather than making a big deal of bed-wetting in the night, make a big deal out of a dry bed in the morning.

From a practical standpoint, it helps to buy a stack of extra sheets and store them at arm's length from your child's bed. Keep a hamper nearby for storing soiled sheets so that you don't have to roam around the house in the middle of the night. It also helps to have a regular laundering routine so that you don't run out of sheets.

Wearing a diaper at night can compound a child's sense of shame, since it is associated with being a "baby." Fortunately, most disposable diaper manufacturers now make slip-on, child-suitable pants that resemble shorts or pull-up underwear expressly for the purpose of making nighttime wetting less onerous and nighttime waking less regular (for everyone).

In an effort to control bed-wetting, some parents routinely

When to Get Help for Bed-wetting

If your child is 7 or 8 years old and still wetting the bed, consider seeking advice from your child's doctor, especially if she is showing other signs of sleep problems, such as constant sleep disruption or snoring. Many young children who are usually dry at night start wetting the bed again, which can sometimes be caused by stress or life changes, such as going to a new child-care setting or moving. But, sometimes it could signal a urinary tract infection or the onset of other physical problems. Talk with your health-care provider if your child suddenly changes her bladder or bowel habits to make sure your child doesn't have an infection or other health issue.

awaken their child long enough to have her "go potty" when they're ready to turn in. That may mean carrying your weighty child to the toilet. If you decide to do that, the task should be done as silently as possible with only an adequate night-light in the bathroom so as not to send the signal that it's time to wake up.

Some companies make wet alarms that go off when a child urinates in the bed, but some alarms are positively unsafe with a tangle of wires, exposed batteries, sharp clothing clips, and other features of poor and unsafe design. And bed-wetting usually happens in the middle of the night when your child is so deeply asleep that she may not respond to the alarm (but you will!).

There are other causes for night wetting besides a full bladder. For example, night wetting that extends beyond the early years may be hereditary. If either of you were bed wetters, there's a good chance that your child will be, too. Taking a long time to overcome bed-wetting is usually more of a boy's problem than a girl's. Having a new baby in the house or moving to a new neighborhood could both be stressors that spark new bed-wetting episodes. Sometimes, bed-wetting can be a symptom of a mild urinary tract infection that can easily be treated.

The real solution to bed-wetting is very simple. Just wait. Usually, it will abate on its own by the time your child reaches 8. The process is gradual until it dawns on you that there have been no wet sheets in a long time. If bed-wetting doesn't go away by then, your child's doctor may prescribe drugs to reduce urine or expensive machines to alert your child, but waiting is truly the best solution. Whatever you do, don't make bed-wetting a big deal or scold and punish your child for her accidents. It won't stop the wetting. It will only make her feel shame and remorse for something she can't help. And those feelings have a way of implanting themselves in children's psyches for a lifetime.

Sleep Problems When Traveling

Traveling with a toddler can be a real challenge, and you can expect her sleep patterns to be disrupted by the stress of traveling to an unfamiliar environment. It doesn't help to be confined to a car or narrow airplane seat for hours on end.

While some toddlers may nap in an airplane just to escape the noise and confusion, your child may become cranky, squirmy, and miserable for the duration of the trip, only to fall asleep later in the day and resist sleep at her regular bedtime. Don't be surprised if your toddler becomes whiny, demanding, and out-of-sorts. She may regress to babylike behavior—which could include bed-wetting—so take extra precautions when sleeping in guest quarters.

Here are some tips that may help to make travel a little easier:

- **Get enough rest.** If you're driving on a long trip, plan to stop and rent a motel room, in the middle of the day if you have to, so everyone, not just baby, can take a nap.

- **Improvise.** If it's your child's regular nap time and you're not at home, then figure out ways to signal sleepy-time to your toddler, by using a blanket, a toy, or other props to help her let go and succumb to sleep.

- **Take a vacation after your vacation.** Anticipate that you'll not return home fully rested. In fact, you'll be exhausted and your child's sleep schedule will be "off" until she readjusts to being back at home. Don't be surprised if she regresses to more babyish sleep patterns—it's only temporary. Schedule your trip so you have a whole weekend afterward to catch up on rest and relaxation.

Family Upheavals

Toddler sleep can be readily interrupted by family crises, whether it's divorce, illness, or moving. Babies and toddlers are sensitive to family stresses, and one way of showing their distress is to regress into old night-waking patterns, bed-wetting, and tantrum-like behavior when life gets unbearably hectic. You don't have to tell your child that big changes are afoot, she'll be able to read your body language and know something's wrong. And,

unfortunately, most children blame themselves and feel that they're the person causing the problem, even if they're innocent bystanders.

First of all, planning out your family's life change in advance can be a big help to everyone. Even the most well-thought-out change is bound to have some kinks, and when you're overwhelmed, your child will feel the storm, even if you don't verbalize what's going on; it's likely to show up with clinginess, seemingly "spoiled" behavior, and sleeping disruptions.

While some toddlers are highly sociable and adaptable and welcome the exhilaration of changed environments to explore, others are completely unnerved by change. If your toddler already has serious sleeping problems, then it may be *you*, her parents, who will need to adjust to your child's need for protection and balance, and not the other way around.

STABILIZING TODDLER SLEEP

- **Keep routines intact.** If you're in the process of divorce and you're the non-custodial parent, it may be tempting to plan a weeklong vacation with your toddler, or keep her on weekends for your own convenience. But younger children do better with brief but regular visits.

- **Maintain steady routines.** With an impending divorce, try to blend parental visitation into the everyday life of your toddler so that visits happen in a predictable way throughout the week, preferably during the daytime, instead of expecting your toddler to adapt to long separations from one parent or a the stress of overnight visits in an unfamiliar setting.

- **Keep nighttime rules going.** Write down your child's bedtime routines and the rules that go along with them and ask that your child's other parent follow the rules, too, so that your child can feel secure that bedtime stays bedtime.

- **Pace transitions for your toddler's needs.** Be aware of your toddler's reactions to change and to strange new environments. Make transitions as gentle as possible and help her to learn positive strategies for relaxing and letting off steam prior to sleep, such as keeping a glass of water by the bed, gentle back rubbing, old familiar stories, or carrying along a favorite blanket or toy that signals "home away from home."

A Distant Memory

Although it may seem that your toddler-turned-child will never sleep through the night, indeed, she eventually will, and bedtime battles will become a distant memory for most children. Some are simply light sleepers who are easily roused by sounds or who become over-stimulated—just like adults who have trouble winding down for the night. Other children are destined to sleep like logs no matter what the hubbub outside their bedrooms. One thing is for sure, though: Sleep is important, and your job as a parent is to protect that sleep time and space to ensure that your child gets all the rest she needs to be fully functional and alert wherever she is.

Glossary

Sleep-related terms that parents may encounter.

APNEA

The temporary slowing, pause, or complete cessation of breathing. This occurs in all young infants, but more frequently in premature and low-birthweight babies. Sometimes called positional apnea, it may be the result of being placed in a sharply angled, nearly upright position, such as the one provided by a rear-facing infant seat. If a baby is suspected of having positional apnea, a health-care practitioner may suggest ways to pad the car seat or may recommend use of a flat infant bed; these are designed specifically to restrain small babies in fully reclined positions while riding in cars.

APNEA MONITOR

A motion detector that sets off an alarm when a baby ceases to breathe for a period of time. Portable monitors are available for home use but are suggested only for premature and low-birthweight babies with an apnea problem.

APNEA OF PREMATURITY (AOP)

Apnea of prematurity is the cessation of breathing by a premature infant that lasts for more than 15 seconds and/or is accompanied by hypoxia (oxygen deprivation) or bradycardia (when a baby's heart rate slows down to less than 100 beats per minute).

APPARENT LIFE-THREATENING EVENT (ALTE)

A syndrome characterized by symptoms in which a child exhibits some combination of apnea, change in color, change in muscle tone, coughing, or gagging. Though an apparent life-threatening event (ALTE) used to be referred to as "Near-Miss SIDS," later research showed no connection between ALTEs and SIDS.

AUTONOMIC NERVOUS SYSTEM

The part of the peripheral nervous system that controls physical activities that are performed without conscious control, such as heart rate and digestion.

CIRCADIAN RHYTHM

A circadian rhythm is roughly a 24-hour cycle in the biochemical, physiological, or behavioral processes of living beings, including plants, animals, fungi, and cyan bacteria.

CONTROLLED CRYING

Also known as graduated extinction, gradual retreat, or "Ferberizing" (named for pediatrician Richard Ferber), controlled crying is a sleep-training method in which parents let the baby cry for progressively longer intervals before checking on him.

CORTISOL

A corticosteroid hormone produced by the adrenal gland that increases blood pressure and blood sugar and reduces immune responses.

DEEP SLEEP

A sleep state in which the body remains still and seemingly unresponsive to outside stimuli.

EPIDEMIOLOGY

The study of factors affecting the health and illness of populations.

FOREMILK

The milk released at the beginning of a feed, which is watery, low in fat, and high in carbohydrates relative to the creamier milk that is released as a feed progresses.

GHRELIN

A hormone produced in the human stomach and pancreas that stimulates appetite.

HEPA FILTER

A high-efficiency particulate air filter that can remove at least 99.97 percent of airborne particles 0.3 micrometers (μm) in diameter.

HINDMILK

Milk released in the later part of a breastfeeding session, which is higher in fat and gives a baby a greater sensation of fullness. Fat content of human milk varies from feed to feed, but within a given feeding it rises steadily.

HYPNAGOGIC HALLUCINATIONS

A sensory experience that happens in between wakefulness and sleep. Common hypnagogic hallucinations are seeing geometric patterns, hearing buzzing or hissing noises, or a falling sensation followed by a muscle twitch.

HYPOTHALAMUS

The hypothalamus links the nervous system to the endocrine system via the pituitary gland. The hypothalamus is located below the thalamus, just above the brain stem. The hypothalamus is responsible for certain metabolic processes and other activities of the autonomic nervous system, including body temperature, hunger, thirst, fatigue, anger, and circadian cycles.

LEPTIN

A protein hormone that plays a key role in regulating energy intake and energy expenditure, including appetite and metabolism.

LIGHT SLEEP

A quiet sleep state often marked by momentary bursts of arm and leg movements.

LOW BIRTHWEIGHT

An infant with a birthweight of less than 2,500 grams (or 5 pounds 8 ounces).

MELATONIN

A naturally occurring hormone found in most animals; this hormone is important in the regulation of the circadian rhythms of several biological functions.

NARCOLEPSY

A neurological condition most characterized by excessive daytime sleepiness, in which a person falls asleep during the day at inappropriate times.

NEURON

Responsive cells in the nervous system that process and transmit information by sending chemical signals. Neurons are the core components of the brain, the vertebrate spinal cord, the invertebrate ventral nerve cord, and the peripheral nerves.

NIGHT TERRORS

A sleep disorder most common in children ages 2 to 6 during the non-REM stage of sleep, characterized by extreme terror and a temporary inability to regain full consciousness. Unlike nightmares, the child is not fully asleep when they occur, and episodes may be followed by a brief period of amnesia.

NOCTURNAL ENURESIS

Nocturnal enuresis is also called involuntary urination (or bed-wetting) at night by a child who has outgrown diapers. Primary Nocturnal Enuresis (PNE) is when a child has not yet stayed dry on a regular basis. Secondary Nocturnal Enuresis is when a child or adult begins wetting again after having previously stayed dry.

NON-RAPID EYE MOVEMENT (NREM) SLEEP

A collective term for sleep stages 1 through 4, in which there's little or no eye movement, and dreaming is rare.

PETROCHEMICAL

A chemical product made from the raw materials of petroleum or other hydrocarbon origin. Some examples include bisphenol-A, acetone, and benzene.

PREMATURITY

When a baby is born sooner than 37 weeks after the beginning of the mother's last menstrual period (LMP).

PRONE POSITION

The stomach-down position. Sleeping in the prone position is thought to increase an infant's risk of SIDS.

RAPID EYE MOVEMENT (REM) SLEEP

A stage of sleep characterized by rapid movements of the eyes and also by low muscle tone.

SLEEP STUDY

Also known as a polysomnogram, usually used to diagnose or rule out obstructive sleep apnea or other sleep disorders. Sleep studies usually take place overnight in a sleep lab. Electrodes are attached to a patient and data is recorded and analyzed.

SUDDEN INFANT DEATH SYNDROME (SIDS)

The sudden death of an infant under 1 year of age that remains unexplained after a thorough case investigation, including performance of a complete autopsy, examination of the death scene, and review of the clinical history.

Resources

There are thousands of Web sites that discuss infant and adult sleep. Unfortunately, though, most either sell medications or advertise baby go-to-sleep programs—usually a variation of "crying it out"—to desperate parents. Here are some Web sites and organizations that provide reliable information on sleep topics:

TOPIC	NAME	DESCRIPTION	CONTACT INFORMATION
Apnea	American Sleep Apnea Association	Non-profit organization dedicated to educating the public about sleep apnea and serving people with the disorder	www.sleepapnea.org; 202-293-3650
Crib Safety	Consumer Federation of America	Not-for-profit consumer's organization concerned with product safety	www.consumerfed.org; 202-387-6121
	Consumer Reports	Consumers Union provides free articles on baby products and subscription-only access to baby product ratings	www.consumerreports.org
	U.S. Consumer Product Safety Commission	Federal agency with current information on product recalls	www.cpsc.gov; 800-638-2772
Night Terrors	Night Terrors Resource Center	Provides information and resources for individuals and families with sleep terrors	www.nightterrors.org
SIDS	American SIDS Institute	National non-profit health-care organization dedicated to the prevention of sudden infant death and the promotion of infant health	www.SIDS.org; 800-232-7437

TOPIC	NAME	DESCRIPTION	CONTACT INFORMATION
SIDS	Alliance of Grandparents, A Support in Tragedy (AGAST)	All-volunteer organization dedicated to those who have lost a grandchild to SIDS	www.agast.org
	Back to Sleep Campaign	Promotes placing babies on their backs for sleeping to lower the risk of sudden infant death syndrome (SIDS)	www.nichd.nih.gov/sids/; 800-370-2943
	Centers for Disease Control and Prevention (CDC)	Government organization that is an excellent resource for up-to-date health information	www.cdc.gov
	First Candle	A national nonprofit health organization for parents, caregivers, and researchers to advance infant health and survival	www.firstcandle.org
	Sudden Infant Death Syndrome Network	A nonprofit voluntary agency dedicated to eliminating SIDS, providing support to affected families, and raising public awareness	www.sids-network.org
Sleep, General	National Sleep Foundation	A nonprofit organization dedicated to improving the quality of life for Americans who suffer from sleep problems and disorders	www.sleepfoundation.org
	Sleepnet	An educational site devoted to consolidating sleep information	www.sleepnet.com

Endnotes

1 The Sleepy Fetus

1. Birnholz, Jason C. "The development of human fetal eye movement patterns." *Science* 213(4508): 679–681.

2 Newborns in "The Fourth Trimester"

1. Czeisler, Charles A., Jeanne F. Duffy, Theresa L. Shanahan, Emery N. Brown, Jude F. Mitchell, David W. Rimmer, Joseph M. Ronda, Edward J. Silva, James S. Allan, Jonathan S. Emens, Derk-Jan Dijk, and Richard E. Kronauer. "Stability, precision, and near-24-hour period of the human circadian pacemaker." *Science* 284 (June 25, 1999): 2177–2181 [DOI: 10.1126/science.284.5423.2177 (in Reports)].

2. Billiard, M., and A. Kent. "Physiology, investigations, and medicine." *Sleep*, Spring 2003.

3. Ardura, J., J. Andrés, J. Aldana, and M. A. Revilla. "Development of sleep-wakefulness rhythm in premature babies." *Acta Paediatrica* 84(5) (1995): 484–489.

4. Morganthaler, Timothy I., et al. "Practice parameters for the clinical evaluation and treatment of circadian rhythm sleep disorders." *Sleep* 30(11) (Nov. 2007): 1445–1459.

5. de Weerth, Carolina, Robert H. Zijl, and Jan K. Buitelaar. "Development of cortisol circadian rhythm in infancy." *Early Human Development* 73(1): 39–52.

6. Hale, Thomas W., Ph.D. *Medications and Mother's Milk: A Manual of Lactational Pharmacology*, 13th ed. Amarillo, Texas: Pharmasoft Medical Publishing, 2008.

7. Mennella, Julie A., Lauren M. Yourshaw, and Lindsay K. Morgan. "Breastfeeding and smoking: Short-term effects on infant feeding and sleep." *Pediatrics* 120(3) (Sept. 2007): 497–502.

8. Batty, G. David, Geoff Der, and Ian J. Deary. "Effect of maternal smoking during pregnancy on offspring's cognitive ability: Empirical evidence for complete confounding in the US National Longitudinal Survey of Youth." *Pediatrics* 118(3) (Sept. 2006): 943–950.

9. Ainsworth, M. D. S., and M. C. Blehar. "Developmental Changes in Behavior of Infants and their Mothers Relative to Close Bodily Contact." Meeting of the Society for Research in Child Development, April 1975.

3 Where Should Baby Sleep?

1. Final Report, 2004 Sleep in America poll, conducted on behalf of the National Sleep Foundation, Washington, D.C.

2. http://www.mamasource.com/, retrieved July 21, 2008.

3. Keller, Meret A., and Wendy A. Goldberg. "Co-sleeping: Help or hindrance for young children's independence?" *Infant and Child Development* 13(5): 369–388.

4. Hogg, Tracy, and Melinda Blau. *Secrets of the Baby Whisperer: How to Calm, Connect, and Communicate with Your Baby.* New York: Ballantine, 2005.

5. Wright, Robert. "Go Ahead—Sleep With Your Kids." http://www.slate.com/id/2020, posted Friday, March 28, 1997.

6. Mao, Amy, Melissa M. Burnham, Beth L. Goodlin-Jones, Erika E. Gaylor, and Thomas F. Anders. "A comparison of the sleep–wake patterns of cosleeping and solitary-sleeping infants." *Child Psychiatry and Human Development* 35(2) (2004): 95–105. [DOI: 10.1007/s10578-004-1879-0].

7. Reite, Martin, and J. P. Capitanio. "On the Nature of Social Separation and Social Attachment," *The*

Psychobiology of Attachment and Separation. New York: Academic Press, 1985, pp. 228–238.

8. Coe, C. L., S. G. Wiener, L. T. Rosenberg, and S. Levine. "Psychoendocrine aspects of mother-infant relationships in nonhuman primates." Department of Psychiatry and Behavioral Sciences, Stanford University School of Medicine, Stanford, California, 1987.

9. Drago, Dorothy A., and Andrew L. Dannenberg. "Infant mechanical suffocation deaths in the United States, 1980–1997." *Pediatrics* 103(5) (May 1999): p. e59.

10. Horsley, T., T. Clifford, N. Barrowman, S. Bennett, F. Yazdi, M. Sampson, D. Moher, O. Dingwall, H. Schachter, and A. Côté. "Benefits and harms associated with the practice of bed sharing: A systematic review." *Archives of Pediatric and Adolescent Medicine* 161(3) (March 2007): 237–245.

11. Parent survey reported in September 2008 issue of *Babytalk* magazine.

12. "Toxicology and Carcinogenesis Studies of Decabromodiphenyl Oxide (CAS No. 1163-19-5) In F344/N Rats and B6C3F1 Mice (Feed Studies)," The National Toxicology Program, The National Institute of Environmental Health Sciences.

13. de Weerth, Carolina, Robert H. Zijl, and Jan K. Buitelaar. "Development of cortisol circadian rhythm in infancy." *Early Human Development,* 73(1): 39–52.

14. Coleman-Phox, Kimberly, Roxana Odouli, and De-Kun Li. "Use of a fan during sleep and the risk of sudden infant death syndrome." *Archives of Pediatric and Adolescent Medicine* 162(10) (2008): 963–968.

4   Six-Weeks: The Crying Peak

1. Barr, Ronald G. "The 'colic' enigma: Prolonged episodes of normal predisposition to cry." *Infant Mental Health Journal.* Vol. 11 (1990): 340–348.

2. Keefe, M. R. "Irritable infant syndrome: Theoretical perspectives and practice implications." *Advances in Nursing Science* 10(3) (Apr. 1988): 70–78.

3. Hunziker, Urs A., and Ronald G. Barr. "Increased carrying reduces infant crying: A randomized controlled trial." *Pediatrics* 77(5) (May 1986): 641–648.

4. Bremne, J.D., and E. Vermetten. "Stress and development: Behavioral and biological consequences." *Developmental Psychopathology* 13(3) (Summer 2001): 473–489.

5. Wolke, Dieter, Patrizia Rizzo, and Sarah Woods. "Persistent infant crying and hyperactivity problems in middle childhood." *Pediatrics* 109(6) (June 2002): 1054–1060.

6. Kuhn, C. M., S. R. Butler, and S. M. Schanberg. "Selective depression of serum growth hormone during maternal deprivation in rat pups." *Science* 201 (1978): 1034–1036.

7. Hargrove, Thomas, and Lee Bowman. "Conference Questions Adult Sleep with Babies." Scripps News Special Report, April 16, 2008. http://scrippsnews.s10113.gridserver.com/node/684 [71].

8. Hunt, C. E., and Fern R. Hauck. "Sudden Infant Death Syndrome." In Robert Kliegman (ed.), *Nelson Textbook of Pediatrics,* 18th ed. New York: Saunders, 2007.

9. Spiers, Philip S., Lynn Onstad, and Warren G. Guntheroth. "Negative effect of a short interpregnancy interval on birth weight following loss of an infant to sudden infant death syndrome." *American Journal of Epidemiology* 143(11): 1137–1141.

10. Coleman-Phox, Kimberly, Roxana Odouli, and De-Kun Li. "Use of a fan during sleep and the risk of sudden infant death syndrome." *Archives of Pediatric and Adolescent Medicine* 162(10) (2008): 963–968.

11. Halloran, Donna R., and Greg R. Alexander. "Preterm delivery and age of SIDS death." *Annals of Epidemiology* 16(8): 600–606.

12. Saririan, Shahrzad, and Fern R. Hauck. "New recommendations to

reduce the risk of SIDS: What should we advise parents?" *American Family Physician* 74(11) (Dec. 2006), 1839–1840.

13. "Evaluation of child care practice factors that affect the occurrence of sudden infant death syndrome: Interview conducted by public health nurses." *Environmental Health and Preventive Medicine*, Springer Japan, ISSN 1342-078X (Print), 1347-4715 (Online), 6(2) (July 2001): 117–120. [DOI 10.1007/BF02897957].

14. Schellscheidt, J., A. Ott, and G. Jorch. "Epidemiological features of sudden infant death after a German intervention campaign in 1992." *European Journal of Pediatrics*, Springer Berlin/Heidelberg ISSN 0340-6199 (Print), 1432-1076 (Online), 156(8) (July 1997): 655–660.

15. Hunt, C. E., and Fern R. Hauck. "Sudden infant death syndrome." *Canadian Medical Association Journal* 174(13) (June 2006): 1861–1869.

16. Haglund, B., S. Cnattingius, et al. "Sudden infant death syndrome in Sweden, 1983–1990: Season at death, age at death, and maternal smoking." *American Journal of Epidemiology* 142(6) (1995): 619–624.

17. Franco, Patricia, Nicole Seret, Jean Noël Van Hees, Sonia Scaillet, Françoise Vermeulen, José Groswasser, and André Kahn. "Decreased arousals among healthy infants after short-term sleep deprivation." Pediatric Sleep Unit, University Children's Hospital, Free University of Brussels, Brussels, Belgium, and Pediatric Sleep Unit, Clinique St. Joseph, Liège, Belgium. Also published in *Pediatrics* 114(2) (August 2004).

18. Opdal, Siri H., and Torleiv O. Rognum. "The sudden infant death syndrome gene: Does it exist?" *Pediatrics* 114(4) (Oct. 2004): pp. e506–e512.

19. Savino, F., E. Bailo, R. Oggero, V. Tullio, J. Roana, N. Carlone, A. M. Cuffini, and L. Silvestro. "Bacterial counts of intestinal lactobacillus species in infants with colic." *Pediatric Allergy and Immunology* 16(1) (Feb. 2005): 72–75.

20. Saavedra, J. M., A. Abi-Hanna, N. Moore, and R. H. Yolken. "Long-term consumption of infant formulas containing live probiotic bacteria: Tolerance and safety." *American Journal of Clinical Nutrition* 79(2) (Feb. 2004): 261–267.

21. Evanoo, G. "Infant crying: A clinical conundrum." *Journal of Pediatric Health Care* 21(5): 333–338.

22. Kirjavainen, Jarkko, Liisa Lehtonen, Turkka Kirjavainen, and Pentti Kero. "Sleep of excessively crying infants: A 24-hour ambulatory sleep polygraphy study." *Pediatrics* 114(3) (Sept. 2004): 592–600.

23. Williamson, A. M., and A. M. Feyer. "Moderate sleep deprivation produces impairments in cognitive and motor performance equivalent to legally prescribed levels of alcohol intoxication." *Occupational and Environmental Medicine* 57 (2000): 649–655.

24. Gay, Caryl L., Shih-Yu Lee, and Kathryn A. Lee. "Sleep patterns and fatigue in new mothers and fathers." *Biological Research for Nursing* 5(4) (2004): 311–318.

25. Runquist, Jennifer J. "Persevering through postpartum fatigue." *Journal of Obstetric, Gynecologic & Neonatal Nursing* Jan/Feb 2007: 28–37.

26. Corwin, Elizabeth J., Jean Brownstead, Nichole Barton, Starlet Heckard, and Karen Morin. "The impact of fatigue on the development of postpartum depression." *Journal of Obstetric, Gynecologic & Neonatal Nursing* 34(5) (2005): 577–586.

27. Runquist, Jennifer J. "A depressive symptoms responsiveness model for differentiating fatigue from depression in the postpartum period." *Archives of Women's Mental Health* 10(6) (Dec. 2007): 267–275.

28. Mooallem, John. "The Sleep-Industrial Complex." *The New York Times Magazine*, Nov. 18, 2007.

5 Three to Four Months

1. Harrison, Yvonne. "The relationship between daytime exposure to light and night-time sleep in 6-12-week-old infants." *Journal of Sleep Research* 13(4) (Dec. 2004): 345–352.

2. Specker, B. L., et al. "Sunshine exposure and serum 25-hydroxyvitamin D concentrations in exclusively breastfed infants." *Journal of Pediatrics* 107 (1985): 372–376.

3. Clemens, T. L., J. S. Adams, S. L. Henderson, and M. F. Holick. "Increased skin pigment reduces the capacity of skin to synthesise vitamin D3." *Lancet* 319(8263) (Jan. 9, 1982): 74–76.

4. Elias, Marjorie F., Nancy A. Nicolson, Carolyn Bora, and Johanna Johnston. "Sleep/wake patterns of breast-fed infants in the first 2 years of life." *Pediatrics* 77(3) (March 1986): 322–329.

5. WHO Working Group on Infant Growth. "An Evaluation of Infant Growth: A Summary of Analyses Performed in Preparation for the WHO Committee on Physical Status: The Use and Interpretation of Anthropometry." Geneva: World Health Organization, 1994, p. 160.

6. United States Breastfeeding Committee Statement on the Importance of Breastfeeding/Human Milk Feeding in the Prevention of Obesity. Raleigh, N.C.: United States Breastfeeding Committee, 2003.

7. Stirnimann, F. *Psychologie des neugeborenen Kindes*. Zurich: Racher, 1940.

6 Four to Six Months

1. Macknin, M. L., S. V. Medendorp, and M. C. Maier. "Infant sleep and bedtime cereal." *American Journal of Diseases of Children* 143(9) (Sept. 1989): 1066–1068.

. . . Keane, V., et al. "Do solids help baby sleep through the night?" *American Journal of Diseases of Children* 142 (1988): 404–405.

2. Elias, Marjorie F., Nancy A. Nicolson, Carolyn Bora, and Johanna Johnston. "Sleep/wake patterns of breast-fed infants in the first 2 years of life." *Pediatrics* 77(3) (March 1986): 322–329.

3. Ibid.

4. Armstrong, K. L., R. A. Quinn, and M. R. Dadds. "The sleep patterns of normal children." *Medical Journal of Australia* 161(3) (Aug. 1, 1994): 202–206.

5. Sher, A., et al. "Sleep difficulties in infants at risk for developmental delays: A longitudinal study." *Journal of Pediatric Psychology* 33(4) (2008).

6. Cubero, J., D. Narciso, S. Aparicio, C. Garau, V. Valero, M. Rivero, M. Esteban, R. Rial, A. B. Rodríguez, and C. Barriga. "Improved circadian sleep-wake cycle in infants fed a day/night dissociated formula milk." *Neuro Endocrinology Letters* 27(3) (June 2006): 373–380.

7 Six to Nine Months

1. Mindell, Jodi A., et al. "Behavioral treatment of bedtime problems and night wakings in infants and young children." *Sleep* 29(10): 1263–1276.

2. Bremne, J. D., and E. Vermetten. "Stress and development: Behavioral and biological consequences." *Developmental Psychopathology* 13(3) (Summer 2001): 473–489.

3. Post, R. M. "Transduction of psychosocial stress into the neurobiology of recurrent affective disorder." *American Journal of Psychiatry* 149 (1992): 999–1010.

4. Wolke, Dieter, Patrizia Rizzo, and Sarah Woods. "Persistent infant crying and hyperactivity problems in middle childhood." *Pediatrics* 109(6) (June 2002): 1054–1060.

Index

Adult sleep
  brain waves in, 18–19
  naps, 18
  stages of, 17–19
  waking body changes and, 19
Albuterol, 21
Alcohol, 22, 90, 94
Allergies, 81–83, 129
Alpha-fetoprotein (AFP), 77–79
Alprazolam (Xanax®), 21
Amphetamines, 21–22
Apnea, 23, 77, 181, 185
Apnea monitor, 181
Apnea of prematurity (AOP), 181
Apparent life-threatening event
    (ALTE), 17, 181
Autonomic nervous system, 181

Baby's room. *See also* Bassinets; Bed
      sharing; Cribs; Places to sleep
  buying baby furniture, 7–8, 50–52
  items to include in, 59–62
  monitors in, 62, 63
  night-lights in, 64
  preventing nasal congestion in, 61
  rocking chairs/gliders in, 60, 64
  scent soothers in, 64
  soothers for, 62–64
  sound machines and CDs in, 62–63
  tips for setting up, 59–62
Banging head and crib, 160
Bassinets
  co-sleepers, 45
  features, 50, 57–58
  informal survey on sleep locations
      and, 31, 32, 33
  pros and cons, 57–58
  safety issues and comments, 34
Beds. *See* Bassinets; Bed sharing;
      Cribs; Places to sleep
Bed sharing
  bed-crib safety controversy, 41–42

biology of mother-baby closeness
      and, 38–39
  breastfeeding and, 38, 42, 47, 48
  co-sleepers/sleeping and, 45, 47–48
  extended, 150–151
  history of, 33–37
  how and when to stop, 46–47
  independence and, 37–38
  informal survey on sleep locations
      and, 31–33
  intimacy, sex life and, 44–45
  negatives and safety concerns,
      39–43, 44–46
  not working, 133–135
  parenting issues and, 45
  pediatricians and, 42–43
  positives, 38–39
  reasons to stop, 140–141
  reluctantly, sleep training and, 152
  safety checklist, 43–46
  safety issues, 35, 39–43
  SIDS and, 35, 38–39, 40, 43
  sleep positioners and, 45–46
  transitioning out of, 139–141. *See*
      also Sleep training
  when not to do, 40
Bedside sleepers, 34, 45, 50, 58
Bed types. *See* Bassinets; Bed sharing;
      Cribs; Places to sleep
Bed-wetting, 175–177, 178
Bonding with baby, 6–7, 16, 42. *See*
      also Closeness
Bottle-fed babies. *See* Formula and
      bottle feeding
Bouncy seat, 33, 34, 88
Brain
  of baby, compared to adult, 14–17
  development, 5, 13, 15–16, 131
  sleep problems and development,
      131
  of three-month-olds, 100–102
  in utero development, 5

Brain *(continued)*
    waves, stages of sleep and, 18–19.
        See also Rapid eye movement
        (REM) sleep
Breastfeeding
    affecting sleep, 14, 20, 103–105
    bed sharing and, 38, 42, 47, 48
    bedside sleepers and, 58
    bottle-fed baby sleep compared to,
        102–105
    caffeine and, 93
    colic and, 80, 81, 82, 84
    cribs and, 49
    crying baby and, 67, 68, 69
    on demand, instead of schedule, 27
    extinction method and, 143
    foremilk, 25, 182
    formula combined with, 14
    herbal teas and, 22
    hindmilk, 25–26, 182
    milk components, 132
    newborn schedule, 13, 17
    at night. *See* Nighttime feedings
    night feeding for four to six month
        old babies, 128–132
    nursing baby to sleep, 89
    pacifiers and, 90
    pumping milk and, 86, 94
    schedule/frequency, 13, 14, 17, 27,
        143, 145, 151
    in side-lying position, 39
    SIDS and, 73, 75
    sleep differences compared to
        formula, 103–105
    sleeping through night and, 143,
        145, 151
    smoking and, 23
    stimulants/sedatives and, 21–23, 69,
        93, 108
    storing breastmilk, 78
    vitamin D, sunlight exposure and,
        101–102
Brompheniramine (Dimetane®,
    Dimetapp®), 22

Caffeine, 22, 93, 176
Car seats, 31–32, 35, 99, 111, 121

Castor oil, 22
CDs and sound machines, 62–63
Cetirizine (Zyrtec®), 22, 123
Charting day/night patterns, 113–116
Chlordiazepoxide (Librium®), 22
Chlorpheniramine (Chlor-Trimeton®),
    22
Chlorpromazine (Thorazine®), 22
Circadian rhythms, 5, 14–15, 103, 118,
    181
Citalopram (Celexa®), 23
Clemastone (Tavist®), 23
Closeness, 36, 38–39, 67–68, 69
Cluster feeding and fussing, 67–68,
    105, 130
Cocaine, 22, 73, 75
Codeine, 23
Colic
    allergies to cow's milk and, 81–83
    benign long-term effects of, 83
    cause unknown, 79
    comforting strategies, 85
    defined, 79
    eliminating dietary causes of, 82
    finding cause of, 85
    gastroesophageal connection, 84–86
    getting support, 86
    gut flora and, 80–81
    important points to remember, 84
    overview of, 79–80
    parenting style and, 83
    physiological effects of, 80
    questions and answers, 86–90
    screaming-baby emergency plan,
        85–86
    sleep cycles and, 83–84
    soy-milk-based products and, 82–83
    taking breather from, 85–86
    untreatability of, 86
    what we know about, 80–86
Comforting strategies, 85. *See also*
    Handling baby
Congestion, preventing, 61
Controlled crying, 121, 181
Cortisol, 16, 39, 116, 182
Co-sleepers/sleeping, 45, 47–48
Co-sleeping, 47–48

Cow's milk, allergies to, 81–83
Cradles, 50
Cribs
    assembling, 52, 53
    banging, 160
    bed-crib safety controversy, 41–42
    breastfeeding and, 49
    climbing out of, 161
    falling out of, 60, 174
    informal survey on sleep locations
        and, 31–32
    mattresses for, 8, 53, 54–55, 56
    mattress support, 52
    moving to bed from, 174–175
    non-full-size, 35, 49–50, 51
    organic mattresses and bedding,
        56
    picking, 49–50
    playtime, sleep time and, 54
    pros and cons of, 48–49
    resources, 185
    safety issues and comments, 35
    safety shopping checklist, 51–52
    safety tips, 52–54
    sheets and mattress pads, 56–57
    shopping checklist, 50–52
    taking time to buy, 7
    tent or dome over, 161, 175
    toys and, 54, 63, 175
    used, safety tips, 8
Crying. See also Colic
    action plan for older babies, 158
    closeness and, 36, 38–39, 67–68, 69
    cluster feeding and fussing, 67–68,
        105, 130
    comforting strategies, 85
    constant and shrill, 70
    controlled, 121, 181
    decoding, 25–26, 111
    finding cause of, 85
    handling strategies by personality
        type, 120–123
    illness symptoms and, 70
    inconsolable, 70
    naps and. See Naps (baby)
    responding promptly, 24–25, 68–70,
        87–88

    screaming-baby emergency plan,
        85–86
    six-week peak of, 67–70
    swaddling to calm, 26–27, 28
    types to report to doctor, 70
    uncovering reasons for
        sleeplessness and, 69
    weak and whiny, 70
Crying it out. See Extinction method
    (crying it out)

Day care, 7, 74
Deep sleep
    adults in, 18
    babies waking abruptly from, 76–77
    brain waves in, 18
    defined, 182
    infants in, 17
    lights affecting, 59
    SIDS and, 76–77
    in utero, 6
Dehydration, 15, 176
Delaying tactics, 166
Dextroamphetamine (Dexedrine®,
    Adderall®), 22
Diazepam (Valium®), 23
Diphenhydramine (Benadryl®), 23,
    133
Doctor
    family bed and, 42–43
    not responding to your needs, 152
    reporting crying to, 70
    sharing worries with, 123
    testing factors contributing to your
        fatigue, 92, 133
Doxepin (Adapin®, Sinequan®,
    Zonalon®), 23
Doxylamine succinate (Unisom®
    Nighttime), 23
Dreams. See also Rapid eye movement
    (REM) sleep
    adult compared to baby, 19
    bad, night terrors and, 20, 168,
        172–174, 183, 185
    importance of, 19
Drowsy but awake state, 27–28,
    110–111, 117–120, 139–140, 142

Drugs. *See* Medications; *specific medications*

Early-morning risers, 170
Exercise, importance of, 165–166, 172. *See also* Tummy time
Exhaustion. *See* Sleep deprivation (adult)
Extinction method (crying it out), 121, 142, 143–148, 154

Faded bedtime, 148–149, 153–154
Family upheavals, 178–179
Feeding baby. *See also* Breastfeeding; Formula and bottle feeding
   big differences between breast and bottle, 102–105
   breastfeeding, 14
   on demand, instead of schedule, 27
   food allergies and, 81–83, 129
   importance of sleep cycle, 13–14
   newborns, 13–14
   at night, 38, 47, 48, 49, 87, 89, 104, 128–135
   questions and answers, 131–135
   solids, 105–106, 129
Ferberizing. *See* Extinction method (crying it out)
Fetus. *See also* Pregnancy
   activity stages, 6
   sleep patterns, 5, 6
Fluoxetine (Prozac®), 22
Foremilk, 25, 182
Formula and bottle feeding
   affecting sleep, 14, 89, 103–105
   allergies to cow's milk and, 81–83
   breastfeeding compared to, 102–105
   colic and, 80, 81, 82–83, 86
   controlling formula and air intake, 26
   on demand, instead of schedule, 27
   effects of, 14, 16–17
   excessive crying and, 67, 68
   extinction method and, 143
   neurological changes from, 16
   at night. *See* Nighttime feedings

night feeding for four to six month old babies, 128–132
   rice cereal in bottle, 86, 105–106
   schedule/frequency, 13, 17, 26, 27
   SIDS and, 20, 74–75
   sleep differences compared to breastfeeding, 103–105
   solids and, 105–106
   soy-based formulas, 82–83
   storing breastmilk and, 78
   vitamin D, sunlight exposure and, 101–102
Four-Month Sleep Shift, 127–135
Furniture, buying, 7–8, 50–52. *See also* Places to sleep; *specific bed types*

Ghrelin, 91, 182
Graduated extinction, 141, 142, 143, 148, 154

Hallucinogens, 21–22
Hammocks or motion beds, 7, 36, 50, 58–59, 64, 86
Handling baby, 120–123
Head and crib banging, 160
HEPA filters, 61, 182
Herbal supplements, 92, 95
Herbal teas, 22
Heroin, 23, 73, 75
Hindmilk, 25–26, 182
Hormone activity. *See also* Melatonin
   cortisol, 16, 39, 116, 182
   ghrelin, 91, 182
   growth hormone, 18
   increase in, at three months, 100
   leptin, 90–91, 182
   of newborns vs. older babies and adults, 17
   sleep/wake cycle and, 16
   soy-milk-based products and, 82–83
   stress hormones and crying, 69–70, 145–146
Hydrocodone (Vicodin®), 23
Hypnagogic hallucinations, 17–18, 182
Hypothalamus, 15, 182

Leptin, 90–91, 182
Light sleep
    adults in, 18
    baby sleep cycles and, 20, 24
    brain waves in, 18
    defined, 182
    as stage 1 sleep, 18
    in utero, 6
Low birthweight, 22, 74, 182

Mattresses. *See* Bassinets; Bed
    sharing; Cribs; Places to sleep
Medications. *See also specific*
    medications
    affecting baby sleep, 21–23
    potential sedatives, 22–23
    potential stimulants, 21–22
Melatonin
    colic and, 84
    defined, 182
    initial production of, 16, 100
    keeping room dark and, 59
    optimizing production of, 100,
        101–102, 118, 165–166
    production cycles, 100
    as "sleep" hormone, 16
    supplements, 100
Methamphetamines, 21–22
Methylphenidate (Ritalin®), 22
Mobiles, 54, 120
Momsomnia, 91. *See also* Sleep
    deprivation (adult)
Mother-baby night closeness, 38–39
Motion beds. *See* Hammocks or
    motion beds

Naps (adult), 18, 95–96
Naps (baby)
    Four-Month Sleep Shift, 127–128
    holding baby for, 111–113
    locations for, 108–110
    monitoring length of, 127. *See also*
        Charting day/night patterns
    put-down guidelines, 110–111,
        114
    questions and answers, 110–113,
        152–153

routines for, 99–100, 107–113,
        127–128, 170–171
    signs of tiredness, 117
    toddlers, 170–171
Narcolepsy, 183
Nefazodone HCL (Serzone®), 23
Neurons, 5, 16, 183
Newborns
    brain of, compared to adult, 14–17
    daily feedings, 13–14, 27. *See also*
        Breastfeeding; Feeding baby;
        Formula and bottle feeding
    drowsy but awake, 27–28
    sleep characteristics, 17
    sleep cycles, 13–14, 20–21, 86–88
    swaddling to calm, 26–27
    what happens during sleep, 16
Night-lights, 64
Night terrors, 20, 168, 172–174, 183, 185
Nighttime feedings, 38, 47, 48, 49, 87,
        89, 104, 128–135
Nighttime put-down, 116–120
Nine to twelve months, 157–161
    average sleep patterns, 160
    climbing out of crib, 161
    developmental overview, 157–158
    head and crib banging, 160
    pulling up, 160
    questions and answers, 158–160
    separation anxiety, 157, 159–160
    waking in middle of night, 158
Nocturnal enuresis, 183. *See also*
    Bed-wetting
Non-rapid eye movement (NREM)
    sleep, 6, 183
Nursery. *See* Baby's room; Bassinets;
    Bed sharing; Cribs; Places to
    sleep
Nursing. *See* Breastfeeding

Organic mattresses and bedding, 56
Overheating, 43, 75–76, 101–102

Pacifiers, 76, 89–90, 168
Parents' bed. *See* Bed sharing
Personality type, handling strategies
    by, 120–123

Petrochemical, 183
Physiological changes during sleep,
     15–16. *See also* Brain
Places to sleep. *See also* Bassinets;
     Bed sharing; Cribs
  bedside sleepers, 34, 45, 50, 58
  bouncy seat, 33, 34, 88
  buying baby furniture and, 7–8
  buying beds, 7–8, 50–52
  car seat, 31–32, 35, 99, 111, 121
  chart of, by bed type, 34–36
  co-sleeping and, 45, 47–48
  cradles, 50
  hammocks or motion beds, 7, 36,
     50, 58–59, 64, 86
  informal survey on, 31–33
  moving to bed, 174–175
  overview of, 31
  safety issues by bed type, 34–36
Portable play yards, 32, 33, 36, 170
Positive routines and faded bedtime,
     141, 148–149, 153–154
PPD (post-partum depression), 92
PPF (post-partum fatigue), 90, 92.
     See also Sleep deprivation
     (adult)
Pregnancy
  baby's activity stages during, 6
  baby's sleep patterns during, 5, 6
  employment during/after, 6–7, 9
  planning ahead during, 5–7
  resting during, 8
Premature babies, 14, 20
  apnea in, 181
  rocking chairs and weight gain, 64
  sedating drugs and, 22
  SIDS and, 72–74
  sleep cycles, 183
  sleep hormone development, 100
  wake cycles, 24
Procedural memory, 20–21
Prone position, 26, 74, 183
Pulling up, 160
Pumping milk, 86, 94
Put-downs
  drowsy but awake, 27–28, 110–111,
     117–120, 139–140, 142

nap-time, 110–111, 114
nighttime, 116–120

Questions and answers, 86–90,
     110–113, 131–135, 152–154,
     158–160, 161

Rapid eye movement (REM) sleep
  adults and, 18–19, 91
  babies in, 20–21
  defined, 183
  dreaming and, 19, 20
  excessive crying and, 83
  importance of, 19, 20–21
  NREM and, 6, 183
  as paradoxical sleep, 18
  physiology of, 18
  procedural memory and, 20–21
  smoking affecting, 23
  in utero, 5, 6
Resources, 185–186
Roaming toddlers, 171
Rocking chairs/gliders, 60, 64
Routines. *See* Sleep schedules; Sleep
     training

Scent soothers, 64
Scheduled awakenings, 141, 142, 150
Sensitive babies, 120, 122–123
Separation anxiety, 47, 145, 147, 157,
     159–160
Shopping for baby beds/cribs, 7–8,
     50–52
Signs of tiredness, 117
Six to nine months
  routines for. *See* Sleep training
  sleep patterns, 139
Sleep cycles (adult), 17–19
Sleep cycles/patterns (baby). *See also*
     specific age groups
  charting day/night patterns, 113–116
  circadian rhythms and, 5, 14–15,
     103, 118, 181
  Four-Month Sleep Shift, 127–135
  ignoring "shoulds," 8–10
  newborns, 13–14, 20–21, 86–88
  nine to twelve months, 157–161

physiological changes during sleep, 16
signs of tiredness and, 117
six to nine months, 139. *See also* Sleep training
toddlers, 165
twelve-week-olds, 103–105
varying, colicky babies and, 83–84
wake cycles and, 24
Sleep deprivation (adult), 90–96, 172
dealing with exhaustion, 86–87, 90–96
don'ts, 94
effects of, 154
factors amplifying, 92, 133
momsomnia and, 91
overcoming, 92–95, 122, 133
pervasiveness of, 95
power napping and, 95–96
PPD (post-partum depression) and, 92
PPF (post-partum fatigue) and, 90, 92
testing factors contributing to fatigue, 92, 133
Sleep deprivation (baby)
becoming increasingly hyper, 152–153
developmental problems and, 131
extinction method and, 146–147
SIDS and, 76–77
Sleep hormones. *See* Hormone activity; Melatonin
Sleep positioners, 45–46
Sleep schedules. *See also* Sleep training; *specific age groups*
developing daily routine, 99–100
first four months, 86–88
Four-Month Sleep Shift, 127–135
nap routines, 99–100, 107–113, 127–128, 170–171. *See also* Naps (baby)
nighttime put-down, 116–120
nighttime routine derailers, 150
signs of tiredness and, 117
toddlers, 178–179
too much sleep and, 152

Sleep training
best advice for, 151
compromising for effective training, 152
defined, 141
extended bed sharing, 150–151
extinction method (crying it out), 121, 142, 143–148, 154
graduated extinction, 141, 142, 143, 148, 154
newborns and, 17, 75, 110
overview of, 141–142
and parent education, 142
positive routines and faded bedtime, 141, 148–149, 153–154
questions and answers, 152–154
scheduled awakenings, 141, 142, 150
time to start, 139–141
too much sleep and, 152
Smoking, 5, 23, 40, 41–42, 69, 73, 74
Sound machines and CDs, 62–63
Stages of sleep, 17–19. *See also* Rapid eye movement (REM) sleep
Stimulants, 21–22, 69, 108. *See also specific stimulants*
Stomach
colic and digestive issues, 81, 84, 85, 87
sleeping on, SIDS and, 74
tummy time, 26, 106, 115–116
Storing breastmilk, 78
Sudden infant death syndrome (SIDS), 71–79
age of baby and, 72
alpha-fetoprotein (AFP) and, 77–79
baby monitors and, 63
bassinets and, 57
bed sharing and, 35, 38–39, 40, 43
bedside sleepers and, 58
bed types and, 34, 35, 41
breastfeeding and, 20
couches, armchairs and, 76
cribs and, 35, 53
crying to sleep and, 121
day care and, 74

Sudden infant death syndrome
    (continued)
  deep sleep in morning and, 77
  defined, 183
  ethnic origin and, 76
  factors that may contribute to, 72–79
  facts about, 71–72
  flu season and, 76
  formula feeding and, 20, 74–75
  gender and, 74
  health factors and, 77
  illegal drugs and, 73, 75
  low birthweight and, 74
  overheating and, 43, 75–76
  pacifiers and, 76, 89–90
  prematurity and, 72–74
  preventing, 59
  protecting baby from, 73
  resources, 185–186
  separate sleeping quarters and, 75
  sleep deprivation and, 76–77
  sleep position and, 26
  sleep training and, 75
  smoking and, 5, 23, 40
  statistics on, 71, 74
  stomach-down sleeping and, 74
  teen pregnancy and, 75
  tobacco smoke and, 5, 23, 40, 73, 74
  typical risk factors, 74
  ventilation and, 59, 61, 75
Sunlight exposure, 100–102
Swaddling, 26–27, 28, 43, 76, 85, 120

Three to four months
  brain development and needs,
      100–102
  charting day/night patterns, 113–117
  developing daily routine, 99–100.
      See also Sleep schedules
  feeding and sleep (breastfeeding vs.
      bottle), 102–105
  handling strategies by personality
      type, 120–123
  nap put-down, 110–111, 114
  nap routines, 107–113
  nighttime put-down, 116–120

  questions and answers, 110–113
  tummy time practice, 106
Toddlers. *See also* Nine to twelve
      months
  bad dreams/night terrors, 20, 168,
      172–174, 183, 185
  bed-wetting, 175–177, 178
  challenge of, 165
  delaying tactics, 166
  early-morning risers, 170
  exercise for, 165–166
  family upheavals and, 178–179
  getting support with, 172
  moving from crib to bed, 174–175
  nap routines, 170–171
  not staying asleep, 172
  roaming (containing and
      protecting), 171
  sleep patterns, 165
  stabilizing sleep of, 178–179
  tips for bedtime, 167–169
  traveling and sleep problems, 177–178
Toy basket, 60
Toys
  to avoid, 63
  comforting baby, 123, 175, 178, 179
  cribs and, 54, 63, 175
  dangerous, 63
  early-morning risers and, 170
  for tummy time, 106
Traditional advice ("shoulds"), 8–10
Traveling, sleep problems and, 15, 149,
      177–178
Tummy time, 26, 106, 115–116
Twelve months and beyond. *See*
      Toddlers

Uniquenesses of babies, 122

Ventilation, 59, 61, 73, 75
Vitamin D, 100–102
Vocalizations, 111. *See also* Crying

Wake cycles, 24. *See also* Circadian
      rhythms
Wetting bed. *See* Bed-wetting